─── STEP-BY-STEP ───

MOSAICS

& HOW TO EMBELLISH GLASS & CERAMICS

STEP-BY-STEP

MOSAICS

& HOW TO EMBELLISH GLASS & CERAMICS

165 original and stylish projects to decorate the home and garden, illustrated with more than 1500 step-by-step photographs, templates and easy-to-follow instructions

Contains every technique you need to make attractive and original mosaics, decorative china, painted tiles and stained glass ornaments   edited by SIMONA HILL

HERMES
HOUSE

Contents

INTRODUCTION

Here is the ultimate in craft compendiums: five traditional crafts that each have a long history, brought up to date and made accessible to all, whether experienced or not. The designs in this inspirational collection feature materials that are among the most durable of all: stone, glass and ceramics will not rust, fade or rot, and can withstand years of wear and weather, indoors or out. All have been used decoratively for thousands of years, and many surviving examples

of ancient mosaics, stained glass windows, glassware and pottery look as bright and fresh now as when they were newly created. There is a fascinating contradiction between the delicacy and fragility of glass and ceramics and their ability to endure for centuries, retaining their beautiful colours and luminosity.

Mosaic exploits the hardwearing, impervious qualities of glass and ceramics in a form that is endlessly adaptable. While the technique of building up a picture or pattern from small components can employ many different materials, it is the regular square "tesserae", first manufactured from stone, clay or glass by the ancient Greeks and Romans, that we tend to think of as most characteristic of the form. In Byzantine mosaics glass tesserae became prominent, offering artists an almost limitless range of colours and metallic shades. These beautiful, luminous glass "smalti" are still available today in hundreds of colours and finishes, still manufactured

Left: This mosaic vase, though newly created, has the shape and appearance of an ancient vessel.

Above: With a soft light shining through them, jewel-bright glass tesserae are brought to life, and make excellent candleholders for the home or garden.

Above: Mosaic is weatherproof if properly grouted and great for transforming old and faded outdoor furniture that has seen better days.

using traditional methods. Their hand-cut edges form the surface of the finished work, creating lively reflective effects, and they are traditionally fitted closely together so that their colours look rich and intense.

Glass tesserae are an inspiring material for jewel-like treasures, but other possibilities range from household tiles to sea-washed glass, pebbles and shells. The use of broken plates and dishes, known as "pique assiette", creates charming, informal and subtly coloured designs that are always unique. This is a wonderful way to recycle well-loved but damaged china from your own kitchen, and pretty plates and dishes can be bought very cheaply second-hand. The finished surface tends to be uneven, so it is more

suitable for covering items such as planters and picture frames than for tables, though you could use the centres of plates to create some flat areas for balancing cups and glasses. It's nice to make the most of patterned china: rather than smashing a piece into random shapes you can use tile nippers to nibble around the prettiest motifs and then incorporate them into your design.

A garden mosaic can be anything from a charming, subtle "carpet" of natural pebbles or slate set into paving, to a magnificent pictorial wall feature that is the centre of attraction throughout the year. The colours of a large mosaic will be dominant even in summer, so the design needs to be followed through with planting that

Left: Modern ceramic paints don't need to be fired in a kiln to fix (set) their colours, and are available in many colours.

Below: Stained glass is a traditional craft, once the preserve of skilled artisans.

enhances its effect. A garden of white flowers and shady greenery or dark topiary shapes might have a mosaic mural in blues and whites as a focal point, perhaps using old pottery to evoke the style of a 17th-century garden. Among luxuriant palms and flowering plants in hot, tropical colours you could construct a glittering golden fountain or an exuberant panel in vibrant reds and oranges.

Think beyond walls and floors when using mosaic on a large scale: it makes wonderful quirky furniture, and can turn second-hand benches and chairs into exciting original pieces. A mosaic top gives new life to an old garden table, or you can make a new tabletop from durable marine plywood, cut to the size and shape of your choice, and attach it to an existing base. Abstract patterns or designs based on natural forms in fresh, flowery colours look wonderfully inviting under a shady tree

in summer. Mosaic can be used just as effectively on furniture indoors, and here again the technique is perfect for revamping worn but cherished pieces. On a smaller scale, picture frames, mirrors, vases, boxes and lamps are all ideal bases for mosaic, and there are plenty of easy ideas to try in this book.

Ceramic and glass paints are yet another creative way to introduce glossy, brilliant splashes of colour into your home. The second part of the book suggests a host of easily achievable effects, including stencilling, sponging and stamping as well as freehand painting, with which you can turn plain ceramics and glass into jewelbright works of art. They include

Left: Glass paints offer a simple and satisfying way of adding colour to the accessories with which we decorate our homes.

Below: Brand new tiles can be aged with a traditional design and old-fashioned paint colours.

exploit this power, casting delightful shafts of coloured sunlight on to the floor and walls. Stained-glass shades for lamps and candles create equally strong effects for evening. Glazed ceramics sparkle with reflected light, and their concentrated colours and strong contrasts draw the eye. Even small items such as painted tiles or mosaic frames work as visual accents, pulling a decorative scheme together.

designs for tile murals and friezes inspired by historic and folk themes, as well as simple ideas for dishes, cups and plates and glassware that would fit easily into the most modern interior. Many of the smaller items shown here would make outstanding gifts, which would be especially well received if you take care to plan designs that suit the decorative style of your friends and relatives, perhaps even matching the colour scheme of a specific room.

The smallest amount of pure, rich colour can become the focal point of a decorative scheme, and glass serves this purpose supremely well, not only drawing the eye to its intrinsic colours and patterns, but also filtering light so that, for instance, a green vase on a window ledge can create a cool, shady atmosphere throughout a large interior. Glass decorations expressly designed to hang in a window or from a sheer curtain are a playful way to

All the techniques required are clearly explained, and the projects are graded to give you an idea of the challenge involved, so you can try your hand at simple pieces before embarking on more ambitious ideas or devising your own original creations.

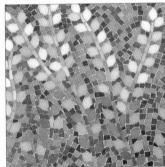

MOSAICS

Durable and adaptable, mosaic is a medium that can find a place in any home or garden, whatever its style. The techniques of mosaic have been successfully applied to many different materials and surfaces, from the vast tile-covered spires of Gaudí's Sagrada Família cathedral in Barcelona to the delicate Roman-inspired micro-mosaics of the 18th and 19th centuries, in which the tesserae are incredibly small. The following pages include a brief history of the art of mosaic and a detailed discussion of the various kinds of tesserae and their preparation, the equipment you will need and suitable adhesives and grouts. A number of different techniques are used for assembling and fixing, and your choice will usually depend on the size and location of the mosaic. There are also suggestions of design themes and help with planning, plus a host of inspiring and varied mosaic projects for you to try.

Glorious
Mosaics

We know that the ancient art of mosaic was practised extensively throughout history because so many impressive examples have survived. It is a remarkably durable and versatile medium – in public places, on the outside of buildings in the playground or park, and in more domestic situations in private homes and gardens. Also beautiful and decorative, mosaics that are created for our enjoyment now are a legacy for the future.

Mosaics have been made by many civilizations who discovered the technique independently of each other. They are unusual in having survived long enough for us to enjoy hundreds of years later.

A History of Mosaic

Most of us will be very familiar with mosaic as an art form, and perhaps the image most often conjured up is that of Roman floors and walls. However, although the term "mosaic" originates from Italy, the art form itself certainly existed long before Roman times and has been practised in various ways by subsequent cultures and civilizations.

Today we have access to a huge variety of work from a multitude of sources, to which we can look for our inspiration. Perhaps the reason we so often associate mosaic with the past is

the durability of the materials used to make them, for example stone, glass or ceramics. Consequently, many ancient examples have survived centuries of upheaval, and can still be seen today.

Western Europe

The earliest surviving mosaics were made in about 3000BC by the Sumerians in ancient Mesopotamia, now known as Iraq. These consisted of arrangements of coloured clay pegs that were pressed into wall surfaces. Later, the Egyptians used fragments of

coloured materials and semi-precious stones to decorate walls and to inlay furniture, decorative objects and items of jewellery.

Ancient Greece is the earliest civilization known to have used natural stones and pebbles in varying colours to create permanent designs, and it was probably the originator of what we today think of as "mosaic".

The Romans built on this technique, standardizing practices by cutting natural stone into regular cubes. They also used fired clay and some glass for special effects. Another Roman innovation was the use of cements and mortars. These made their mosaics astonishingly durable, and as a result there are many surviving examples of floor and wall mosaics throughout countries that were once part of the Roman Empire.

In their mosaics the Romans used an extraordinarily varied range of styles and subjects – from realistic, observed studies of everyday life to naïve garden mosaics, and from classical depictions of the gods to purely decorative designs and geometric borders. These early mosaics were executed in the

Left: This image of Neptune and Amphitrite is from a house in Herculaneum and has survived a volcano in AD79, and all the subsequent years.

Right: The stars in this Byzantine vaulted roof in the Mausoleum of Galla Placidia, Ravenna, Italy, still shine as brightly as when they were created, 5th century AD.

natural colours of the materials they were made from: greys, terracotta, ochre, white, dull blues and greens.

The growth of Christianity introduced new subject matter, but techniques and colours remained broadly unchanged until the Byzantine era, usually dated as beginning with the reign of the Emperor Justinian in Ravenna, about AD527. This was to be a very rich and innovative period in the history of mosaic, exemplified by the beautiful, luminous creations adorning Byzantine churches.

At this time, Ravenna was a wealthy imperial town and the main trading link between East and West. It is here that the best examples of Byzantine mosaic can be found, and the influence of Eastern art is apparent in the designs, such as the large Egyptian eyes, flattened shapes and ordered poses. This iconoclastic style was rendered with a new kind of tessera, or mosaic tile – glass "smalti". Glass, which previously had been used sparingly for highlights, now became the main component of mosaics. It was fired with metallic oxides, copper and marble, or had gold and silver leaf sandwiched between layers of glass. This new material gave mosaic artists access to a large palette of luminous colours. The technique of setting the pieces into the mortar bed at varying angles achieved wonderful effects with the reflective qualities of glass.

During this period, the art of mosaic making was superseded by fresco painting. The mosaics that did continue to be created tended to be copies of paintings – a tendency that persisted right up to the 20th century. As a result, the mosaicist had become a master craftworker and copyist rather than an original artist, which meant that mosaic did not develop as an art form in Western Europe for a long time.

At the beginning of the 20th century, however, the Art Nouveau movement gave artists a new direction, and mosaic began to be seen again as an artistic medium that could be celebrated for its own qualities. Pure pattern re-emerged and forms were simplified and stylized.

Mosaic was given a further boost with the onset of modernism. The best-known exponent of mosaic in this era was the architect Antoni Gaudí (1852–1926). He covered the large exterior surfaces of his buildings, both plain and formed, with irregularly shaped coloured tiles. He also commissioned prominent modern artists of the time, such as Kokoschka, Klimt and Chagall, to make designs for the mosaics that clad his buildings. Examples of his mosaics in Barcelona, Spain, include the façade of Casa Batlló, the spires of the (unfinished) Sagrada Família cathedral, and the serpentine benches on the terrace of the extraordinary Parc Güell.

Above: This undulating mosaic-covered lizard is a fountain designed by Antoni Gaudí, Parc Güell, Barcelona, Spain.

Josep Maria Jujol, a collaborator of Gaudí, is also interesting for the ceramic medallions that he made for the ceiling of the Hypostyle Hall in Parc Güell. He set brilliantly coloured

Right: This turquoise mosaic mask represents Quetzalcoatl, the feathered serpent god of ancient Mexico, c.1500. The pieces of precious stone would have been attached to a carved wooden base.

Below right: Roof of Casa Milà, La Pedrera, Barcelona, Spain, showing chimney pots and ceramic structures designed 1906–10 by Antoni Gaudí.

mosaic pieces (tesserae) against ceramic fragments, such as bases of bottles, cups and dishes, all arranged in patterns of stars and spirals.

Central America

The history of mosaics is not confined to Western Europe. Long before the arrival of Europeans in Central America, the Aztecs and Mayas had developed mosaic techniques separately from the rest of the world. There, mosaic was not used to convey images or systematic patterns, as was the tradition in Europe. Rather, it was used simply to embellish three-dimensional forms, very beautifully, using tesserae made from fragments of precious materials, most often coral and turquoise. These objects were often of a votive or ceremonial nature, such as skulls, weapons and carved snakes, and were encrusted with a variety of precious materials to give them beauty and importance.

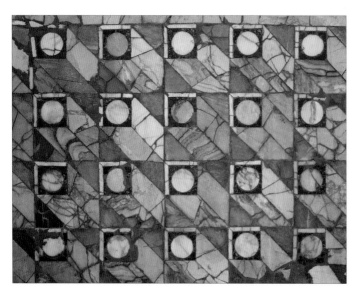

Islamic mosaic

Mosaic is also an important component of Islamic art. The designs are closely related to the buildings in which they are set and seem to rise naturally from the architecture. A fine example of the Islamic mosaic tradition can be seen in the 14th century palace of the Alhambra in Granada, Spain. Muslim craftspeople still construct complicated geometric mosaics today.

Other influences

Many cultures use mosaic-like effects to adorn buildings and objects. In African art, for example, everyday objects are often studded with tacks or covered in coloured beads. The effect is that of mosaic, although the method by which the pieces are attached differs from the traditional technique.

The handwoven carpets of India and Turkey are in many ways comparable to the medium of mosaic. The patterns are made up of individual units of colour, and these can be very useful as inspiration for designs.

Today, mosaic artists draw their inspiration from many different cultures and traditions, combining these influences with techniques and ideas that have developed in Europe.

Interesting exponents

Some of the most amazing examples of mosaic have, however, been made by people who had no formal arts training and who developed their work away from the public eye, often begging their materials from anywhere they could. Raymond Isidore, a manual worker in Chartres, France, covered his entire house and garden with intricate mosaics made from broken ceramics.

His nickname, *Picassiette* (the French for "scrounger"), is now the name used for this style of mosaic. One of the best examples of this type

Above left: Coloured stone mosaic, 9th–10th century AD, from the palace at Divanyolu, Istanbul, Turkey.

Above: Some of Nek Chand's creations, The Rock Garden of Chandigarh, India.

Opposite: Dancing – part of an installation by Nek Chand in India.

of art is Nek Chand's rock garden in Northern India. Like Raymond Isidore, Nek Chand had a humble day job: he was a transport official in the nearby city of Chandigarh. Over the course of 18 years, however, he worked in secret on a clearing he made in the jungle. He built structures and sculpted figures, covering everything in a mosaic made from the city's discarded urban debris and from stones found on nearby hillsides. Forty years on, his incredible garden covers more than 11 hectares (27 acres) and attracts over 5,000 visitors a day.

Inspiration

Mosaics may have a history that reaches back before Roman times, but the inspiration behind the designs can come from the everyday world around us. Designs can be influenced by our surroundings, from people and animal life to landscapes and art. These influences can affect not just the motifs but also the choice of colour and texture, and the type of materials to be used. All these things will affect the movement and feel of the final piece of mosaic.

Modern mosaicists work in all manner of styles and bring immense flair to the art. Some draw on traditional influences and methods, while others break new ground in their use of size, shape and materials.

Contemporary Mosaic

There has been a renewed interest in mosaic among the general public, and mosaic is now being applied to all kinds of objects in the decorative arts and sculpture, for private enjoyment, and to decorate public places. You can see the effectiveness of mosaic as a hardwearing design element in locations as varied as railway stations, swimming pools, bars and shopping centres, as well as private homes.

Mosaic artists all around the world derive inspiration from many sources, including nature, animal and plant forms, as well as from the repeating or geometric patterns typical of Roman, Celtic and Cubist art. The bold and abstract art of 20th century artists, such as Picasso and Matisse, has also influ-enced the work of many current mosaic artists. Some employ traditional materials in exciting new ways and others incorporate more unusual materials and textures in their work.

The scale of work varies from small portable panels and accessories to patios and large expanses of floor as well as murals and immense sculptures. French artist Niki de Saint Phalle (b.1930) spent 1979–96 creating a fabulous mosaic Tarot Garden in Garavicchio, Tuscany, Italy, which unites sculpture and mosaic in fantasti-cal figures, using brightly coloured tiles, glass and mirror. Sculptural mosaics are currently popular among young artists, but many prolific mosaic makers work on panels, murals and indoor pieces.

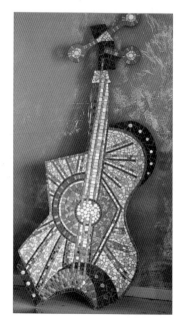

Above: This freestanding sculpture is a funky, brightly coloured guitar by mosaic artist Elizabeth De'Ath.

Left: Mosaic is an applied art that can complement contemporary interiors. This design for a mirror frame was worked out on paper first, before committing to the final design.

Opposite: A pyramid sculpture created with chicken wire and cement by artist Celia Gregory. The mosaic is made from small pieces of rectangular mirror and stained glass.

The depiction of the human form can take many guises. It can be realistic, as the Romans chose, or it can be more abstract. Likewise, birds, animals and fish can be naturalistic or stylized.

Humans and Animals

Figurative mosaic in the hands of an expert may lend itself to great detail and intricacy. In such mosaics, the contours of the face and body are skilfully rendered through the way in which the tesserae are cut to size and positioned for their shape – notably to show the jut of the chin, cheekbones and brow. Tesserae are chosen to suggest the modelling of the features, for their gradations of colour and tone and to show the way light and shade fall on the face or body.

Ancient Roman images of the living world are mostly realistic, though sometimes they convey a quirky sense of humour. Animals in art have often served a symbolic purpose, for example dogs can indicate fidelity. Birds were a common Roman subject, especially doves at a fountain, which suggested harmony and peace.

In Byzantine times, mosaic was largely confined to religious or imperial subjects and was concerned to show figures such as emperors, Christ, God, the Virgin Mary and the saints in an idealized, and therefore essentially stylized, way. Forms were made slender, elongated and more elegant, faces became regular and expressionless, and gestures and rituals (such as benediction) were formalized and ritualized. It is a style that continues to inspire mosaicists today.

Moving with the times
In later centuries, including the Renaissance and Victorian eras, mosaics remained largely classical and representational in inspiration.

During the 20th century, however, there was a move towards the abstract representation of human figures. This

Above: Satyr and Maenad – *a highly detailed replication by Salvatore Raeli of a 2nd century mosaic panel from the House of the Faun, Pompeii, Italy.*

style of depicting people was practised by many artists, including Pablo Picasso, Henri Matisse and Marc

Chagall, whose styles and superb workmanship lent themselves well to mosaic, with the emphasis on outline and colour rather than detail, and the free rendition of line and form.

Modern depiction

The current revival of interest in mosaic often displays a more naturalistic approach, revelling in the beauty and detail of the natural world. Nature can be depicted in numerous ways. For example, a bird could be the main focus within a panel or roundel, or be a stand-alone image on a plain background, such as a garden wall. How the mosaic is executed will depend on the artist's own style. Animals and birds can be treated in a symbolic manner, or they can be allegorical or humorous, realistic or naturalistic. They can appear in outline against a one- or two-colour background, or in silhouette, or have two- or three-dimensional effects. More unusual materials can be added to give detail, texture and depth.

Often animals, birds and insects will form part of a larger mosaic; when they do there needs to be enough tonal contrast in the work to allow the images to stand out, and colours must be chosen carefully. Birds and insects are challenging subjects, but the potential for using vibrant colour is endless, especially with bright plumage. With regard to the human form, today's mosaic artists can choose to depict this in many ways, varying from ethnic art to the vibrant, contemporary approach of the strip cartoon.

Below far left and centre: Takako Shimizu's cobweb and spider brilliantly convey the delicacy and transparency of the web. The well-camouflaged mosaic bat has texture and a three-dimensional quality.

Below: A rabbit panel by Claire Stewart shows the broad outlines of the animal's body against a simple background.

The ocean and the teeming variety of life found in it have provided the mosaic artist with a rich source of inspiration for centuries. Likewise, landscapes, whether naturalistic or abstract, appear often in mosaic.

The Natural World

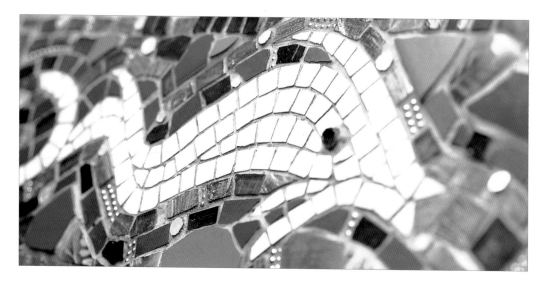

Marine themes are popular choices for bathroom mosaics. Splashbacks, tiled panels, floors and walls can all be decorated with dolphins, fish and shells. The recreation of landscapes will tend to be seen in large-scale mosaics, such as wall panels, or even whole walls.

Marine life

Many mosaic materials, especially the intense and vibrant material smalti, are wonderful for recreating the beautiful colours of fish and the many shades of the ocean – azure, emerald, turquoise and aquamarine. Marine themes offer wonderful opportunities for mosaic artists to experiment with exciting and vivid colour.

Marine life, including dolphins, fish, octopuses, starfish and seaweed, can create a flowing mosaic design, full of action and energy. The impression of water, light and movement can be conveyed effectively and with surprising economy in the way in which the tesserae are laid. Artists can also intersperse the mosaic with iridescent and reflective materials, such as mirror, to highlight certain areas and create a glistening scene.

Mosaics inspired by sea life are often very graphic and highly patterned. In fact, the scales on fish often look like mosaics themselves, and mosaic artists can depict this natural patterning with intricate detail.

Above: A detail from a picture frame by Norma Vondee, showing a classical-style dolphin. The white tiles highlight an area of the body, making it appear to glisten.

Landscapes

As with any painting, the creation of a landscape begins with the composition. It needs to be planned and sketched out, and the order of work and colours and tones of the tesserae need to be considered in advance.

Landscapes can, at first glance, appear to be faithful to reality, but most will involve a certain amount of stylization, of tidying up, of selecting particular subjects for the foreground and background, of highlighting

Right: A close-up of a soft coral smalti mirror frame decorated with sea creatures, by Norma Vondee.

Below right: Roman mosaic provided great inspiration for artists throughout the last millennium. This reproduction, using tiny pieces of marble and stone, depicts sea creatures that were intended to look as if they were swimming around a classical water feature.

details and of trying to create a feeling of distance and three-dimensional space. Images are built up by laying lines of regular or cut tesserae around images such as trees or hills, and backgrounds can include other patterns. A mosaic landscape is like a pixellated image that has to be viewed from a certain distance for it to be in focus.

Mosaic landscapes in earlier centuries were often very detailed, showing the subtle undulations of hills, the movement of water and the gradations of blue in the sky, but images do not have to be naturalistic to be effective. Some contemporary mosaic artists take inspiration from naive art and the surreal landscapes of de Chirico, and they have produced scenes that make full use of mosaic's textural and graphic qualities. Such works suggest a complete landscape rather than showing highly detailed images and objects.

For the mosaic maker, plants and flowers are appealing subjects. They soothe the senses, are easy to look at, are universally popular and valued, and can be depicted in many different artistic styles.

Plants and Flowers

Natural plant forms are a very popular theme in mosaic, and plants are often woven into the designs of mosaic borders. They can flow around a panel or large mural, creating wonderful rhythm and activity, which adds interest and depth to a design. Plant forms can be depicted in a very elegant and stylized manner.

Contemporary mosaicists often use the medium's graphic qualities to produce remarkable work based on natural forms. Bold colours and chunky textures can combine to create vivid three-dimensional images. Plants and flowers are also excellent individual images, perhaps best for table tops and panels, as the petals, leaves and stems lend themselves well to flowing ornamentation. Trees, especially the tree of life, are a common theme in mosaic.

The images could be depicted in subtle materials, such as marble, and have delicate, soft-toned flowers, or they could be bold and graphic and less representational, using funkier colours and materials, such as vitreous glass and mirror. Ceramic tiles can give a warm, earthy feel to mosaic pictures of plants.

Left: Tree of Life – *a panel with a border of hand-painted Mexican tiles by Helen Baird. Trees are a popular source of inspiration in mosaic.*

Above: These simple tiles take their inspiration, colour and shape from the bright sunflower.

Above right: Detail of part of the bush from Bird on a Bush, a marble mosaic using soft, warm variegated tones, by Salvatore Raeli.

Right: This garden ornament by Rebecca Newnham shows how well natural plant forms can be expressed abstractly.

Far right: The knobbly textured surface of a pineapple is vividly conveyed by Norma Vondee.

Many mosaics make use of non-representational geometric and abstract patterns of one form or another. The range of motifs is almost limitless, and designs with repeated patterns are ideal for borders.

Geometric and Abstract

By their nature, geometric patterns are very well suited to the art of mosaic. The basic outline is simple and ideal for the shape of tesserae, and shapes can be repeated as often as is needed. The repetition is not monotonous; quite the opposite. The effect can be soothing and pleasing to the eye, and variations can be achieved through different colourways.

Pattern

A repeated pattern is an effective way of linking spaces: for instance, a path and hall floor could both be in a simple chequerboard pattern, the path in, say, black and white, and the hallway in blue and white. The transition from

outdoors to indoors is conveyed by the change in colourway. Although the two areas are relatively small, a continuity of pattern makes the overall space seem larger.

There are many standard geometric patterns to choose from, such as the Greek key, which remains ever popular, the intertwining, flowing rope designs of Celtic art, or the sinuous calligraphic motifs of Islamic or Arabic art. Geometric shapes frequently occur in 20th century art, and the blocks of colour of Mondrian, for example, would translate well into a mosaic project.

Above: Patchwork mosaic is reflected in the sides of this sunken pond feature. Patterns in ponds are best kept simple because of the constant movement of the light playing on the water.

Left: Triangles – an ungrouted mosaic in vitreous glass by Emma Biggs. Irregular and asymmetrical in design, the black and white triangles give intensity to the subject of colour and form.

Opposite: Echoes of the art of Paul Klee are visible in this geometric birdbath in tones of blue. The grid effect is offset by the changes in colour.

Design

Once you have your inspiration, next comes the practical part of the design.

Before embarking on a project consider its situation and the materials to use

in order to make it durable enough to survive. Also the intended use should

be taken into account. For instance, a mosaic designed as a flooring will need

to be smooth and without edges to trip up on and waterproof so it can be

cleaned. All these elements will affect the final design that you decide upon.

The wide choice of materials available means that designing a mosaic is a highly personal process. You need to consider such aspects as size, location, function and colour before starting work.

Practicalities

Above: Square tiles are the basis of most mosaic work and can be laid whole or clipped into tesserae of the desired shape and laid in a variety of ways.

Left: Fairies – a beautiful abstract image of three fairies made from mirror and iridescent stained glass by Celia Gregory.

All you need to do is be clear about what you want to achieve and how you want to realize it. Do this, and materials, colour and style will marry happily with setting, mood and size to give you a mosaic of which you are proud. Before committing tesserae to adhesive, consider the following points.

When you are designing with mosaic, you have the liberty to use just one material, such as smalti, or to combine as many as you wish. Sometimes, this freedom can make it harder to reach decisions. Of course, no object exists in a vacuum and there will be other factors to consider when creating your designs.

Your mosaic may be intended for a predetermined place within a room or open-air space, surrounded by other objects. It may also be used for a specific purpose, such as to contain water. Your designs should also take into account the fact that mosaic is long-lasting and the colours virtually permanent. Unlike textile, paper or even paint, stone, glass and ceramic do not disintegrate; nor do they break easily or fade. Once the setting medium is hard, changes cannot be made. These qualities are the great strengths of mosaic, but they also mean you cannot go over your work and cover it up.

Function

Always consider the main function of the mosaic: is it to be practical or decorative? Most mosaic is hardwearing and water-resistant, which makes it quite safe to use for items such as splashbacks behind the bathroom basin or kitchen sink, or for the floor of a hallway, garden room or patio. If the work is to withstand wear and tear from feet or soap and water, think about which materials will be best suited to your needs: glass, for example, is not so suitable for the passage of feet, bikes and perhaps the odd piece of garden equipment. However, if a purely decorative effect is what you are after, clearly these considerations do not apply and your choice is wider.

Location

Consider where the mosaic is to be positioned. Every aspect of the design – whether it is simple or complex, abstract or representational, the size, the colours to be used and the materials – is influenced by which room of the house the mosaic is intended for, or its position in the garden.

Focal point

Decide whether the mosaic is to stand out from or blend in with its surroundings. Will it be the focal point of a decorative or planting scheme, or is it to go with established furniture or features? Your answers will determine how strong the design needs to be.

Mood

Consider the impact and mood the mosaic is to create. It is worth being clear at an early stage just how much of

a centrepiece you want your mosaic to be, as it is a strong medium that can easily upstage its surroundings. The mosaic can be as bold as you like, but its style should have a link with its situation. For example, a bright geometric mirror frame will jar in a guest bedroom that is decorated in soft florals; likewise a large panel in bright folk art reds and oranges might swamp a tiny but sophisticated all-white courtyard garden.

Above: The earthy tones of this lamp stand complement the dusky yellow lampshade. Its spiral design is eye-catching, yet soothing, so it does not dominate the room.

Size

You need to decide on the size of the mosaic. Ensure that the design is in scale with the overall size: a tiny pattern will look out of place in a large mural, while a big pattern will look just as wrong in a tiny space.

Remember, too, that patterns or designs look larger the closer they are to your eye level. Look at one of the illustrations in this book at eye level, then put the same page on the floor; you will see how much detail is lost. Operate on a "less is more" principle and take out superfluous detail for smaller-scale pieces or those that will be viewed only from afar.

When designing a mosaic for either an interior or exterior space, there are some important factors to consider.

points to consider for EXTERIORS

• What is the mosaic for?
• Where is it going to be sited?
• Do you want it to blend in with established plants and garden features, or will it be the centrepiece from which all else flows?
• Are the colours suitable for its purpose, size and location?
• Is the mosaic the right size for its specific purpose: not so small that it is lost, nor so big that it dominates the space?
• If it is to convey information, such as a house name or number, is the design clear enough and uncluttered with detail to enable it to be viewed from a distance?

Above: The hot colours of this small water feature by Tabby Riley suit the exotic planting around it.

Above: A dull brick wall is enlivened by an impressionistic mosaic of two cockerels by Takako Shimizu.

To aid you in your planning and preparation and to help you avoid making time-consuming mistakes, there are some questions in the boxes to consider. These will help you to be clear about the purpose of your design, taking into consideration if it is a purely decorative or practical mosaic.

Mosaic is a bold medium and you can cover large areas with it and create dramatic effects. Indoors, especially, it will be a strong feature. You want it to be striking but, if it is large, not to overpower its surroundings. Bear these considerations in mind when beginning to plan work on design, colour, materials and size.

Being so durable means that mosaic is ideal for out-of-doors, where wind, rain and frost would quickly see off a less hardwearing medium. When considering your initial design, make sure your mosaic fits within its environment.

Light

Bear in mind the nature of daylight where you live: essentially blue in temperate areas and more red in tropical parts. Take some tesserae outside to see how natural light alters their colours.

There is no reason why you cannot use strong, hot colours in temperate areas, but be aware of how vibrant they can look. Mosaics in brilliant reds and oranges need to be carefully placed in temperate gardens. If allowed to peep from under lavish green planting, they can add a touch of drama and humour, and are good for shady areas, dark courtyard gardens or a particular "room" in a large garden, perhaps set among hot-toned flowers. Using cool blues and greens in warmer settings can, conversely, create an area of calmness and tranquillity.

Siting

Clever positioning is part of a successful mosaic, where all aspects of its design (subject, pattern, framing, colour, texture and size) come together in the right setting. You might like to

points to consider for INTERIORS

- What is the mosaic's function?
- Which room is it going in?
- Is the room's colour scheme being built around the mosaic?
- If not, does the mosaic fit in with the existing scheme?
- Is the design you like appropriate to the room where you intend to place the mosaic?
- Are the weight of the object and the material used appropriate to its function and position?
- What happens if you decide to redecorate your home?
- Is the mosaic portable (wall-mounted, for instance, or on furniture)?
- If not, what will happen if you later want to move it to another place, or take it with you when you move into different accommodation?

choose a design that is appropriate for the site, for example food in the kitchen, or vines in the dining room.

When you are working in a room on a ceiling or floor, consider the viewing lines. If the mosaic is to be seen at an angle, make sure it gives the best view. If the piece is in an architectural setting, make sure that the design is sympathetic to its surroundings.

Mosaic-framed mirrors should be sited adjacent to windows, not opposite them, to achieve the best effects. Subtle colours should be positioned with care so the colours are enhanced, not lost by glare or bright light.

Above: In a restrained modern setting this very striking mirror frame, designed by Marion Lynch, is all the ornamentation you need.

Scale

The size of your design is important, so this must be borne in mind when planning, and detail that will be lost at a distance must be eliminated.

The importance of size applies equally to the actual size of the tesserae you are working with. Choose sizes that will look right for their intended position: they must not be so large that they cannot cope with the design or pattern you want; neither should they be too small or they will tend to look untidy and ineffective, reducing a strong design to something weaker and with less impact.

Colour is one of the most fundamental elements of any mosaic design and has a profound effect on our response to the work. In addition, the way light, real or artificial, falls on these colours is hugely important.

Using Colour

When deciding which colours to use, you should have some samples to place in the setting you have in mind. Here you can see how the natural light falls on them. The closer to the window they are, the stronger the colours will look. If they are set on a wall between two windows and against the glare of daylight, however, quite the opposite happens and they will appear darker. What is more, the same shade of red will look slightly different when placed flat on the floor and when hung vertically on the wall. Also, as anyone who has tried to match colours under fluorescent lighting or has caught sight of themselves in an elevator mirror will know, the light source can profoundly affect some colours. For this reason, colour samples should be viewed in all the types of light in which they will be seen (daylight, tungsten bulb, halogen, neon and so on), and consideration should be given to how the light changes at different times of the day.

Hot and cool colours

What we perceive as colourless white light is divided into the colours of the spectrum – red, orange, yellow, green, blue, indigo and violet. These divide broadly into hot colours (red, orange and yellow) and cold (green, blue and indigo). The shades that centre around violet (a mixture of red and blue) tend to be cooler or warmer, depending on the proportion of red to blue: mauve and lilac incline to cool, maroon and purple to warm.

In addition, colours are either predominant or recessive: in other words, some catch the eye more than others. It is a question not just of light and dark, but of which colours attract the eye first, and which colours are seen second. If you glance casually at a selection of colour images you will notice that your eye instinctively goes to some colours first. You will probably find that it alights immediately on any reds, oranges or yellows, or any strong, clear colours (in an all-blue room, for instance, the eye goes first to the brightest shade of blue). Only after that does it move to the more recessive tones, the blues (or softer shades of blue in our all-blue room), the greens and the browns.

So, when deciding which colours to use, you need to bear in mind the visual effect they will have. A palette of warm colours – reds, oranges and

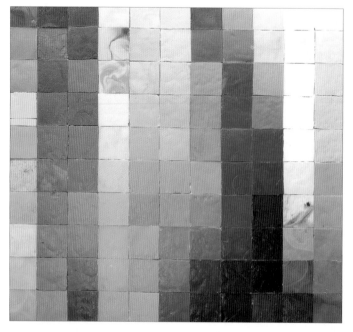

Left: This is a small indication of the vast range of colours and hues of smalti that are now widely available to the mosaic artist .

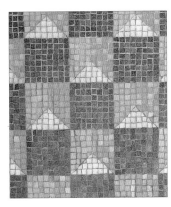

Above: Using darker and lighter colours throws different elements of a design into relief and brings others to prominence.

Above: A strong colour used against a light background stands out more clearly than white on a coloured background.

Above: The use of colour alone can produce entirely different results from the same pattern.

yellows – will create a warm impression. They will also be strong, dominating their surroundings. And because they draw the eye, they will make spaces seem smaller. This need not be a disadvantage – an entrance hall in warm tones will seem extrawelcoming on a cold winter's night, and a north-facing bathroom can have the chill taken off it and be made to feel cosy and inviting by using colours from the warm end of the spectrum – but they could make a small room seem cramped.

The cool colours of blues, greens and indigos, coupled with the "hard" effect of mosaic, may make a cold room seem more so. Along with browns, they are also recessive, so they will be well suited to making small spaces seem larger, provided you do not opt for too many dark tones, which will make areas seem more confined. So, soft blues, greens and lilacs would be a good choice for a mosaic at the end of a small garden.

When it comes to dark and light colours, received wisdom is that a dark area stands out more when surrounded

by light-toned colours. This will happen if the colours are not too bland (too much magnolia, cream or beige can be dull). However, it can often be as successful to play up the dark aspect by choosing a similar tone of another colour. The secret is to make the colour deep but rich, such as dark scarlet, blackcurrant, peacock blue, racing green or chocolate brown. Boldness pays off. Whichever colour you do choose, note that if using large areas of the same colour, varying the tone and sizes of the mosaic pieces adds interest.

Matching colour to style

Another very important aspect of colour is that the palette you choose must match the style of the design if the whole is not to look incongruous. For example, a folk art pattern would not suit a combination of chrome yellow, black and silver, while an Art Deco design would work less well in primary blue, red and yellow. Similarly, a realistic floral mosaic will be most successful executed in colours as close as possible to the real plant, while a piece inspired by the work of Tiffany asks for his characteristic delicate turquoises, lavenders, chartreuse greens and soft pinkish whites.

Matching colour to surroundings

You will need to take into consideration the items that will surround your mosaic. However much you may want it to provide a focal point, it needs to bear some relation to the existing colour scheme in the room or it will simply look out of place.

By studying the furniture, walls, and fabrics in the room you can tell if there is an overall colour scheme. You can then blend your mosaic with it, perhaps picking up on some of the colours in a particular item.

Whether it is to go on the wall, be placed on the floor, or sit on another item, a mosaic panel needs to relate to

Above: Decorative mosaics can be used as accessories to coordinate with existing schemes and fittings. For example, this marine-inspired mirror frame echoes the coral marble sink unit.

Left: Ideas and designs derived from the sea, such as this starfish, often look best in blues, greens and sandy shades.

the wall or floor colour. Perhaps the background colour could be one or two tones lighter or darker than the walls or floors. Perhaps its design could echo the colour of the tiles in a tiled hall, or its frame could replicate other picture frames in the room.

Right: The colours of the mosaic tiles have been carefully chosen to echo the vases on the windowsill.

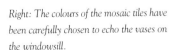

Cool and warm light

The fact that the quality of light varies depending on which country you live in becomes particularly relevant when considering the garden. In temperate latitudes, the light, even in midsummer, tends to be blue.

In the Mediterranean and tropical parts of the world, the light is significantly warmer and redder. This explains why the colours of Provence, Italy or Santa Fe in New Mexico – ochres, terracottas and earth tones with splashes of cobalt blues and rust reds – look so right there but do not always translate so well in temperate zones. By contrast, the soft greens, browns and grey-blues that suit cloudy skies can look too subdued and washed-out in stronger sunlight.

White and dark grout

In mosaic, the gaps between the pieces are as much a part of the design as the tesserae themselves, and these gaps are filled by a grouting medium. The effect of the mosaic varies dramatically depending on the colour of grout chosen: a white grout will make the overall effect very much lighter; a dark

grout is deep and sombre but can create contrast. It is well worth testing out a small sample to decide which effect you want. See the section on grouting, on page 70, for four examples of the same tiles finished with different coloured grouts.

Above: The choice between white or dark grouting will affect the overall appearance of the mosaic.

Below: Soft, earthy, rain-washed colours suit the quality of light in temperate gardens and match their surroundings well.

The element of contrast adds drama and movement to a design, and is necessary to satisfy the eye and keep it interested. It can be introduced in many different ways, not just in the choices of colour.

Using Contrast

In mosaics, creating contrast ensures that a design remains attractive and intriguing. It is easily achieved by mixing materials and varying their texture, changing the colours and sizes of the pieces, and by introducing elements of surprise, such as gold or silver, glass, mirror and strangely shaped pieces. The fall of light and the opacity of the work also have effects.

You can also achieve contrast by making a soft, sinuous design out of an intrinsically hard material. Mixed media mosaics create the vital element of contrast simply through their mixture of materials.

Size and shape

Tiles are usually cut into quarters, but they can, in fact, be cut into numerous shapes, including squares, rectangles, triangles, and, with practice, even semi-circles and wedge shapes. Varying tile sizes and shapes within patterns and various areas of the design is a way of creating contrast.

For example, a round table top could have a circular central section of large, unstructured, broken household tiles, and a contrasting border of neatly laid tiles in a more formal design, or with distinct shapes, such as triangles or repeating squares.

Shaping mosaic

Their usually square shape and hard texture means that mosaic tesserae are well suited to geometric or angular design. However, there is no reason at all why you cannot deliberately play up the visual differences between squares of clay or glass and sensuous curves and arcs. On some of Antoni Gaudí's extraordinary houses in Barcelona, Spain, the undulating walls and roofs flow like ocean waves, covered in gleaming tiles and mosaic.

Colour

Using colour is a simple but effective way of providing contrast. An obvious example would be a floral mosaic in which the flower is brilliantly coloured and the background is plain, perhaps palest green.

Using just black and white is the most extreme contrast, or you could limit yourself to one or two dark and light colours to focus on how the tiles are cut and laid, and experiment with patterns in individual areas.

If a bright, vibrant look is desired, you could use combinations from opposite sides of the colour wheel, such as scarlet with blue or purple with yellow. However, contrasts do not have to be extreme to work; shades of the same colour, or a palette of related tones, can be just as effective.

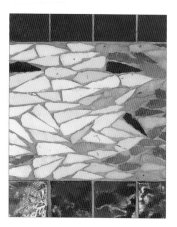

Left: Shape and colour both give contrast here, as a river of pointed shards flows between a retaining border of square tiles.

Right: Within this soft natural colour palette, contrast comes from the juxtaposition of the star with the circle and the black and white unglazed tiles.

Varying materials

A touch of the unexpected is an ideal way of enlivening a design. A matt chequerboard in black and white can be transformed by silver or glass tesserae placed at random intervals, while a pebble pool surround may be brought to life with a few beautifully shaped shells. Similarly, a monochrome mosaic can be changed beyond recognition by the addition of a panel made of broken patterned china in either the same or a contrasting colour.

Above: The mirror juxtaposes a swirling pattern with the plain mirrored centre, while the small table top contrasts a plain surround with a vibrantly coloured centre.

Right: This elegant alcove was created using rectangular stone mosaic by Robert Grace. The side wall contrasts with the other surfaces as the tesserae are laid in a more haphazard manner. The gold mosaic panels are of the Madonna, a Byzantine replica, and the Young Patrician, *both by Salvatore Raeli.*

You can create almost any pattern or shape you want with mosaic, once you have gained some experience of cutting and working with the medium. Outlines, rhythm and variety, and shading are all vital elements.

Using Pattern

If you are a beginner, it is sometimes better to think of mosaic as a medium that is most effective in broader outline rather than fine detail. Unlike drawing or painting, mosaic can become less effective the more it is weighed down with detail; instead, a few bold outlines can be filled in with patterns and shapes. Pattern alone can be the focus of a mosaic.

Simple outlines

If you are a good draughtsperson and you can draw or paint, you may find that your initial attempts at design may not be quite right for mosaic, as you will be tempted to add too much detail by way of shading, moulding and modelling.

To start with, you may like to study the work of cartoonists, who can evoke people, places and whole landscapes with a few lines of the pen. A facial expression may be conveyed with single strokes for eyes, brows, mouth and so on; movement is also minimally expressed. Equally, you could examine the cut-outs in the late work of Matisse to see how brilliantly he captured the contours of the human body

Left: Arch Air Condensed – *detail of a bee from a recycled china mosaic by Cleo Mussi. The background patterns are as vivid as the bees.*

Top: This detail shows various ways of changing direction and outlining movement.

Below: This mosaic table top by Salvatore Raeli shows how the pattern dictates the direction of the tiles.

Top: Here the pattern is created by the different sizes and shapes of the pieces.

Below: Bold, strong patterns can be made by using larger, clipped pieces of tiles – shape and pattern become one.

Top: The lines here are laid in curves, to give a sense of movement.

Below: This intricate design by Cleo Mussi uses the direction of the pieces to emphasize the pattern.

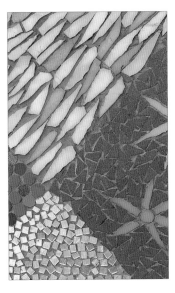

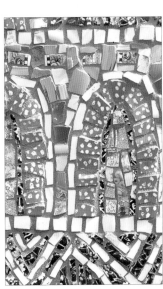

in movement with pieces of coloured tissue paper. It is worth experimenting with this "less is more" principle.

If you prefer to adapt an existing design, all you need to do is trace the basic shape, hold it away from your original to make sure the outlines are sufficient to show what you want to portray, then make your outlines the right size. This is easy with modern photocopiers that enlarge or reduce.

Forming patterns

The art of laying tesserae to form images and patterns is called *opus* (*opera* is the plural). There are no strict rules to adhere to, as each artist develops his or her own style, but there are a few things to consider. A fan shape is frequently seen in mosaic,

and this gives pattern and interest to a background, especially if you are laying just one colour. A pair of compasses will help to draw the curves. Rows of straight square tesserae laid like brick-work can also fill large areas.

When laying circular mosaics, guidelines should be drawn with a large pair of compasses. If the design comes to a central point, then tesserae cut at angles will be needed to work the centre. This can be fiddly and involve using tiny pieces. Alternatively, you could cover the central point with a large piece of tile and work around it.

Rhythm and variety

These are essential elements of pattern. When the lines of tesserae flow around a particular subject or group of

Above: The simple, but elegant, circular design of these table tops by Rebecca Newnham echoes the shape of the objects and focuses the eye on the material.

subjects and create rhythm and movement, it is called *opus vermiculatum*. Images can also be outlined in the background colour or in a distinct colour to help emphasize them and define their shape and pattern. Laying two or three lines of tiles around a shape will also add clarity to the design. Lines of tesserae can be laid to flow in directional lines, leading the eye to or around a design: this is called *andamento*.

Random patterns of tiles can be used to add variety to a mosaic. Sometimes this is necessary to fill

awkward or asymmetrical shapes. You can vary the interstices, or spaces between the tesserae, depending on the effect you require.

Geometric shapes are ideal for creating rhythm in mosaics and they will not become monotonous. Squares or oblongs, checks, chevrons, circles, swirls or spirals, Greek key, interlocking or separated – all are intrinsically pleasing to the eye and have an inbuilt sense of movement. This is why these motifs have remained so popular across the world and through the ages.

Shading with pattern

Often, you will need to convey some variation in shading and change of colour in a mosaic. You may stagger lines of colour in alternate rows to create fingers of colour or introduce some tonal shading so the change is not too abrupt. This often occurs in patterns

using subtle colours. Some degree of moulding or shading is vital in representational mosaics, and this can be achieved by varying the size and/or the shape of the mosaic pieces, as well as their colour, to suggest the contours of a face (nose, eyes, chin, brow), the body and limbs, or the shape of a flower.

Left: It is possible to create wonderful patterns with square mosaic tesserae. The lines in this piece are laid in curves that give a great sense of movement.

This is a skilled procedure. Be sure to practise carefully beforehand, laying out your pieces like a jigsaw puzzle on a piece of cardboard, well away from any setting medium, until every piece is in the right place.

Grout lines also play a part in helping the rhythm and flow of a design. Straight lines give a more formal, structured effect and curved lines help to give a feeling of movement. The widths and colours of the lines can vary.

Below: Here, light falls on the eyes and nose – facial features that are skilfully conveyed through a varied use of pattern and colour.

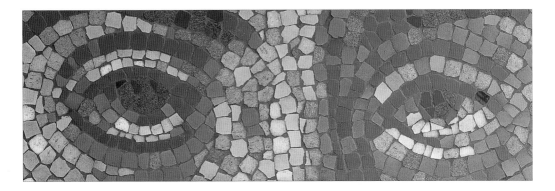

Texture can be one of the most interesting, exciting aspects of mosaic. Even on a flat panel, the depth of tile can vary and many materials can be used to vary the surface and create sparkling shapes and textural schemes.

Using Texture

Different materials have their own inherent qualities. Clay or ceramic have an even surface but have a slight organic roughness. Metal is hard and angular. Wood is rough but warm to the touch. Stone is smoother and cooler in its effect, while smalti and glass are the most responsive to light.

Mixed media

Combining two or more different materials is a way of adding drama, pattern and variety. Mixed media can achieve all kinds of exciting textural effects. Inserting pieces of broken china in an otherwise plain design adds not just colour and pattern: the broken pieces have a different texture and the fractured edges add spots of roughness to the even surface. You can contrast ceramic, which is slightly textured, with glass, which is smooth, or metal with stone. If you experiment

Above: Iridescent, multi-faceted beads, shells and glass all contribute to the varied texture of this dramatic, sculptural garden wall head by Takako Shimizu.

Left: A detail of a mosaiced garden seat, which provides durable external seating, designed by Celia Gregory. The stones make rough, textured breaks in the smoother blue and gold sections of the seating area.

with combinations of various textures, however, do not overload the mosaic with too many at the expense of clarity.

Setting

The texture should be chosen according to the purpose of the mosaic. A splashback, kitchen countertop or cabinet door needs to throw off grease and water, not hold them. A floor or garden path should not be slippery underfoot, nor should it be so uneven that people risk tripping when they walk on it. There is also an aesthetic aspect to choice of texture, so that it suits its setting. A rougher texture might look right in a farmhouse kitchen, but smoothness looks better in a more classical setting. The hardness of metal is ideal in a contemporary loft-style interior, while stone and pebbles are a natural choice for a garden.

Right: A close-up of Norma Vondee's beautiful panel shows how the artist has depicted the sharp, spiky texture of a pineapple and included ridged glass along with rough and smooth ceramic pieces.

Below: The uneven qualities of river-washed glass are very subtle in this mirror frame by Celia Gregory. Within the mosaic are trinkets of china, some of which come from pieces of Tudor pottery.

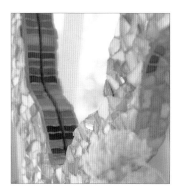

Materials and Techniques

Mosaic is a versatile art form with great potential for personal creativity, and the range of materials available is visually exciting, colourful and tactile. And, as mosaic becomes more popular, the choice of material continues to grow. Planning projects and preparing the materials carefully enables you to create the mosaics you want, and this is followed by the vital grouting and cleaning stages, after which your mosaic is ready to be displayed.

The subtle colours of marble, the opacity of smalti and the sheer opulence of gold leaf make these invaluable materials. These three types of material give a luxurious appearance to any mosaic.

Marble, Smalti and Gold Leaf

Each mosaic material has its own qualities that will influence the colour, style, look and texture of the finished piece. You can choose to work in just one medium or mix materials to create interesting texture and variety. Marble, smalti and gold leaf can work together to produce sumptuous results.

Marble

This is a natural material; it was used in Graeco-Roman•times and is still associated with the luxurious qualities of modern Italian mosaics. Its hard and durable qualities make it excellent for use on floors. Marble is also a subtle material: it represents sheer beauty and natural elegance, and has a depth and timeless quality beyond any other material.

Above right: Marble comes in large slabs that can be cut into squares by hand to produce a more authentic style of mosaic.

Above far right: Smalti has been made for over 2,000 years. It is opaque and creates a wonderfully textural finish to mosaic.

Right: Machine-cut marble in regular squares on mesh or paper backing is effective for covering large areas.

Far right: A selection of tiles with gold and silver leaf twinkle with luxury and magic.

The colours are soft and the variations in tone are subtle: white, chalky pinks and rose, through to delicate greens, blues and blacks. Polishing intensifes the colours. When marble is cut, it has a crystalline appearance and the grains vary according to which part of the world the stone has come from.

For use in mosaics, marble is generally cut from rods with a hammer and hardie (a type of anvil). It is an expensive material, and this limits its use to the finest quality of mosaic.

You can also buy marble that has been machine-cut into regular squares. These squares are laid on to a paper backing, which can be soaked off. The handmade characteristic of the mosaic is lost in this form, but its quality is not impaired, and this is a cheaper form that can be used to cover large areas quickly.

Smalti

Traditionally made in Italy, smalti is opaque glass that is available in a great variety of colours. It is individually made, and the thickness, colour and size vary slightly each time. Each round slab, called a *pizze*, is made from molten glass fired with oxides, metals and powdered marble. Once it has cooled, it is cut into tesserae. It is often sold by the half kilo (1¼lb). *Smalti filati* are threads of glass rods of smalti used for micro-mosaics.

Designs made from smalti have a slightly uneven characteristic that creates a brilliant reflective surface. This bumpiness means that smalti mosaics are often not grouted and cannot be used on floors. Smalti comes in a superb range of colours, and any irregularities create character.

Gold leaf

This is the most opulent tile available to the mosaic artist. It is expensive, yet irresistible, and nothing can surpass its reflective quality. It can be used sparsely in a mosaic and still have a great impact and effect. The tesserae have a backing glass, which is usually

Above: Storing tiles in glass jars is a colourful and practical way to see what you have in stock.

turquoise, yellow or green. Then there is a layer of 24-carat gold leaf, which is protected with a thin layer of clear or coloured glass called the *cartellina*. The gold tesserae can have a smooth or bumpy surface.

Different variations are available with silver or copper leaf, a thin film of gold alloy or other metals. The colours of tile, ranging from deepest gold to vivid blues and greens, are formed when either the *cartellina* or the backing glass is altered.

With their luminous quality, wide range of colours and great choice of surface texture, glass tiles are invaluable to the mosaic artist. Ceramic tiles, which are widely available, offer additional textural variation.

Glass and Ceramic Tiles

These are usually made from vitreous glass and glazed and unglazed clay or porcelain, and come in small, regular tiles. They are laid on to mesh or brown paper to make up sheets measuring approximately 30 x 30cm (12 x 12in), which can be used to cover large areas without the tiles having to be laid individually. The range of materials is always expanding and there is a huge variety of colours and shapes to choose from.

Glass tiles

Vitreous glass is the most commonly used mosaic glass. Its production has been standardized, and it is therefore cheaper than smalti and more accessible to the amateur. It comes in sheets, and the individual tile is a regular square about 2 x 2cm (¾ x ¾in). The

Right: Vitreous glass tiles come on sheets of mesh or brown paper, which are soaked off in warm water. The individual tiles can be clipped into smaller squares.

Above far right: Vitreous glass is a commonly used material; there is a lovely selection of colours. They are easy to clip with mosaic tile nippers.

Far right: Ceramic mosaic tiles come in many shapes and colours, and different kinds of textures.

sheets can be used whole to cover large areas or split into sections for individual mosaics.

Glass is available in a wide variety of colours. The famous Bizzaria range has a grainy quality to the glass and offers a beautiful selection of tiles that have copper blended into the glass, creating a reflective quality that the other tiles can lack. Cutting the individual tiles into four creates the classic square tesserae; the glass is easy to clip and offers extensive potential for intricate design.

There is a now also a new range of glass mosaic made in France. The colours are more rustic than Bizzaria. The glass is smooth and the concentration of the colour is even throughout, appearing like plastic. When these glass tiles are blended with the other glass ranges, they provide the mosaicist with a beautiful palette.

Glass is liable to chip or crack, so tile manufacturers have developed several types of sheet mosaic that are suitable for floors: these are non-slip and non-absorbent and meet many of the regulations associated with commercial properties.

Glass tiles can be shiny, round, square, bumpy, thick, thin, smooth or textured, and come in many different colours. Tiles for mosaic artists are like sweets for children: it is difficult to know which ones to choose. Stored in clear glass jars, the colourful array can be quite spectacular.

Ceramic tiles

Mosaic ceramic tesserae are round or square and are made from porcelain. They are good for creating texture, as they can be glazed or unglazed: a combination of the two creates surface interest. The colour is uniform in unglazed tiles, and the surface is likely to be matt and more porous than glazed tiles. Ceramic tiles are inexpensive and widely available.

Above: Display your mosaic tesserae in groups of colours in clear glass jars. You can easily see what you have available to use, and the gradations of tone and shade.

All the materials mentioned so far build an image using mainly squares. Broken-up household tiles, smashed china and mirror and pieces of stained glass, however, create mosaic pictures in a very different style.

Tiles, China, Mirror and Glass

Shiny household tiles, broken pieces of china, in all colours and shapes, pieces of reflective mirror and shimmering stained glass all bring a new creative freedom to mosaic making.

Household tiles

Glazes on household tiles can be shiny, which enables you to play with the reflection of light in the design. When smashed up into irregular shapes, they are fantastic for working into abstract designs. The random shapes of the pieces also make them excellent for covering three-dimensional and sculptured surfaces. They are easy to handle and allow a freedom in expression that some regular square tiles lack, especially when working over curves.

Household tiles can reflect the contemporary aspect of mosaic. They offer enormous variety and versatility to the mosaic artist and it is possible to cover large areas cheaply with them.

China

The use of broken china is a wonderful way to recycle and make something beautiful out of otherwise useless items. A mosaic created with broken china is completely individual because no two pieces are likely to be the same.

China and crockery are not really suitable for intricate designs, but are wonderful for working with patterns

and texture. The curving nature of the material gives the final mosaic a textured finish. Odd pieces of pottery with quirky handles, lids and patterns can add some humour to a mosaic.

Mirror

You can buy mirror in sheets made up of small squares, or rectangles, or in large sheets that need to be smashed up. Mirror works very well scattered through a coloured mosaic. It also produces a fantastic effect when covering entire surfaces, especially sculptured forms. You can generally get offcuts from a glazier for free.

Stained glass

Walking into a stained glass supplier is like walking into an Aladdin's cave.

Above and above left: Plain household tiles are easy and cheap to obtain and can be easily cut to shape. They are good for sculptures and can be useful when you require the mosaic to be water-resistant.

Not only is there the most beautiful array of colours, but the glass has a wonderful shimmering quality to it, rather like beautiful jewels. There is even a stained glass that is iridescent and reflects light like mother-of-pearl.

Some types of stained glass are pieces of art in themselves. They can be used to cover whole surfaces for a luxurious finish or used in small areas to highlight details in a picture or an abstract pattern. Using stained glass in a mosaic design will create something extra special.

Right: The uneven quality of broken cups and plates creates texture, and the patterns and designs are also interesting to play around with in your own designs.

Below and below centre: Stained glass offers a beautiful array of colours and textures, and possesses wonderful reflective qualities. Each sheet of glass could be a piece of art in itself, and when it is broken up into small fragments provides a fantastic mosaic material.

Below far right: Recycling broken ceramics to use in mosaic is an inventive and cheap source of materials. Collect pieces, and sort them by colour and pattern.

When making decorative mosaics, you can use both traditional materials and more unusual found and collected objects, ranging from shells and washed glass from beaches, to glass jewels and semi-precious stones.

Mixed Media

Using a variety of materials can bring personality and originality to mosaic designs. Mixed materials are particularly effective in sculptural mosaics and for creating a variety of textures and depth in two-dimensional work. It is also fun to gather a collection, such as natural materials from beaches or rivers, or old china from second-hand or thrift stores. There are no boundaries to what can be used, and it can be challenging to experiment with new methods and new materials.

Pebbles

Some of the earliest known mosaics were made from pebbles, and there is still a strong tradition in making pebble mosaics in Greece. In Lindos, Rhodes, you can find many pebble doorsteps and pavements.

Pebbles from the sea or rivers can be found in many subtle colour variations. They have a certain simplicity that is easy on the eye. They are long-lasting and it is possible to seal them, which makes them appear wet and the colours richer. Pebbles are traditionally used to cover large areas in gardens. They offer good drainage, and the simple designs look good without being overpowering.

Left: Glass beads with a flat metallic back used for making jewellery are brilliant for bringing a sparkle to mosaics.

Top: Stone, marble and slate can be cut into small pieces to create natural, subtle yet textural, mosaics.

Top: Small pieces of washed glass can be added to mosaics for effect. Their soft colours give a gentle look.

Top: Glass, plastic and antique beads all work well in mosaics, adding texture and colour to the work.

Above: Shells come in beautiful soft colours and are traditionally used in grottoes or garden follies.

Above: Washed glass and old pottery can often be found on a riverbank. Both will add character to a mosaic.

Above: Pebbles are good for creating simple, lasting designs and have natural muted tones and textural qualities.

Shells

Seashells, in their teeming variety of shapes and colours, have provided inspiration for craftspeople for centuries. The Chinese used mother-of-pearl for inlaying. Shells bedded into lime cement line the grottoes of Italian Renaissance gardens, and 18th-century European country house owners adorned their garden follies with them.

Salvaged materials

The edges of washed glass and pottery that have been smoothed and rounded by years of erosion in the water can be found on beaches and riverbanks. The effect of the water also softens the colours to create a gentle mosaic material. Collected or salvaged materials could include anything from old coins to forks and spoons. Metal foil, building blocks or even dice can be used.

Beads and jewels

Glass beads and jewels catch the light and twinkle. Their unevenness creates texture, which emphasizes the detail in a mosaic. Antique beads often have peculiarities within the glass that make them distinctive. You can buy jewels created for jewellery making that have a flat back, which makes them easier to lay, and placed in a mosaic they will add glints of colour.

Creating a design is fun, and collecting ideas in a scrapbook will be very useful for inspiring your projects. The design will affect your choice of materials, colours and style and the most suitable method of application.

Planning Projects

Take inspiration for your designs from books, magazines, other artists, nature or any other source that stimulates you. Keep any pictures or images that grab your attention for reference later. Stick them in a scrapbook and make notes about what you liked.

Drawings

The initial drawing will be only a guideline for your mosaic. Keep it simple and clear, with strong lines. If you cannot draw, trace an image or cut out a photocopy, and enlarge or adjust it to a suitable size and draw around it. It may be a good idea to make a few copies, so that you can try out different colour schemes before buying the tiles.

When you start applying the tesserae, your ideas may change as you work. This is all part of the evolutionary process of responding to the materials and their colour and texture.

It is not usually necessary to make all the design decisions at the beginning of the project. Creativity is a journey; allow the space during the process for new ideas and additions to unfold. When thinking about your design, bear in mind the colours, textures and contrast of the materials. Also, bear in mind how much time you want to spend on your mosaic, as this may influence the intricacy and complexity of the design.

Starting out

If the task is site specific, make an accurate template with graph paper or brown paper and/or take measurements before you start the detailed planning and work. Make clear notes while you are on site so it is easy to decipher the figures and information gathered when you are in your studio. It may help to photograph the site, too.

If you are a beginner, it is best to start with basic techniques and a small project, such as a pot stand, terracotta pot or small wall panel. As you become more confident, you can be more ambitious and explore your creativity.

Choosing tiles

The appearance of the mosaic is totally dependent on the materials you use. The design may even revolve around using a certain tile, the unique quality of which is your source of inspiration. Discovering how different materials work alone and with each other is an exciting aspect of mosaic artistry that takes time to master.

There is a fantastic range of tiles from all over the world in different colours, glazes and textures. You can use stone, with its soft colours, or choose from a lavish range of stained glass. There is no shortage of choice.

Aside from aesthetic decisions, there are various factors to take into account when choosing. The cost could be a consideration; for example marble is a very beautiful and durable material, but it is very expensive, while porcelain is a much cheaper alternative.

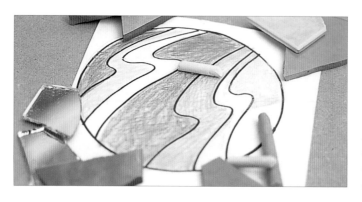

Left: It is useful to make a simple line drawing first using a soft pencil, then emphasize the lines with a black pen and shade in the colours to be mosaiced.

Above: There is a huge range of mosaic tiles to choose from. Vitreous glass tiles, shown here, are best suited to indoor work.

Left: Tile sample boards are a useful way of choosing colours and tiles for a project. Tile suppliers have a wealth of knowledge, and it is important to check with them that the tiles you choose suit the project you are undertaking.

Qualities of tiles

Not all tiles are suitable for all situations, so it is vital to make the right choice if your mosaic is to last. Each tile and material varies, so check their qualities and uses when you buy them.

Glass tiles or stained glass would be damaged quickly if positioned on a floor and exposed to high heels. Glazes also come in varying levels of hardness; a soft glaze would restrict the tile use to inside. A harder glaze can be used on the floor, and a frost-proof tile can be used outside. The fired clay that lies under the glaze also has its own individual qualities, such as absorbency, which can affect whether the tiles are suitable for a shower or bathroom.

choosing the right technique

Each project is different and no task is approached in exactly the same way. You need to decide which technique to use and the suitable fixing agents that are required. Here are some questions that you should consider before starting:

- Where is the piece to be finally positioned?
- Will you work directly, for example on to the pot?
- Will you choose a semi-indirect method, for example on to mesh, which is good for a floor panel?

- Is the site accessible, or is it easier to make the mosaic off-site?
- How durable does the mosaic need to be?
- Does the mosaic need to be water-resistant, waterproof, weather- or frost-proof?

While a small project could be made in the kitchen, it is advisable to allocate a special space in which to work, giving you a clean area for drawing and a workbench or table for doing the mosaic.

Creating a Workspace

The workspace is your own creative environment, so some wall space should be allocated for displaying your finished mosaics and any images that inspire you. Shelving will be needed, to store books, files, tools and materials, and a water supply is essential.

Posture

The most comfortable way to mosaic is definitely working at an easel or a table. It is important to have the seat or stool at a suitable height. It is worth spending time getting this right so that a good posture can be maintained and you can avoid shoulder and back strain.

Lighting

Ideally, the table or workbench should be placed near a natural source of light. Daylight is the best way to see true colour. When light is limited or when you are working at night, daylight bulbs are ideal. It is best to have more than one light source to avoid shadows.

Storage

When organizing materials, it is a good idea to build shelving and store tiles in glass or clear plastic jars, so it is easy to see how much stock you have and all the different colours. Tools are expensive and rust easily, so keep them clean and dry. Adhesives and grouts solidify if they get wet, so they must all

safety

These are sensible precautions you can take to avoid injuring yourself:

- Wear goggles when cutting materials to avoid getting fragments in your eyes. Hold the mosaic tile nippers away from your face.
- Wear a face mask when cutting wood or mixing powder to avoid inhaling fine powder into sinuses and lungs.
- Wear hardwearing gloves when cutting wire and use rubber or latex gloves when mixing up powders, and also when grouting, cleaning or sculpting. Your hands

be stored in a damp-free area, preferably in sealed containers. Most chemicals have a limited shelf life and can go off, so should be checked regularly.

Large mosaics

When working on a mosaic that is too big for a table or easel, you should work on, or at least prepare the design on, the floor. You will need a hard

Left: Larger projects can be planned on the floor or in an area where it is possible to see the whole design.

will get dry and sore if they come into contact with water and adhesives for too long. It is also recommended to wear thin latex gloves when making mosaics. Take care, and keep antiseptic cream, plasters and hand cream on your shelving.

- Hold mosaic tile nippers at the far end of the handle to avoid hand blisters.
- Always clean and vacuum the work area regularly to avoid an unnecessary build-up of dust.
- Create your mosaic with awareness of the safety of those around you, as well as yourself.

surface, so if the floor is carpeted, use a large piece of wood. If you are using mesh or brown paper, you should draw up the design and get a clear under-standing of the whole image. Then you can cut the image into fragments and work in sections on the workbench.

If you need to see the whole design develop, it is best to work on the floor and protect the surrounding surfaces with plastic sheeting. This can be hard on the back, so you should take regular breaks and have a good stretch.

Preparing for work

Once you have chosen where and how to work and what to mosaic, you should gather all the required tools and materials together, mix enough fixing agents for the immediate work

and prepare a good range of tiles before commencing.

Keep the work area clean, sweeping away loose fragments regularly. It also makes good sense to keep coloured tiles in some kind of order, placing different tiles, colours and shapes in separate small piles, for ease of use. When working with cement-based adhesive, clean off any excess while it is damp; if left overnight, the cement will harden and become very difficult to remove from the surface it is on.

Cleaning up

Sweep up or vacuum at the end of each session, as fragments get every-where and can be sharp. Cleaning and reorganizing will also make the next day's work much easier. If different

Above: Good light, a work surface and seating at the right height for good posture are essential for comfortable and productive mosaic making.

Above left: Gloves, goggles and face masks should be worn to protect against any injury or harmful inhalation caused by sharp chips or ground glass or tile.

cement-based adhesives and grouts are allowed to mix in the drains, this can cause serious blockages and endless problems. When cleaning mixing bowls that held these materials, there-fore, always scrape out and throw away as much excess as possible, before washing away the residue. Placing gauze over the plug can avoid the need to clean the drains regularly.

The materials for a mosaic usually need some form of preparation for the work. Tiles can be smashed, nipped or sawn, glass cut and marble or smalti reduced to the correct size pieces by a hammer and hardie.

Preparing Materials

By preparing and clipping the materials you will be using before you start the mosaic – in the same way as a painter would mix a palette of paints – you will be free to concentrate on laying the mosaic design.

Sheet mosaic

Many mosaic tiles come on sheets, either on fibreglass mesh or on brown paper; the tiles are about 2cm (¾in) square and the sheets are approximately 30cm (12in) square. These are useful for laying a large area.

When making smaller mosaics using sheet mosaic, you should take the tiles off their backing. To remove the tiles from sheets formed with brown paper or mesh, soak the whole sheets in clean warm water. When the glue has dissolved, the tiles will slip off the backing material easily.

Smashed ceramic tiles

Antoni Gaudí is famous for his extensive use of mosaic in his fairytale buildings in Barcelona. They are very colourful and predominantly use ceramic tiles smashed into small fragments. Ceramic tiles come in an enormous range of colours, tones, textures and glazes, and are suitable for both interior and exterior use, as many are frost-proof. They are fun and easy to work with.

Clipping tiles

Mosaic tile nippers are the essential tool for any mosaicist, and are good for clipping most materials. With practice, intricate shapes can be achieved.

The mosaic nippers should be held at the end of the handles for the best possible leverage. The rounded side of the head is placed over the tile, which need be inserted only a few millimetres. To cut the tile in half, the nippers are positioned in the centre of the tile with the head pointing in the direction the cut is needed. Holding the opposite edge of the tile between thumb, fore-

finger and index finger will stabilize it. The ends of the handles are then presssed together.

Goggles are essential, as initially the tiles seem to fly all over the place. With practice, however, it becomes possible to control the cuts, and the fingers support the bits in place. If the cut goes astray, the excess can be nibbled away on the edge of the tile.

Cutting and sawing tiles

A hand tile cutter is the tool traditionally used for cutting tiles, and it is available from do-it-yourself stores. It

smashing ceramic tiles

1 Wearing goggles and protective gloves, smash the tiles with a small hammer, aiming at the centre of the tile. To make these fragments smaller, gently smash with a hammer in the centre of each fragment.

2 Pieces can fly all over the place if you hit the tile too hard, so for protection, cover the tiles with a cloth and wear goggles. Use the mosaic nippers to shape the ceramics into the size and style required.

Right: Glass and mirror can be cut with a glass cutter. The surface is scored lightly, using a metal rule as a guide, then broken.

Far right: A hammer and hardie are used to break thick materials, such as stone and smalti, into pieces.

will cut straight lines on tiles, though its use is limited to ceramic tiles with a soft clay base.

Hard floor tiles or stone need to be cut with a wet tile saw. This specialized piece of equipment is essential for certain tasks, such as cutting thin strips of marble, which are then made into the correct size for mosaicing with a hammer and hardie. It is possible to hire wet tile saws.

The saw cuts the material with a metal disc that is revolved by a motor and kept cool with water. As the tile hits the blade, the water can spray out, making this quite a messy but effective technique needing protective clothing.

Cutting glass

A glass cutter is used for cutting straight lines or large shapes in stained glass and mirror.

Right: (from the top) Tile cutters, for cutting straight lines; a tile scorer; mosaic tile nippers, for cutting tiles into shapes; a craft (utility) knife; and a glass cutter for cutting glass and mirror.

The surface should be scored lightly with the cutter, then the ball of the cutter used to tap the underside gently; it will crack along the line. Tile nippers are good for making smaller cuts and detailed shapes.

Goggles and gloves should be worn when handling glass and mirror, since even the smallest splinters cut easily.

Cutting stone and smalti

A hammer and hardie are the traditional tools for cutting stone and smalti, both of which are too thick for modern tile clippers. The material is held over the chisel between the thumb and forefinger and the hammer swung down on to this point. With practice, accurate cutting is obtained.

Mosaics can be laid on to a variety of different surfaces, and, as long as the correct procedures are followed, they will be hardwearing and waterproof and have a professional-quality finish.

Preparation and Fixing

Traditional mosaics were laid on to a cement bed. Now, we can also mosaic on to all sorts of different surfaces, such as wood, old furniture, plaster, ceramic, terracotta or fibreglass.

Bases

Unless working with a sculptured form, you should work on to a flat, even surface for a professional-quality mosaic. Uneven surfaces should be sanded down. If working on to cement, a new surface should be laid; self-levelling cement is an easy option.

The base or surface should be rigid. For example, floorboards are flexible, and any mosaic laid on them will lift if there is movement. So a thin layer of wood should be cut to fit and screwed in evenly to cover the entire surface.

Wood is a very good base, but if the mosaic is going outside or will come into contact with water, the wood must be exterior grade, such as marine ply.

Priming surfaces

Most working surfaces, such as wood, concrete, terracotta urns, old furniture or plaster, are porous, so the surface must be sealed with diluted PVA (white) glue (see box below). This greatly improves the sticking power of adhesive and makes the final mosaic more hardwearing and waterproof.

Before sealing, it is important to ensure that the surface is clean of all loose debris and hair. Smooth surfaces, such as wood or fine plaster, should be scored with a sharp implement, such as a bradawl or craft (utility) knife. On more slippery surfaces, such as plastics or existing tiles, a special two-part resin primer can be brushed on to provide a key. It creates a surface to which an adhesive can easily attach.

Diluted PVA glue can also be used to coat terracotta pots in order to make them frost-resistant.

Fixing methods

Once the surface has been properly prepared, there are various ways to fix the tiles. Choosing which technique to use depends partly on where the mosaic is situated and partly on personal preference. The direct method involves placing the material straight on to the working surface. The indirect method involves creating the mosaic off-site, then installing it. Two semi-indirect methods are worked on to paper or mesh off-site and then fitted into the cement on-site, so combining aspects of both methods.

Traditional stone and smalti mosaics were laid straight on to a bed of cement. Modern materials, however, are often much thinner, and need to be stuck as well as embedded.

priming wood

1 Take a craft (utility) knife and score the surface of the wood, creating a key. This improves the grip between the tiles and the adhesive.

2 Mix up PVA (white) glue with water in a ratio of 1 part glue to 3 parts water. Apply this evenly with a dense sponge or a paintbrush.

Right: You will need some, if not all, of these tools to prepare surfaces and apply adhesive. Clockwise from top left: hard bristle brush, paintbrush for glue, notched trowel, hammer, chisel, flexible knife, dustpan and brush, rubber spreader and adhesive applicator.

Direct method

This method involves simply sticking the tesserae, face up, on to the base, which has been covered with a layer of cement-based tile adhesive. It is good for working on to wood or sculpture forms, when working with smashed ceramic tiles, washed glass, tiles of different heights, or when covering large areas. It is also good to work directly into adhesive because it avoids having to spend extra time fitting and allows the design to develop in the environment where the mosaic is situated.

The direct method is easiest to start with and recommended for beginners.

Indirect method

Originally, this technique was devised as a way of making large-scale mosaics off-site, so that they could be moved ready-made, then laid in position. The design would be sectioned into manageable areas, and each area made into a slab. It is equally useful, however, for mosaics that cannot be laid directly due to an awkward location.

working with cement-based tile adhesive

1 Mix white cement-based tile adhesive with water in the ratio of 2½ parts powder to 1 part water, until you have a smooth consistency. Choose and prepare the tiles you are going to use. Apply adhesive to the base with a flexible knife.

2 Stick the tesserae into the adhesive, ensuring good contact by pushing them in with your fingertips. If you use too much adhesive, the excess will squeeze through the gaps and get messy, but if you use too little, the tesserae will fall off.

A wooden frame is made to the size of the finished slab, and greased internally with petroleum jelly. The mosaic is appplied to a piece of brown paper marked with the dimensions of the slab, using the semi-indirect brown paper method (see right).

When the tesserae are dry, the frame is placed over the paper and dry sand sprinkled over the design and nudged into the crevices with a soft brush. The frame is then filled with mortar. The surface is smoothed, then covered with damp newspaper and polythene (polyethylene) sheeting and left to dry slowly for five to six days.

When the mortar is dry, the slab and frame are turned over and the brown paper dampened with a wet sponge, then peeled away. The frame is unscrewed and the slab removed.

Brown paper method

This reverse technique involves gluing the tesserae into position off-site, then setting them into adhesive on-site, cutting up the sheets of mosaic if needed.

When using this technique, the tesserae are glued face down on brown paper with PVA (white) glue; if they are uneven in any way, the irregularity will occur on the underside of the mosaic, making this method ideal for mosaics requiring a smooth surface.

The front of the mosaic is invisible during the design process, so this method is limited to tesserae that are coloured right through.

Once the mosaic sheet is pressed into the waiting adhesive, and been left to dry for 24 hours, the brown paper is soaked off with a wet sponge.

Mesh method

In this second semi-indirect method, fine-weave fibreglass mesh acts as a perfect base for the mosaic. The tesserae are stuck face up on to the mesh, so it

the direct method using PVA glue

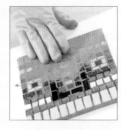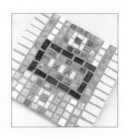

1 Cut a piece of wood to the desired size. Clip a selection of tiles into quarters and halves. Experiment with the tesserae; the design does not need to be complicated.

2 Once you are happy with the design, use a small brush to apply the PVA (white) glue to the back of the tesserae, and stick them in place and leave to dry.

3 Mix up some grey powder grout with water in the ratio of 3½ parts grout to 1 part water. Apply with your fingertips, wearing rubber (latex) gloves.

4 Wipe down the surface with a damp sponge to remove all traces of grout on the tesserae. Once the grout is dry, polish the tiles with a dry, soft cloth.

Left: The completed mosaic, on its brown paper base, needs to be cut into sections that can be handled easily.

is possible to see the mosaic design developing and taking shape. If the mosaic is large, it can be cut up and transported easily. When the tesserae are secure on the mesh, it is pressed, face up, into the adhesive and left to dry.

Cement-based tile adhesives

There is a vast range of modern cement-based tile adhesives for use on both direct and indirect mosaics. They come in a variety of shades, mainly white and grey. Your choice of colour will be influenced by what colour you want to grout in: grey for grey, black or dark colours; white for lighter shades.

Medium-strength adhesive comes in tubs ready-mixed, which is fine for decorative pieces or if the mosaic does not need to be particularly waterproof.

Most large tile companies have their recommended range of cement-based adhesive and additives. It is worth asking which materials are most suitable for the job you are undertaking. There is a variety of products for all situations, from exterior frost-proof, cement-based adhesives through to flexible liquid additives, such as admix, which can be added for extra protection against movement or to make the adhesive suitable for a shower.

PVA glue

This is good for sticking tiles directly on to wood, when it should be used undiluted. For priming or sealing, dilute PVA (white) glue 3:1 with water. It is water-based, so its use is limited to internal use only. It dries slowly, so tiles may be repositioned.

Epoxy resin glue

This is a strong glue made up of two separate components: the hardener and the resin. It is good for use in underwater locations or in damp places, but it has a limited working time and is sticky and toxic, so a face mask should be worn. Epoxy resin glue is useful when working with the direct method as it sets in just four hours, reducing drying times drastically.

Right: This soft mesh is used for subtle relief work, while chicken wire is more effective for larger-scale sculpting. Big exterior sculpting can be formed with bricks or breezeblocks (cinderblocks) then covered with a layer of tile adhesive.

Far right: In the mesh method, the mosaic pieces are glued, face up, straight on to the fibreglass mesh.

Grouting is incredibly satisfying: it unifies the mosaic and blends the images and colours. Designs that felt garish or too busy are softened, and patterns that work with movement come to life.

Grouting

On a practical level, grouting is when the gaps between the tiles are filled with a cement mortar that has a different quality to the adhesives. The process strengthens the mosaic and makes it waterproof. Grouting ensures that mosaic can be a functional art form that can be used in swimming pools, showers, water features, external wall murals or lavish floors.

Grout comes either ready-mixed or in a powder and in a variety of colours. There are also powdered stains that you can add to create almost any colour you want. The colour you choose will have a profound effect on the colours and look of the finished mosaic. Some of these differences can be seen in the four panels below. The grid of grey grout overpowers the neutral tiles, and the white grout is also very strong. The cream grout works well with the white tiles, as there is balance, while the beige grout warms the white tiles.

Note that white grout will blend with pale tiles, lighten darker colours and contrast blacks, while black grout will deepen blacks and blues, make reds and greens really rich and contrast with white. The qualities and varieties are endless, giving you great scope for creativity.

Grouting is a messy job, especially if stains are used, so clothes and surroundings should be well protected and rubber gloves should be worn to protect the hands.

When to grout

The finished mosaic should be grouted when the tile adhesive is dry. Before

Right: These four panels of neutral vitreous glass mosaic were grouted in four different shades: clockwise from top left, beige, grey, cream and white.

Below: Grout comes in different colours, which can dramatically alter the finished look of the mosaic.

being grouted, small mosaics can be gently shaken to remove loose adhesive, and any loose tiles can be re-adhered. On larger-scale mosaics, light vacuuming can be effective.

On a large-scale project, the whole surface should not be grouted in one go, because when you start to clean off the grout, the first areas may have already dried. One section should be grouted at a time, then cleaned off before the next section is begun. The grout should be left to dry for 24 hours until it is completely hard.

Above: For grouting and cleaning your mosaics, you will need a mixing trowel, a grout spreader, some cleaning cloths, a sponge, a bowl and protective sheeting.

Above: Wear rubber gloves and grout your mosaic using a rubber spreader. Rub the grout into any gaps using your fingertips.

grouting and cleaning

1 When the mosaic is being laid, adhesive can squeeze through the gaps between the tesserae. Scrape this away with a blade or craft (utility) knife. Then ensure that the mosaic is clean.

2 Wearing rubber gloves, mix together the powdered grout and clean water in a bowl. Follow the manufacturer's instructions to achieve the right consistency.

3 Apply the grout over the mosaic, using your fingers, a grout spreader or a rubber spreader. Push the paste into the gaps and smooth it evenly over the whole surface.

4 Wipe away any excess grout with a damp sponge. After 10 minutes, any remaining excess grout can be rubbed away easily with a dry cloth. (If left much longer, remove with a nail-brush or paint scraper.)

Once the colours and the design of the mosaic have been revealed by the cleaning process, attention must be paid to where and how to present the finished work, how to light it and how to maintain its beauty.

Finishing Your Work

If the tesserae of the mosaic have a shiny glaze, the grout will have come off easily with the sponging process. Matt porcelain, however, holds the grout, making it harder to clean.

It is possible to buy an acid called patio cleaner, used by builders for cleaning cement off brickwork. When diluted with warm water, it is very effective for removing resilient grout. If sponged or poured on to the mosaic, it will make a fizzing noise as it eats away at the grout left on the surface of the tiles. After a few minutes, the dirty water can be sponged away. Resistant areas can be removed with a paint-scraper or abrasive paper, before being polished with clean cloths.

Sealing

Stone and pebbles look richer when sealed, appearing slightly wet and retaining their subtlety of tone without the addition of a varnish or shine to the surface. Sealants come in matt or shiny varieties.

Beeswax can be rubbed on to matt tiles to give them a deeper colour. Terracotta tiles need to be treated with linseed oil. This is flammable, so always dispose of cloths that the oil comes into contact with carefully.

Siting

There are no hard-and-fast rules about where to site your mosaic; it is a matter of judgement and common sense,

which you must learn to trust. Asking someone to hold the mosaic in place so you can have a look is always wise. You can usually tell when the site is right. If you are unsure, you can swap with your helper to ask their opinion.

Aside from the positioning of the mosaic, the colour of the surrounding walls must be taken into consideration. You do not want the walls to clash with the mosaic, or for them to overpower it.

Hanging

A small mosaic can be hung like a picture, using wire and picture hooks. Hanging a larger, heavier mosaic, however, requires more thought.

Far left: This colourful panel is lightened by the white grout, and the glazed tiles laid in a Gaudí-style mosaic have a fresh flowing feel. To clean, first spray the mosaic with glass cleaner. Any proprietary window cleaner will do. If you do not have this, use some water with vinegar added to reduce smearing.

Left: Polish with a clean dry cloth, preferably a lint-free one, and you should achieve a good shine on the glass and the glazed ceramic tiles. The colours weave into each other, while the mirror and glass balls make shimmering focal points within the mosaic.

It is important to find out whether the wall you intend to fix the mosaic to can hold the weight. Plasterboard (gypsum board) will not, so if it is a partition wall, the mosaic must be fixed to a supporting strut.

When fixing into brick or plaster, you will need to drill holes, using a drill bit that is compatible with the size of screw you have chosen. The correct position for the fixings should be marked on the wall with a pen. Wall plugs (plastic anchors) should be placed in the drilled holes to give the screws something to grip on to, then the mosaic can be hung in place.

Mosaic panels can also be fixed to the wall with mirror plates. Protruding mirror plates are fitted to the wood at the edge of the panel and then the mirror plates are screwed to the wall. Those with a keyhole opening are fitted to the back; they then slot over screws inserted into the wall.

Lighting

Mosaics nearly always look their best in natural light, with its soft tones. Yet the night-time light is important and needs consideration.

A mosaic could be lit with a spotlight fixed on the ceiling or a traditional picture light. It is important not to over-light and bleach out the colours and subtle reflective quality of

the tiles. Different colours and wattages of bulb, as well as different angles and distances, should all be tried.

Maintenance

The best way to maintain a mosaic is to clean it regularly, so avoiding the build-up of resilient dirt. A floor mosaic should be swept and mopped with a gentle cleaning agent, making sure the dirty water is removed properly. Decorative mosaics should be dusted and cleaned using glass cleaner and a dry cloth. Bathroom mosaics should be cleaned as any other tile.

Above: These are some of the tools you may need when siting and installing your mosaic. Clockwise, from top right: saw, hammer, abrasive paper, wire (steel) wool, U-shaped hooks, pliers, screwdriver, picture wire, picture hooks, hanging hooks, screw eyes, screws, wall plugs (plastic anchors) and eraser.

If the mosaic has got really dirty, the patio cleaner referred to opposite should be used, though it may be necessary to re-grout after cleaning. If the correct maintenance steps are taken, the mosaic could last for a millennium.

Ornaments

Ornaments are not just the frippery that they are made out to be. Often they are useful objects that we need to have around the house or garden, but that can be disguised or decorated in such a way as to make them a pleasure to have around. Even those objects which are solely decorative do perform a psychological function in brightening up our everyday lives. All the projects have been graded from one to five, one being the easiest.

Ornamental items offer a limitless supply of design opportunities for the mosaicist: from simple objects, such as a plant pot or letter rack, to more advanced items, such as a lamp base, vase or fire screen.

Indoor Ornaments

Mosaic is an effective disguise for many everyday objects, transforming the mundane or mass-produced into something original. Containers, in particular, make excellent subjects for mosaic decoration. Plant pots, terracotta urns, candle-holders, vases and bowls are just a few suggestions.

Smaller ornaments

Excellent hunting grounds for objects to mosaic – such as picture frames, plain wooden boxes, old pots and bowls – are car-boot (garage) sales, junk (thrift) shops and even house clearance auctions. "Job lot" boxes of assorted odds and ends can be picked up extremely cheaply. These do not require a huge commitment in terms of time, effort or cost of materials, making them good items on which to practise your ideas and techniques. The objects can be functional or purely decorative.

A letter rack, house number plaque, pot stand or a china tile would be ideal choices to start with, since they are regular in shape, can be laid flat and are easy to work with. A set of mats or coasters would be an easy way of experimenting with colour and patterns before embarking on larger projects. Some decorative spheres, in a wide range of patterns and colours, a

Below left: Gentle spiralling bands of mosaic cover this tall terracotta urn.

Below centre: Pots of fresh herbs in the kitchen become decorative objects in their own right.

Below right: Squares of textured coloured glass cast beautiful patterns when a candle is lit in this mosaic candle-holder.

Above: This large, striped, stained-glass mosaic bowl was made by Martin Cohen.

group of cheerful plant pots and simple mirror frame would expand your repertoire a little, while still being fairly simple projects that are easy to work.

A contemporary mosaic bowl can be made by buying a shallow, light, wooden, metal or plastic shape to which you can adhere mosaic on the inside only. This will give you a stable base on to which to add your pattern.

Larger ornaments

Once you have gained confidence, you may feel ready to try some items that are more ambitious in terms of scale or complexity.

A tray for the kitchen gives scope for quite a large design, with a ready-made border formed by the sides. A floral lamp base for the sitting room worked on a breezeblock (cinderblock) combines both artistry and some basic wiring, while a spiral lamp stand makes use of an old carpet tube.

The cosmic clock – at home in any room – could be an inspiration for many different clock designs. A hole must always to drilled to allow for the spindle to be pushed through to the front, and the mosaic design must avoid tiling over this hole. The surface decoration needs to be designed to allow for the function of the clock and the movement of the hands.

Looking to the bedroom, the floral trinket box transforms a plain wooden box into a work of great beauty.

One of the most popular subjects for mosaic is the mirror frame, and the variety of effects shown in this chapter gives an indication why. Mirrors are useful objects both for practical reasons and decorative ones.

Mirror Frames

Mirror frames can be bought ready made, or they can be made from many diverse materials that can be customized with mosaic. They can be flat or include three-dimensional or sculptural elements. They can also be as extravagant or simple as you want. They provide an excellent platform for self-expression, and you can explore combinations of colour and texture to create collage-like effects.

Right: This large, curved mirror was inspired by a Gustav Klimt painting, reflected in the shape of the design. Its use of flowing lines of gold smalti, broken up in a rhythmic pattern, makes a very decorative and individual piece, designed by Norma Vondee.

Below: A pair of complementary circular mirrors are given extra interest by having the mirrors placed off-centre.

Left: Two differently toned variations of the same style mirror echoing the soft, warm tones of the wooden floor.

Opposite: This large, curvaceous mirror by Celia Gregory was made from washed glass collected from the banks of the River Thames, and contrasts with the angular shape of the fireplace. The soft greens beautifully complement the whites and neutral tones of the room.

Only the most minimalist of gardeners wishes to exclude any suggestion of ornament from their garden. Containers, in particular, are an ideal choice for mosaic and provide a welcome splash of colour in any garden.

Garden Ornaments

Mosaic seems quite at home in a garden, adding a touch of colour to a dull area, or providing a dramatic focal point. Blue colour schemes are ideal to complement the surrounding green.

Pots and containers

Mosaic can be applied to many kinds of garden containers, from night lights, window boxes and chimney pots to the largest urn. The most commonly covered containers are, however, ceramic pots. Use a frost-resistant terracotta pot as a base where you can, and if it is not glazed, you must varnish the inside to stop moisture seeping through from

the inside and pushing off the tesserae. This is important if the pot is to be used for plants that are left outside. It is also advisable to use water- and frost-resistant cements and grouts.

There is also a wide range of excellent plastic containers available that accurately replicate almost any kind of finish you care to name, from verdigris, terracotta and copper to stone, but have the advantage of being lightweight. Mosaic can be applied to add detail and personalize any of these types of pot. Once a pot is covered in mosaic, no one will know that the base is plastic rather than terracotta.

An elaborately carved or shaped antique-style container, in real or simulated stone, may need a different treatment to simple plant pots. Large urns look good partially covered with mosaic, as it highlights the contrast between the pot and mosaic, but tesserae should be chosen to enhance the base colour. Urns make stunning focal points and add a sculptural feel to any garden.

Considerations to take into account concern the appearance of not only the container but also the plants. Your design and chosen colour palette should complement the environment. For example, a restrained geometric design would suit a clipped topiary box tree, but a more vibrant, abstract design would harmonize with bright red geraniums.

Surroundings

In any garden, the plants must be the first feature. You do not want any decoration to "shout" at the plants or detract from their beauty. When planning your design, therefore, you must make the surrounding plants your first consideration, so that your mosaic design echoes their beauty.

Left: A bright urn, and accompanying birdbath, with strong colours and designs are ideal for dark or shady courtyards.

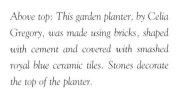

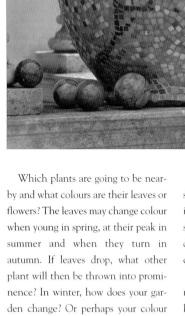

Above top: This garden planter, by Celia Gregory, was made using bricks, shaped with cement and covered with smashed royal blue ceramic tiles. Stones decorate the top of the planter.

Above: In a predominantly green space, brightly patterned ceramic pots by Cleo Mussi add interest.

Above right: This traditional garden urn is decorated with unusual modern faces in subtle, muted tones.

Which plants are going to be near-by and what colours are their leaves or flowers? The leaves may change colour when young in spring, at their peak in summer and when they turn in autumn. If leaves drop, what other plant will then be thrown into prominence? In winter, how does your garden change? Or perhaps your colour scheme is subdued, with grasses and low-maintenance shrubs or evergreens. In this case, do you want ornaments to blend in or stand out?

Out of doors, even under cloudy skies, light is ever-changing and so very important. Will your mosaic be in shade, dappled shade or full sun? What does it look like under different weather conditions, from bright sun to rain?

For all these considerations, you need to choose whether you want to keep to gentle shades and natural tones or opt for bold, bright colours that have impact. Either way, mosaic will complement the natural surroundings and allow your plants to shine.

Made with tesserae cut from brightly coloured tiles and small pieces of mirror, this striking number plaque should be clearly visible from a distance. A larger plaque could be made to display a house name.

House Number Plaque

you will need

12mm (½in) thick chipboard (particle board)

saw

felt-tipped pen

PVA (white) glue

paintbrushes

ceramic household tiles: yellow, mid-blue and dark blue

mirror

tile nippers

tile adhesive

flexible knife

black tile grout

grout spreader

sponge

waterproof exterior paint

wall fastening

screws

screwdriver

soft cloth

clear glass polish

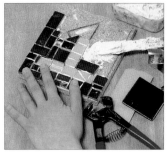

1 Cut a piece of chipboard to size, depending on the length of the house number required. The one used here is 18 x 15cm (7 x 6in). Draw the house number on the chipboard, making sure it is at least 1.5cm (⅝in) wide. If you wish, you can also mark the intended positions of the mirror. Paint the chipboard – front, back and sides – with diluted PVA glue. Leave to dry thoroughly.

2 Cut the tiles and mirror into small pieces using tile nippers. First tile the number with the yellow tesserae you have cut, sticking them on the base, a small area at a time, with tile adhesive. Then tile the area around the number in both shades of blue, cutting and applying small pieces of mirror to the marked positions. Wipe off any excess tile adhesive and leave the plaque to dry for 24 hours.

3 Cover the surface with black tile grout, filling all the gaps between the tesserae so no moisture can penetrate to the chipboard base. Spread the grout along the edges of the plaque, then leave to dry for about 10 minutes. Sponge off the excess grout and leave to dry for a further 24 hours. Paint the back with an exterior paint and fix a clip for hanging. Polish the plaque with a soft cloth and clear glass polish.

As well as protecting your table top, this mosaic pot stand will brighten up any meal time. The geometric shape is integral to the pattern in which the brightly coloured tesserae are laid.

Pot Stand

you will need

12mm (½in) thick chipboard (particle board), 30 x 30cm (12 x 12in)

pencil

metal ruler

PVA (white) glue

paintbrush

jigsaw (saber saw)

abrasive paper

ceramic household tiles: yellow, dark blue and lilac

tile nippers

mirror

tile adhesive

flexible knife

black tile grout

grout spreader

sponge

felt

scissors

soft cloth

clear glass polish

1 Using the template provided, carefully mark the proportions of the pot stand on to the piece of chipboard; use a metal ruler to make sure the lines are straight.

Prime both sides of the chipboard with diluted PVA glue and leave to dry. Cut around the outline of the design using a jigsaw. Sand down any rough edges and prime with diluted PVA glue. Leave to dry.

2 Using tile nippers, cut the tiles into small pieces that will fit inside the shapes you have drawn. Here, small pieces of mirror have been added to the dark blue sections, and small pieces of the dark blue tiles have been included in the lighter areas. Fix them in position with tile adhesive, using a flexible knife. When the surface is covered, sponge off any excess adhesive and leave to dry for 24 hours.

3 Fill the gaps between the tesserae with black tile grout. Rub the grout into the sides of the stand as well, then leave to dry for about 10 minutes. Wipe off any excess grout with a sponge, then leave to dry for 24 hours. Paint the sides of the pot stand with diluted PVA glue. Cut felt to size and stick it to the back of the stand with PVA glue. Finish by polishing the top with a soft cloth and clear glass polish.

A mosaic door plaque adds a distinctive touch to your home and will withstand all weathers. Plan the design carefully so that you have space between the numbers and the border to fit neatly cut tesserae.

Door Number Plaque

you will need

scissors
craft paper
floor tile
pencil
metal ruler
vitreous glass tesserae: turquoise, black and yellow
PVA (white) glue
glue brush
tile nippers
cement-based powdered grout
notched spreader
sponge
cement-based tile adhesive
lint-free cloth

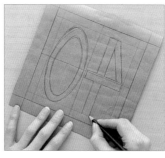

1 Cut a piece of craft paper the same size as the tile. Mark the border and number in reverse on the shiny side of the paper. The border is one tessera wide. There should be room between the border and numbers to insert a quarter-tessera neatly.

2 Dilute the PVA glue to a 50/50 solution with water. Glue the flat (or right) sides of the turquoise tesserae on to the border of the craft paper, with a single black tessera at each corner of the plaque.

3 Cut some black tesserae with the tile nippers to make rectangles. Glue the black rectangles flat-side down over the paper numbers.

4 Cut the yellow tesserae into quarter-squares. Lay them around the straight edges of the numbers, using the tile nippers to cut to size as necessary. Glue them flat-side down as before. Place quarter-square yellow tesserae all around the curved edges of the numbers, cutting as necessary.

5 Mix the grout according to the manufacturer's instructions. Grout the mosaic with the spreader, removing the excess with a damp sponge. Leave to dry. Spread a layer of tile adhesive over the floor tile and key (scuff) with the notched edge of the spreader.

6 Place the grouted mosaic paper-side down on a flat surface. Place the floor tile on top, matching corners and edges. Press the tile down, wipe away excess adhesive and leave to dry.

7 Using a sponge and water, soak the paper on the front of the mosaic. Leave for 15 minutes.

8 Lift one corner of the paper to see if it comes away cleanly. If it does, peel the paper off carefully. If it proves difficult, leave it to soak a little longer and then try lifting it again.

9 Wipe away any surplus glue. Re-grout the plaque, including the sides. Remove excess grout with a damp sponge, then polish the surface with a dry, lint-free cloth.

This lantern is made by using a plain drinking glass as the base for a mosaic of tiny stained-glass squares, applied around the outside – a good way to use up glasses you're not too fond of.

Mosaic Lantern

you will need

indelible black felt-tipped pen

metal straightedge

pieces of stained glass: blue, green, red and yellow

glass cutter

ultraviolet glue

heavy-based glass tumbler

spatula and bowl

tile grout

black acrylic paint

sponge scourer

night-light

1 Using an indelible black felt-tipped pen and a metal straightedge, mark a neat grid of squares on each of the different coloured pieces of stained glass. Each square needs to measure 1cm/⅜in.

2 Cut the glass into 1cm/⅜in-lengths by scoring the glass with a glass cutter, using the straightedge as a guide. Tap underneath the score line with the ball end of the glass cutter, and then snap the glass apart gently between both thumbs.

3 Score the glass strip into 1cm/⅜in squares. Turn the strip over so the score lines face the worktop and tap each score line with the ball end of the glass cutter. The glass should break easily into squares.

4 Using ultraviolet glue, stick the glass mosaic pieces around the glass tumbler, working from the top to the bottom. Leave a gap of 2mm/1⁄16in between squares to allow for grouting.

5 In a bowl, mix 30ml/2 tbsp of tile grout with 25ml/1½ tbsp of cold water and a 5cm/2in length of black acrylic paint. Stir until it forms a smooth, dark grey paste.

6 Using a spatula, press the grout into the gaps between the mosaic pieces. Remove any excess with the spatula, then allow to dry.

7 When the grout is dry, use a damp sponge scourer to clean any remaining smears of grout from the surface of the mosaic pieces.

8 When the lantern is clean, place a night-light in it. Never leave burning candles unattended and always keep them out of the reach of children.

A plain terracotta pot is decorated with squares of brightly coloured tesserae and mirror glass, set in white tile adhesive. This project is very simple to do – you could decorate several matching pots.

Jazzy Plant Pot

you will need

small terracotta plant pot
yacht varnish
paintbrush
vitreous glass tesserae
tile nippers
mirror glass
white cement-based tile adhesive
mixing bowl
flexible knife
sponge
abrasive paper
soft cloth

1 Paint the inside of the plant pot with yacht varnish. Leave to dry. Cut the tesserae into neat quarters using tile nippers. Cut small squares of mirror glass the same size, also with tile nippers. Continue cutting the tesserae until you have enough pieces, in a variety of colours, to cover your pot completely.

2 Mix a quantity of tile adhesive as recommended by the manufacturer. Working from the bottom of the pot, spread a thick layer over a small area at a time using a flexible knife. Press the tesserae into the tile adhesive in rows, including the pieces of mirror glass. Leave to dry overnight.

3 Mix some more tile adhesive and rub all over the surface of the mosaic. Fill any gaps in between the tesserae, then wipe off excess adhesive with a damp sponge before it dries. Again, leave to dry overnight.

4 Use abrasive paper to remove any lumps or spills of tile adhesive that may have dried on to the surface of the tesserae, and to neaten the bottom edge of the pot.

5 Mix some more tile adhesive and smooth it all over the rim of the pot. Leave until completely dry, and then polish the finished mosaic well with a soft cloth.

As we turn the soil in our gardens, broken and weathered pieces of china and glass are uncovered and can be used to make decorative mosaics. Weathered green glass is set in tile adhesive for these hearts.

Mosaic Hearts

you will need

heart-shaped pastry cutter

petroleum jelly

green garden wire

scissors

thick cardboard

ready-mixed tile adhesive

bowl of water

weathered pieces of glass or china

1 Coat the pastry cutter with petroleum jelly to make removing the finished mosaic easier. Cut a short length of wire to make it into a loop. Position the loop at the top of the heart with the end of the wire bent up inside the mould. Place the mould on the cardboard and half fill with tile adhesive. Smooth the surface of the adhesive with wet fingers.

2 Arrange the pieces of glass or china on the surface of the adhesive.

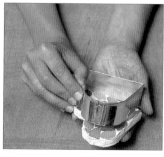

3 Leave to dry for 24 hours or until it feels solid to the touch. Gently remove from the mould.

Plant pots are a good choice of project for a beginner. The straighter the sides, the less cutting and trimming of tiles there will be as you work down towards the pot base.

Mediterranean Garden Pot

you will need
terracotta flower pot
mosaic tiles
tile adhesive
old kitchen knife
tile nippers
goggles
squeegee
mosaic tiling grout
cloth
scourer

1 Clean the pot and allow it to dry. If it is terracotta it may take a while. Butter each tile with adhesive using a knife and apply to the side of the dry pot. To fit the lower rows, you will need to trim the tiles with tile nippers.

2 Leave the adhesive to dry, then grout the mosaic.

This design relies on the various effects that are created by the juxtaposition of colours and textures. It can quite easily be adapted but should be kept simple for the best effect.

Mosaic Bottle

you will need
wine bottle
silicone sealant
pencil or pointed stick
vitreous glass tesserae, including white
tile nippers
cement-based tile adhesive
mixing container
soft cloth
sandpaper (optional)

1 Clean the bottle, rub off the label and dry thoroughly. Dab silicone sealant on to the bottle using a pencil or pointed stick to form a simple line drawing, such as a series of swirls.

2 Cut white vitreous glass into small pieces, about 2mm/¹⁄₁₆in and 4mm/⅛in, using tile nippers. Stick these tesserae to the lines drawn in silicone sealant, then leave overnight to dry.

3 Choose an assortment of colours from the vitreous glass and cut them into quarters. Some of the quarters will have to be cut across the diagonal, so that they can fit snugly between the white swirls. Stick these to the bottle in a series of bands of colour with the sealant. Leave overnight to dry.

4 Mix up some cement-based tile adhesive and rub the cement into the surface of the bottle. Make sure all the crevices between the tesserae are filled, otherwise the tesserae are liable to pull away, as the silicone sealant will remain rubbery. Wipe off excess cement with a dry soft cloth and leave overnight to dry.

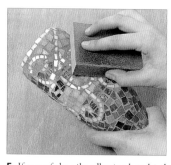

5 If any of the tile adhesive has dried on to the surface of the tesserae, sand the bottle down. For a really smooth and glossy finish, polish the bottle with a dry soft cloth.

If you would like to introduce mosaic to an outdoor setting but are daunted by a large project, these tiles are the perfect solution. They can be left freestanding or be fixed to a wall as an interesting feature.

China Tiles

you will need

plain white ceramic household tiles

PVA (white) glue

paintbrush

pencil

selection of china

tile nippers

tile adhesive

acrylic paint or cement stain

tile grout

nailbrush

soft cloth

1 Prime the back of a plain tile with diluted PVA glue using a paintbrush and leave to dry. Draw a simple, rough design on the back of the tile using a soft pencil.

2 Using tile nippers, cut a selection of china into small pieces that will fit into your design and arrange these in groups according to their colour and shape.

3 Dip the tesserae into tile adhesive and press them, one by one, on to the tile, using the drawing as a guide. Make sure there is enough adhesive on the tesserae; when they are pressed on the tile, glue should ooze out around them. When the tile is covered, leave it to dry overnight.

4 Mix acrylic paint or cement stain with the tile grout. Rub the grout into the surface of the mosaic with your fingers, making sure all the gaps between the tesserae are filled. Leave to dry for 10 minutes.

5 Scrub the surface of the tile with a stiff nailbrush to remove all the excess grout, which should come away as powder. When clean, leave the tile to dry for 24 hours. Finish by polishing it with a dry, soft cloth. Repeat for any other tiles you want to make.

This sunflower mosaic is simple to make and, if you have enough china, you could make several plaques to brighten up an outdoor wall. Collect bright fragments of china in a harmonious blend of colours.

Sunflower Mosaic

you will need

pencil

5mm/¼in thick plywood sheet

coping saw or fretsaw

medium- and fine-grade sandpaper

bradawl or awl

electric cable

wire cutters

masking tape

PVA (white) glue, diluted

white undercoat paint

paintbrush

tile nippers

china fragments

mirror glass strips

tile adhesive

grout

mixing container

cement dye

nailbrush

soft cloth

1 Draw a simple sunflower on the plywood. Cut it out with a saw and sand any rough edges. Make two holes in the plywood with a bradawl or awl. Strip the electric cable and cut a short length of wire. Push the ends of the wire through the holes from the back and fix the ends with masking tape at the front. Seal the front with the diluted PVA glue. Seal the back with white undercoat paint.

2 Using tile nippers, cut the china and mirror strips into irregular shapes. Stick them to the plywood using tile adhesive. Dip each fragment in the tile adhesive and scoop up enough of it to cover the sticking surface; the tile adhesive needs to squelch out around the edge of the mosaic to make sure that it adheres securely. Leave the adhesive to dry thoroughly overnight.

3 Mix up the grout with cement dye, as directed by the manufacturer. Press a small amount of wet grout into the gaps on the mosaic. Leave to dry for about 5 minutes. Brush off any excess with a nailbrush. Leave again for 5 minutes and then polish well with a clean, soft cloth. Leave overnight to dry.

Personal letters and correspondence often have a tendency to be lost or misplaced in a busy household. This simple design for a boldly coloured letter rack could be a decorative solution.

Love Letter Rack

you will need

3mm (⅛in) and 12mm (½in) thick MDF
(medium-density fiberboard)
or plywood sheet
pencil
jigsaw (saber saw)
PVA (white) glue
paintbrushes
wood glue
panel pins (brads)
pin hammer
vitreous glass mosaic tiles
tile nippers
white cellulose filler
grout spreader
sponge
abrasive paper
red acrylic paint

1 Enlarge the templates provided for the front and back pieces. Stick the templates on to the thinner piece of MDF or plywood. Then draw a base on the thicker piece. Cut them out with a jigsaw. Prime the surfaces with diluted PVA glue. When dry, draw three hearts on to the front panel. Stick the pieces together with wood glue and secure with panel pins.

2 When the glue is dry, select two slightly different tones of red vitreous glass tiles for the heart motifs. Using tile nippers, nibble the tiles into precise shapes to fit your design. Fix the tesserae in position on the front panel of the letter rack with white cellulose filler.

3 Select the colours of vitreous glass for the background. Trim the tiles to fit snugly around the heart motifs and within the edges of the letter rack. Fix them to the base as before. Leave the rack to dry overnight.

4 Smooth more filler over the mosaic using a grout spreader. Rub the filler into all of the gaps with your fingers. Rub off any excess filler with a damp sponge and leave to dry.

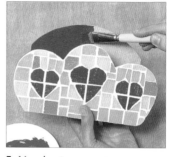

5 Use abrasive paper to remove any filler that has dried on the surface of the mosaic and to neaten the edges. Paint the parts of the letter rack that are not covered with mosaic with red acrylic paint. Leave to dry.

Fragments of plain and patterned broken tiles have been incorporated into the design of these plant pots. You could also use pieces of old plates, which are readily available second-hand.

Plant Pots

you will need
terracotta flower pots
PVA (white) glue and brush (optional)
acrylic paint
paintbrush
chalk or wax crayon
plain and patterned ceramic tiles
tile nippers
tile adhesive
flexible knife
tile grout
cement stain
cloth
nailbrush
soft cloth

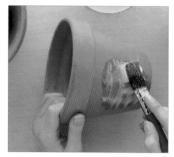

1 If the plant pots are not frost-resistant and are intended for outdoor use, seal them inside and out with a thick coat of diluted PVA glue. This will help to keep out any water that might seep into the porous pot, making it vulnerable to frost damage. Allow to dry.

2 Paint the inside of the pots with acrylic paint in your chosen colour. Leave to dry. Using chalk or a wax crayon, roughly sketch out the design for the tile pieces on the unpainted outside of the pot. Keep your designs as simple as possible and in keeping with this small scale.

3 Using tile nippers, snip small pieces of tile to fit within your design. Using a flexible knife, spread tile adhesive on to small areas of the design at a time. Wearing rubber gloves, press the tesserae in place, working on the outlines first, then the background. Leave for 24 hours.

4 Mix the tile grout with a little cement stain. Spread the grout over the pot with a cloth, filling all the cracks between the tesserae. Wipe off any excess grout. Allow the surface to dry thoroughly.

5 Brush off any dried-on grout with a nailbrush. If there are stubborn parts of grout that will not come off at first, you might try wire (steel) wool, paint scraper, or patio-cleaner. Allow the mosaic to dry thoroughly for at least 48 hours, then polish with a dry, soft cloth.

Squares of coloured glass cast beautiful patterns at night, when the candle is lit in a darkened room. Practise the glass-cutting technique first on scraps of clear glass.

Stained-glass Candle-holder

you will need

pencil

ruler

graph paper

sheets of textured coloured glass

glass cutter

pliers

clear all-purpose adhesive

clear glass candle-holder

tile grout

flexible knife

sponge or soft cloth

1 Using a pencil and ruler, draw a grid of 4cm (1½in) squares on graph paper.

2 Place each sheet of coloured glass over the grid. Following your drawn lines, score vertical lines with a glass cutter (see page 448).

3 Using pliers, and holding the glass carefully, snap the glass along the scored lines into neat, evenly sized pieces.

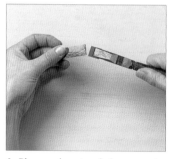

4 Place each strip of glass over the paper grid, score horizontal lines and snap off the squares with the pliers, until you have enough squares to cover the candle-holder.

5 Stick the squares of glass in neat rows around the candle-holder with clear adhesive, alternating the colours, and leaving a tiny gap between each tile. Using a flexible knife, spread the tile grout over the mosaic, filling all the gaps. Rub the excess grout off with a damp sponge or soft cloth. Leave to dry completely before using.

These mosaic spheres can be used as unusual garden ornaments, or a bowlful could make a striking table centrepiece. Select fragments of china to complement your tableware or garden.

Decorative Spheres

you will need

10 polystyrene (Styrofoam) or wooden spheres

PVA (white) glue

paintbrush

pencil

selection of china

mirror

tile nippers

tile adhesive

vinyl matt emulsion (flat latex) or acrylic paint

tile grout

nailbrush

soft cloth

1 Seal the polystyrene or wooden spheres with diluted PVA glue. Leave to dry. Roughly draw a simple design on to each sphere using a pencil. A combination of circular motifs and stripes works well, but you can experiment with other geometric shapes and abstract designs.

2 Cut the china and mirror into pieces using the tile nippers. Combine different sizes of tesserae to fit the design. Stick them to the spheres with tile adhesive. Leave to dry overnight.

3 Add a little coloured vinyl matt emulsion or acrylic paint to the tile grout and mix well. Wearing rubber gloves, rub the grout into the surface of each sphere, filling all the cracks between the tesserae.

4 Leave for a few minutes until the surface has dried, then brush off any excess grout using a stiff nailbrush.

5 Leave to dry overnight, then polish with a dry, soft cloth. Allow the spheres to air for a few days before you arrange them.

A terracotta planter can be embellished with pieces of tile, which are further enhanced by being grouted in a colour chosen to complement them. If the planter is frost-resistant, it can safely be used outdoors.

Decorative Planter

you will need

ceramic mosaic tiles in several colours

tile nippers

notched trowel

tile adhesive

terracotta planter

putty knife

tile grout

cement stain

rubber spreader

nailbrush

soft cloth

1 Snip the tiles into small pieces with tile nippers. You will need a selection of small squares of a single colour to create the borders, and random shapes in several different colours to fill the space between them. Use the notched trowel to apply tile adhesive generously to the sides of the planter.

2 Using a putty knife, apply a small amount of tile adhesive to the back of the single-coloured square tesserae. Position them on the planter to form two straight lines parallel with the horizontal sides of the planter, making a border at the top and bottom edges of your pot.

3 Fill in the central design in the same way with the randomly cut tesserae, mixing the colours to make an abstract design. Leave fairly large gaps of a consistent size between the tile pieces, as thick bands of coloured grout are part of the final design. Leave to dry for 24 hours.

4 Mix the tile grout with a little cement stain. Using the rubber spreader, apply grout all over the surface of the planter, pressing right down between the tesserae. Wipe the spreader over the surface of the planter to make sure the grout is evenly applied. Allow the surface to dry.

5 Brush off any excess grout with a nailbrush, then leave to dry for 48 hours. Polish with a dry, soft cloth.

It is hard to believe that this beautiful, shell-encrusted frame started life as a plain wooden one. Texture is built up using neutral-coloured shells, such as limpets and cockles, embedded into tile adhesive

Grotto Frame

you will need

assorted shells in neutral colours

wooden frame, prepared
and sanded

white tile adhesive

small palette knife

PVA (white) glue and brush

blue limpet shells

small coloured shells

frosted glass beads

tweezers

small clear glass beads in 3
toning colours

large matchstick

emulsion (latex) paint: white

paintbrush

1 Attach the shells to the frame using white tile adhesive and a small palette knife. Allow the shells to overlap the edges at the top and sides of the frame to disguise its square shape and to create a grotto-like effect.

2 Continue to cover the frame around the inside edge, allowing the shells to overlap the edge as before.

3 Fill in the gaps between the shells with smaller shells.

4 Select knobbly shells to cover the side and top edges of the frame; attach them with adhesive as before. Leave to dry for several hours.

5 Use PVA glue to stick on decorative blue limpets and small coloured shells.

6 To add colour and texture, glue on frosted glass beads, using tweezers to position them.

7 Mix the clear glass beads into some glue. Using a large matchstick, add blobs of this mixture in the gaps between the shells on the frame. Leave the glue to dry.

8 Paint the back of the frame white. If the frame is free-standing, it is important that the back looks attractive, so finish by attaching a few more shells to the top of the frame.

For this flowerpot, which combines both the functional and decorative qualities of mosaic, a design and colours have been chosen that reflect the flowers to be planted in it. Squares of mirror add reflections.

Part-tiled Flowerpot

you will need

ready-glazed, high-fired
ceramic flowerpot
chalk or wax crayon
selection of china
tile nippers
tile adhesive
flexible knife
tile grout
cement stain
nailbrush
soft cloth

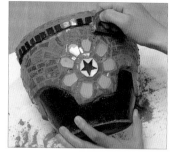

1 Draw a simple design on the pot, using chalk or a wax crayon. Cut appropriate shapes from the china using tile nippers. Use tile adhesive to fix the tesserae to the pot, spreading it with a flexible knife. Work first on the main lines and detailed areas, applying the adhesive to small areas at a time so you can follow the lines of the design.

2 Fill in the larger areas of the design using tesserae in a plain colour. When these areas are complete, leave the pot to dry for 24 hours.

3 Mix the tile grout with a little cement stain, then spread the grout over the pot with your fingers, filling all the cracks between the tesserae. Allow the surface to dry, then brush off any excess grout with a nailbrush. After the pot has dried for about 48 hours polish it with a dry, soft cloth.

This unusual and decorative dragonfly plaque is made from plywood and pieces of old china. Search market stalls for old plates and saucers, and check your kitchen for rejects.

Dragonfly Plaque

you will need

tracing paper

pencil

5mm (¼in) plywood, 50cm (20in) square

jigsaw (saber saw)

bradawl (awl)

PVA (white) glue

paintbrush

acrylic primer

abrasive paper

dark green acrylic paint

cable strippers

electric cable

wire cutters

selection of china

tile nippers

tile adhesive

coloured tile grout

brush

cloth

1 Enlarge the template provided and transfer it on to the plywood. Cut out the dragonfly and make two small hanging holes at the top of the body with a bradawl. Seal the front with diluted PVA glue and the back with acrylic primer. When dry, sand the back and paint with green acrylic paint. Strip some electric cable and cut a short length of wire. Push this through the holes from the back and twist together securely.

2 Cut the china into regular shapes using tile nippers. Dip each piece into tile adhesive, scooping up a thick layer, and press down securely on the plywood to fill in the design. Leave to dry overnight.

3 Press grout into the gaps between the china. Leave it to dry for about 5 minutes, then brush off the excess. Leave for another 5 minutes, then polish with a cloth.

These little star-shaped wall motifs have been created by Cleo Mussi to add sparkling focal points to a garden. They are particularly effective when displayed in clusters or surrounded by lush foliage.

Star Wall Motifs

you will need
3mm (⅛in) thick plywood sheet
pencil
set square (triangle)
ruler
pair of compasses
coping saw or electric scroll saw
abrasive paper
PVA (white) glue
paintbrushes
bradawl or awl
wood primer
white undercoat paint
gloss or matt (flat) paint
wire
wire cutters
adhesive tape
selection of china
mirror
tile nippers
tile adhesive
tile grout
cement stain
nailbrush
soft cloth

1 Draw a star motif on a sheet of plywood, using a pencil, set square, ruler and pair of compasses.

2 Cut out the star using a coping saw or an electric scroll saw. Sand down any rough edges, then seal one side with diluted PVA glue.

3 Make two small holes through the star using a bradawl or awl.

4 Paint the unsealed side with wood primer. Allow to dry, then undercoat and finish with a coat of gloss or matt paint. Allow each coat to dry before applying the next.

▶

5 Cut a short length of wire and bend it into a loop for hanging the star. Push the ends through the holes in the star from the painted side and secure them to the front with adhesive tape.

6 Snip the china and mirror into small pieces using the tile nippers, then arrange these tesserae into groups according to colour and shape.

7 Stick the china and mirror tesserae to the surface of the star, one piece at a time. Take each tessera and dip it into the tile adhesive, or paint some on with a brush, making sure enough is on the tessera to ooze a little from under its edges when pressed on to the base. Cover the surface of the star in this way, then leave overnight to dry.

8 Mix the desired quantity of grout with some cement stain. Wearing rubber gloves, rub the grout into all the gaps between the tesserae. Leave to dry for a few minutes.

9 Using a nailbrush, gently remove all the excess grout. This should brush away as powder; if it does not, the grout is still too damp, so leave to dry for a few more minutes before brushing again.

10 Polish the surface with a soft, dry cloth, then leave to dry for 24 hours before hanging outside.

In this unusual modern design, the coloured grout forms a major feature, with untiled areas left to show it off. Within this design, the tesserae appear as separate decorative elements, rather than parts of a whole.

Funky Fruit Bowl

you will need

soft dark pencil

terracotta bowl

vitreous glass mosaic tiles: yellow, turquoise and white

tile nippers

PVA (white) glue

paintbrush

white glazed ceramic household tiles

matt (flat) coloured glass nuggets

fabric stain

flexible knife

tile grout

rubber spreader

sponge

soft cloth

1 Using a soft pencil, draw freehand spirals on the outside of the bowl, as shown. Each spiral should be about the same depth as the pot. Mark a row of triangles along the edges of each spiral.

2 Using tile nippers, cut the glass tiles into small, equal-sized triangles, to fit the triangles drawn on the bowl.

3 Place a small blob of PVA glue on each pencilled triangle, then press on a glass triangle. Hold the tesserae in place until they stick.

4 Using tile nippers, cut the white ceramic tiles into large triangles of equal size.

▶

5 Apply a thick layer of glue over the inside of the bowl and over the back of each triangle. Press the triangles in place, leaving large gaps between them.

6 Dot blobs of glue at regular intervals around the rim of the bowl and press in the glass nuggets. Leave to dry overnight.

7 Mix the fabric stain with water. You can choose any of the many colours available. Bright primary colours will work well with this design.

8 Gradually add the stain to the tile grout, a spoonful at a time, and mix thoroughly. The final colour of the grout once it has dried will be slightly lighter than its colour when wet.

9 Using a rubber spreader, spread the coloured grout over the entire bowl, evening out the surface. Gently smooth it all over the bowl with your hands. Wipe off the excess grout with a damp sponge. Leave to dry for 1 hour.

10 Polish the surface of the bowl with a dry, soft cloth, removing any residual tile grout.

This unusual design is shown here as a mirror frame, but a similar frame could just as easily be used to frame a photograph or favourite picture. Only two colours are used, although the grouting is a third element.

Squiggle Frame

you will need
9mm (⅜in) thick plywood
jigsaw (saber saw)
PVA (white) glue
paintbrush
glazed ceramic household tiles:
6 blue, 10 black
dishtowel
hammer
pencils
tracing paper
tape measure
carbon paper
thick felt-tipped pen
tile adhesive
admix
tile grout
rubber spreader
sponge
soft cloth
mirror

1 Cut a sheet of plywood measuring 50 x 70cm (20 x 28in) with a jigsaw. Using a large brush, prime the wood by coating it all over with diluted PVA glue. Leave it to dry for 24 hours.

2 Place two blue tiles face down on a dishtowel and fold over the edges. Using a hammer, smash the tiles repeatedly, checking from time to time until they are roughly broken into manageable fragments, keeping the blue and black pieces in separate piles.

3 Draw around the plywood sheet on a large sheet of tracing paper, then draw an inner rectangle of 39 x 60cm (16 x 24in). Enlarge and trace one scroll design using the template provided, then use sheets of carbon paper to transfer your design onto the plywood, flipping the tracing paper to repeat a mirror image another five times. Go over with a thick pen.

4 Mix some tile adhesive with admix, then spread it 3mm (⅛in) thick over a small section of one of the scrolls, removing any excess. Working from the scroll edge out, fill in the blue tiles, and repeat until the frame is covered. Allow 24 hours for the adhesive to dry.

5 Spread some tile grout over the mosaic with a rubber spreader, using a circular motion. Continue until the grout fills all the gaps and is level with the tesserae. Sponge away any surface grout with a damp sponge. Allow to dry for 1 hour, then polish with a dry, soft cloth to rub off any residual grout. Glue the mirror in place.

Small mosaic tiles make an attractive Mediterranean-style frame. To keep the project simple, plan the dimensions of the frame to suit the size of the tiles, so avoiding having to cut and fit odd-shaped pieces.

Mediterranean Mirror

you will need

2cm (¾in) thick MDF (medium-density fiberboard)

pencil

saw

drill

jigsaw (saber saw)

wood glue

white acrylic primer

paintbrush

tile adhesive

grout spreader

vitreous glass mosaic tiles: blues, greens, and yellows

tile grout

soft cloth

mirror

narrow frame moulding

2 ring screws and brass picture wire

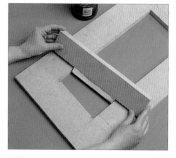

1 Draw a rectangular frame on MDF. Cut it out using a saw. Drill corner holes for the centre and cut this out with a jigsaw. Cut out a shelf and glue it to the frame with wood glue. Allow to dry.

2 Prime both sides of the frame and shelf with white acrylic primer to seal it. Allow to dry. Apply tile adhesive to a small area of the frame, using the fine-notched side of a grout spreader.

3 Apply a random selection of tiles, leaving a 2mm (¹⁄₁₆in) gap between them. Complete the frame, working on a small area at a time. Tile the edges with a single row of tiles.

4 Allow the tile adhesive to dry. Wearing rubber gloves, spread grout over the surface of the tiles with the grout spreader. Scrape off the excess with the spreader and clean off any remaining grout with a soft cloth. Leave to dry thoroughly.

5 Place the mirror face down on the back of the frame and secure it with narrow frame moulding, glued in place with wood glue. Allow to dry.

Screw two ring screws in place on the back of the mirror, more than halfway up the side towards the top, and tie on picture wire securely, to hang it on a wall.

Gently spiralling bands of mosaic look very effective on a tall, elegantly shaped vase. The top and base of the vase are given a marble finish to enclose the rest of the mosaic.

Spiral Vase

you will need

tall vase
yacht varnish and paintbrush (optional)
white chalk
marble tile
piece of sacking (heavy cloth)
hammer
tile adhesive
flexible knife
glazed ceramic household tiles:
pale blue and royal blue
gold smalti
tile nippers
notched spreader or cloth pad
sponge
abrasive paper
soft cloth

1 If your vase is unglazed, seal it by painting all around the inside top lip with yacht varnish. Using a piece of white chalk, draw lines spiralling gently from the rim of the vase to the base. Make sure you have an even number of bands and that they are regularly spaced.

2 Wrap the marble tile in sacking, then break it up using a hammer. Using a flexible knife, spread a thin band of tile adhesive around the top and bottom of the vase, press in your choice of marble pieces and leave to dry overnight.

3 Using a hammer and a piece of sacking, break up all the pale blue and royal blue tiles. Spread tile adhesive over the vase, a band at a time, and press in the tesserae, alternating the two colours. Leave to dry, preferably overnight.

4 Use the tile nippers to cut the gold smalti into small pieces. Using the flexible knife, place blobs of adhesive in the larger gaps between the blue tesserae. Press the gold smalti pieces at random over the blue spirals, checking that they are all level with the rest of the tiles. Leave to dry overnight.

5 Using a notched spreader or cloth pad, rub more tile adhesive in the colour of your choice over the surface of the mosaic, carefully filling all the gaps. Wipe off the excess with a damp sponge and leave to dry overnight. Sand off any adhesive dried on the surface, then polish with a dry, soft cloth.

Semi-precious stones, such as agate and carnelian, can be found on some beaches. To identify them, hold them up to the light and they will glow with shades of warm ochre or deep russet.

Rock Pool Mirror

you will need

paper

pencil

metal ruler

scissors

craft (utility) knife

cutting mat

polyboard

pair of compasses

bradawl or awl

wire

PVA (white) glue and brush

circular mirror glass, 10cm (4in) diameter

masking tape

small sticks

tile adhesive

small palette knife or spreader

small pebbles

semi-precious stones

aquarium gravel

watercolour paints

small artist's paintbrush

palette

1 Enlarge the hexagon template provided. Using a craft knife and metal ruler and working on a cutting mat, cut two hexagons from polyboard. Draw a circle 9.5cm (3¾in) in diameter in the centre of one of the pieces.

2 Cut out the circle with a craft knife, holding the knife at an angle so that the hole has a sloping edge. Keep the cut-out circle.

3 Using a bradawl or awl, pierce two holes in the hexagon. Thread a wire loop through the holes for hanging the mirror and twist the ends together.

4 Glue the mirror glass in the centre of the backing, with the wire loop on the back. Place the other hexagon right side up on top to form a sandwich, and tape together.

5 Cut sticks to fit along the edges of the frame, overlapping them at the corners. Glue in place. Leave to dry.

6 Replace the cut-out circle to protect the glass. Spread tile adhesive over the frame, then arrange the pebbles and semi-precious stones on top, lightly pressing them into the adhesive. Leave the frame to dry.

7 Remove the polyboard circle. Mix the aquarium gravel with PVA glue and fill in the gaps between the stones, especially around the inner edge. Leave to dry. Add a second layer of sticks to the outside edge. Mix water-colour paint with plenty of water and wash over the adhesive.

This design is simple to execute and adds a naïve charm to a plain wooden tray. The semi-indirect method of laying the tiles used here helps to keep the surface of the mosaic smooth and flat.

Country Cottage Tray

you will need

wooden tray

scissors

brown paper

pencil

vitreous glass mosaic tiles in various colours

tile nippers

water-soluble glue

white spirit (paint thinner)

PVA (white) glue

paintbrush

bradawl or awl

masking tape

tile adhesive

notched spreader

sponge

soft cloth

1 Cut a piece of brown paper to fit the bottom of the wooden tray. Using the template provided, draw a country cottage scene in pencil. Plan out the colour scheme for the picture, then, using the tile nippers, cut all of the vitreous glass tiles into quarters.

2 Position the tesserae on to the paper to check your design before going any further. Once you are satisfied with the design, apply water-soluble glue on to the paper in small areas, and stick the tesserae on, face down. Take care to obscure any pencil marks. Trim the tesserae to fit if necessary.

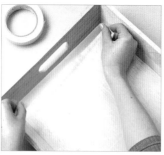

3 Prepare the bottom of the tray by removing any varnish or polish with white spirit. Prime with diluted PVA glue, leave it to dry, then score it with a sharp instrument such as a bradawl or awl. Protect the sides with masking tape.

4 Spread an even layer of tile adhesive over the bottom of the tray, using a notched spreader. Cover the tray completely and spread the adhesive well into the corners.

5 Place the mosaic carefully on the freshly applied tile adhesive, paper side up. Press down firmly over the whole surface, then leave for about 30 minutes. Moisten the paper with a damp sponge and peel off. Leave the tile adhesive to dry overnight.

6 Some parts of the mosaic may need to be grouted with extra tile adhesive. Leave it to dry, then clean off any of the adhesive that may have dried on the surface with a sponge. Remove the pieces of masking tape and then polish the mosaic with a dry, soft cloth.

In this lovely hallway mirror, romantic red hearts and scrolling white lines are beautifully set off by the rich blue background, which sparkles from the inset chunks of mirror glass.

Valentine Mirror

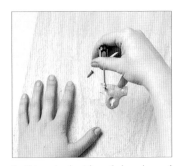

1 Prime both sides of the plywood with diluted PVA glue and leave to dry. Score one side (the front) with a bradawl. Turn the board over and make a dent in the centre about a third of the way down, using a drill. Screw the mirror plate over the dent.

2 Cut a piece of brown paper to the size of the mirror and tape it around the edge to protect the glass. Mark its position in the centre front of the plywood board with a ruler and pencil, and stick it in place with tile adhesive.

3 Draw a small heart in the centre of each border and scrolling lines to connect the four hearts.

4 Using tile nippers, cut the red tiles into small, irregular pieces and the white tiles into regular-sized squares.

▶

5 Spread the tile adhesive over the pencilled heart shapes with a flexible knife and press in the red tile pieces. Repeat for the scroll lines using the white tiles. Scrape off any excess adhesive and leave to dry overnight.

6 Using a hammer, carefully break up the blue ceramic tiles and the mirror tiles into small pieces. It is advisable to wrap each tile in a piece of sacking before breaking up, to avoid the tile shattering or splintering.

7 Working on a small area at a time, spread tile adhesive over the background areas with a notched spreader, then press in the blue and mirror pieces. Leave to dry overnight.

8 Grout the mosaic with tile adhesive, using a rubber spreader to distribute the adhesive over the flat surface and your fingers for the edges.

9 Carefully sand off any lumps of remaining adhesive that may have dried on the surface of the mosaic, using fine abrasive paper.

10 For a professional finish, rub tile adhesive into the back of the plywood board. Remove the protective brown paper from the mirror.

This geometric mosaic uses contrasting colours of glass and ceramic tiles to create a stunning wall panel. Mirror and gold-leaf tiles add an opulent feel. Hang this mosaic where it can be a dramatic focal point.

Mirror Mosaic

you will need

pencil

ruler

9mm (⅜in) thick MDF (medium-density fiberboard), cut to 46 x 46cm (18 x 18in)

paintbrushes

PVA (white) glue

tile adhesive

mirror, cut to 19.5 x 19.5cm (7¾ x 7¾in)

gold vitreous glass tiles in a light and dark shade

matt (flat) ceramic mosaic tiles in light and dark shades

tile nippers

mirror tiles

tile grout

rubber spreader

sponge

soft cloth

1 Using a pencil and ruler, divide the board so that there are seven equal spaces along each edge. Join up your marks carefully to form a grid of squares. Mark the alternate squares with a pencil squiggle to show where the different squares of tones will be mosaiced.

2 Using a large paintbrush, seal the board with a coat of PVA glue diluted 1:1 with water. Allow to dry thoroughly. The PVA will dry clear, so the design will still be visible.

3 Using tile adhesive, stick the main mirror on to the centre of the board so that there are even borders all around it. Leave it to dry.

4 Cut the gold vitreous glass and the two shades of ceramic mosaic tiles in half with the tile nippers. Squeeze the nippers firmly for a clean cut.

▶

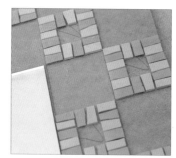

5 Starting on the squares marked with the pencil squiggles, stick the tiles in position, alternating between a light shade of vitreous glass and a light shade of matt ceramic. Leave a slight gap between each piece. Paint un-diluted PVA glue on to each square and stick the tiles to the background to fit within the pencil guidelines.

6 Finish sticking these lighter squares over the entire board, working carefully to ensure the gaps between each piece remain even.

7 Cover the alternate squares over the entire board with two darker colours, one of the matt ceramic, and the other of the vitreous glass, sticking them in position as before and keeping the spacing even throughout.

8 Stick the mirror tiles in the centre of the darker squares using PVA glue as before to create a dark square with a centre of light.

9 Stick squares of the darker vitreous glass tiles in the centre of the lighter squares to create lighter squares with a dark centre. Allow to dry.

10 Spread tile grout evenly over the board with a rubber spreader, making sure the gaps between the tiles have been filled. Smooth a little grout around the edge of the board. With a slightly damp sponge, wipe away any excess grout from the surface and the edge of the board. Leave to dry. Polish with a dry, soft cloth.

In this vivid mosaic, it is important that the tesserae are accurately shaped, with no gaps between them. They are left ungrouted so that tile adhesive dust will not disturb the workings of the clock.

Cosmic Clock

you will need

40cm (16in) diameter circle of wood

strip of plywood, 5mm (¹⁄₁₆in) deeper
than the circle of wood and 130cm
(52in) long

hammer

tacks

black paint

paintbrush

brown paper

scissors

drill

charcoal or black felt-tipped pen

vitreous glass mosaic tiles

PVA (white) glue and brush

tile nippers

tile adhesive

admix

grout spreader

piece of flat wood

sponge

craft (utility) knife

soft cloth

double-sided tape

clock mechanism and hands

picture-hanging hook

1 Position the strip of plywood around the circumference of the circle of wood, and, using a hammer and tacks, cover the edge of the circle to make a neat rim. Paint the rim black and leave to dry. Cut a circle of brown paper to fit inside the rim. Fold it in quarters to find the centre, and make a small hole.

2 Place the paper over the circle of wood and mark the centre through the hole on to the wood. Remove the paper and then drill a hole through the centre of the wood, large enough to allow the spindle of the clock mechanism to rotate freely.

3 Enlarge the template provided, or draw a cosmic design on the brown paper circle, using a stick of charcoal or a felt-tipped pen. (Charcoal is easier to correct.)

4 Snip the glass tiles into tesserae using tile nippers, then stick the tesserae face down on the paper, using PVA glue. Place them as close together as possible, without any gaps in between. Make any further cuts necessary to allow them to fit around the curves in your design.

5 Mix the tile adhesive and admix according to the manufacturer's instructions. Using the fine-notched edge of a grout spreader, spread this over the whole of the board, right up to the edge. Lower the mosaic on to the adhesive and press flat.

6 Smooth over the paper with a flat piece of wood, using small, circular movements. Leave for 20 minutes, then dampen the paper and gently pull it away from the mosaic. Scrape away any adhesive that has come through the tesserae with a craft knife. Leave to dry for at least 2 hours.

7 Carefully wipe any remaining glue from the surface of the mosaic with the sponge and polish with a dry, soft cloth. Using double-sided tape, attach the clock mechanism to the back of the board. Insert the spindle through the hole in the centre and fit on the hands. Fit a picture hook to the back.

This mosaic jewellery box was inspired by the treasures of the Aztecs and Mayas of pre-Columbian Central America, which were decorated with turquoise, coral and jade.

Aztec Box

you will need

wooden box with hinged lid

felt-tipped pen or dark pencil

PVA (white) glue

glue brush

glass nuggets backed with gold and silver leaf

masking tape

fine artist's paintbrush

vitreous glass tesserae

tile nippers

cinca ceramic tiles

sand

cement

mixing container

black cement dye

sponge

soft cloth

plastic bag

1 Draw the design on the wooden box with a felt-tipped pen or dark pencil. The design represents the head of a fierce animal, and the teeth and jaws of the beast are drawn immediately below the opening edge of the lid, using the picture as a guide.

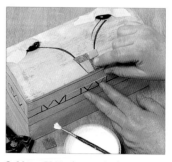

2 Using PVA glue, stick glass nuggets on the box for the eyes. Hold them in place with masking tape to dry. Cut vitreous glass tiles in coral and stick on to the nose and lips. Cut vitreous glass tiles in terracotta and pink for the lips. Use a paintbrush to apply glue to small pieces.

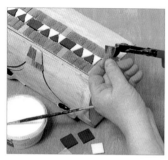

3 Cut triangular black and white tesserae into precise shapes to fit the areas marked for the teeth, then stick them in place.

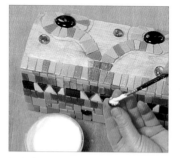

4 Select tesserae in varying shades and use to define the eye sockets and the snout, cutting to fit as necessary. Include a few small nuggets positioned randomly. When tiling around the hinges, leave 1cm (½in) untiled, so the box can be opened. Leave it to dry, then tile the lid in the same way.

5 Mix three parts sand with one part cement. Add some black cement dye. Add water, mixing it to the desired consistency. Rub the cement on to the box surface. Scrape off the excess, rub the box with a slightly damp sponge and polish with a dry cloth. Cover with plastic to dry slowly.

This candle sconce looks beautiful hung on a bathroom wall or in a bedroom. The mirror reflects the candlelight and, together with the small pieces of coloured tile, this gives the mosaic a magical quality.

Candle Sconce

you will need

tape measure

2cm (¾in) thick plywood sheet

pencil

ruler

vitreous glass mosaic tiles

jigsaw (saber saw)

abrasive paper

wire cutters

chicken wire

hammer

U-shaped nails

picture hooks

bonding plaster

PVA (white) glue

sponge

tile adhesive

knife

vitreous glass mosaic tiles, mirror,

washed glass, stained glass,

and amethyst

tile nippers

craft (utility) knife

tile grout

soft cloths

old sheet

drill with rebate (rabbet) bit

mirror plate, with keyhole opening

screwgun or screwdriver

small screws

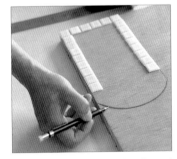

1 Measure and mark out the plywood to a width to fit six whole glass tiles (13cm/5¼in) and length to fit 10 whole tiles (22cm/9in). Use a ruler, working from the corner of the wood and the two straight edges. At the end of this rectangle, draw a semicircle.

2 Clamp the wood on to the edge of a workbench. Using a jigsaw, cut out the shape. Sand the edges of the wood lightly.

3 Using wire cutters, cut out a piece of chicken wire 20 x 50cm (8 x 20in). With a hammer and U-shaped nails, attach one end of the wire to the semi-circle to create a curve. Remove the excess wire using wire cutters or pliers.

4 Fold the wire over and compress it to create the basic shape, fixing the top end to the wood with picture hooks. Mix up some bonding plaster in a bucket into a soft but firm consistency. Pack this into the chicken wire until the structure is filled. Start to create the shape by applying small lumps where there are uneven dips. ▶

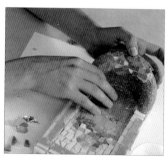

5 When the shape is complete, dip your fingers into water and run them over the surfaces until there is a smooth finish. Leave the plaster to dry for 24 hours, then seal the surface with a thin film of diluted PVA glue, applied with a sponge.

6 Using a knife, apply an even layer of tile adhesive to the outer edges, or border, of the candle sconce. Stick strips of whole vitreous glass tiles (paper side up) on to the border, clipping the last tile to fit and meet the curve at the top of the sculptured holder. Stick further strips of glass tiles on to the sides of the sconce, continuing around the base. Clip the remaining glass tiles and all the other tiles into small pieces.

7 Starting from the top, within the border created from whole tiles, apply tile adhesive and place small, clipped pieces of white tile next to the whole tiles. As the space fills, introduce light pieces of pale blue and green washed glass, working downwards. On the shaped holder, work with richer greens and blues, and include pieces of stained glass and amethyst. Place pieces of mirror randomly to reflect the light.

8 When the mosaic is finished, remove the brown paper on the whole tiles, having moistened it with a damp sponge. Clean the surfaces of the tiles and remove any excess adhesive in the gaps with a craft knife.

9 Apply tile grout over the mosaic, working it into the gaps with your fingers. Gently clean off any excess grout with a damp sponge. After about 10 minutes, use a dry cloth to rub away any excess grout. If it is still wet, leave it for a little while then try again.

10 Place the completed candle sconce face down on an old sheet. Place the mirror plate in position, then mark with a pencil the area under the keyhole-shaped opening. Drill this area so that it is large enough to take a screw head, then screw the mirror plate in position.

A breezeblock makes a safe, solid base for a large lamp. It is covered in a chunky floral design made of floor tiles and marble, with tiny pieces of mirror set into the gaps to catch the light from the lamp.

Floral Lamp Base

you will need
breezeblock (cinderblock)
ruler
soft pencil
drill with a long bit (at least half the length of the block and just wider than the metal rod)
chisel
hammer
lamp power cord
hollow metal rod with a screw thread, cut to the height required for the lamp
tile adhesive
piece of chalk
ceramic floor tiles: shades of yellow for the petals
piece of sacking (heavy cloth)
flexible knife
white marble tiles
mirror
tile nippers
rubber spreader
sponge
dust mask
abrasive paper
soft cloth
copper pipe
hacksaw
lamp fittings
plug
screwdriver
lampshade

1 On one end of the breezeblock, mark diagonal lines to find the centre. Drill a hole right through, turning the block over if necessary to drill from the other end.

2 On one end, use a chisel to cut a deep groove from the centre hole to one edge to contain the lamp power cord. This will be the bottom of the lamp base.

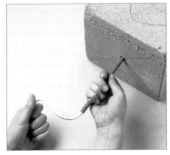

3 Pass the metal rod through the centre hole, with the screw thread at the top, then thread the cord through the rod, leaving a long length at the bottom. Tuck the cord into its groove, leaving enough length to reach an electrical socket. Fill in the groove with tile adhesive to secure the flex. Leave to dry.

4 Using a piece of chalk, draw a large, simple flower design on the sides of the breezeblock. Exclude the bottom of the block. Plan out the colour scheme for your petals, keeping the yellow for the flower centres and white for the background.

▶

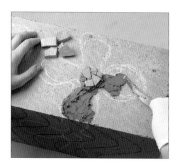

5 Wrap each floor tile in sacking and break it up into pieces with a hammer. Using a flexible knife, spread tile adhesive over each flower shape. Press the yellow tesserae into the adhesive and build up the flower centres. Now start work on the petals, using the other tiles, and continue until they are all covered.

6 Break up each white marble tile in the same way. Working on a small area at a time, spread tile adhesive over the background and press in the marble pieces. Don't worry if your pieces don't butt up to each other. Leave to dry for 12 hours or overnight.

7 Using tile nippers, cut the mirror into small fragments. Insert blobs of tile adhesive into the larger gaps between the tesserae. Then push in the mirror fragments, checking they are level with the rest. Continue inserting mirrored pieces over the base until covered. Leave to dry overnight.

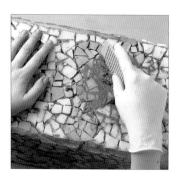

8 Grout the lamp base by scraping tile adhesive over the surface with a rubber spreader. This will bind all the pieces of tesserae together firmly. Use your fingers to smooth it right into the fissures and along the sides of the block. Wipe off the excess tile adhesive with a damp sponge and leave to dry overnight.

9 Wearing a dust mask, sand off any adhesive that may have dried on the surface. Polish with a soft, dry cloth. Finish off by slipping the copper pipe, cut to size, over the hollow rod, so that the screw end is exposed. Attach the lamp fittings, bulb, plug and chosen lampshade.

In this project, vitreous glass mosaic tiles in striking colours are used to decorate a ready-made fire screen. Most of this design uses whole tiles, cut diagonally into triangles.

Mosaic Fire Screen

you will need

ready-made fire-screen base

pencil

ruler

craft (utility) knife

PVA (white) glue

paintbrushes

vitreous glass mosaic tiles

tile nippers

tile grout

nailbrush

wood primer

white undercoat paint

gloss paint

soft cloth

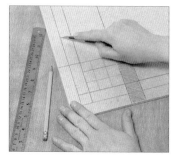

1 Draw the design on to the surface of the screen and its feet. Calculate the space needed to accommodate the tiles required and mark the main areas with a ruler. Score the whole of the surface with a craft knife, then prime with diluted PVA glue and leave to dry completely.

2 Select a range of vitreous glass tiles in the colours you require. Use tile nippers to cut some of the tiles into right-angled triangles for use in the inner border design.

3 Stick the tiles and half-tiles to the base with undiluted PVA glue. Try to make all the gaps between the tiles equal and leave the area that will be slotted into the feet untiled.

4 Tile the edge, then the feet, making sure that they will still slot on to the screen. Leave overnight to dry. Rub tile grout into the entire surface of the mosaic with your fingers, making sure that all the gaps between the tesserae are filled.

5 Leave the grout to dry for about 10 minutes, then remove any excess with a nailbrush. Allow to dry for a further 12 hours, then paint the back of the screen with wood primer, then undercoat paint and finally gloss paint, allowing each coat to dry before you apply the next. Finally, polish the mosaic with a dry, soft cloth and slot on the feet.

A simple spiral was the inspiration for this tall, elegant lamp base. Pieces of mirror have been added to catch the light, and they sparkle when the lamp is switched on.

Spiral Lamp Stand

you will need

cardboard carpet roll tube

5mm (¼in) thick plywood sheet

pencil

jigsaw (saber saw)

drill with a bit just larger
than the metal rod

bradawl or awl

wood glue

shellac

paintbrushes

lamp power cord

hollow metal rod with a screw
thread, cut to the height required

plaster of Paris

ceramic household tiles in three colours

tile nippers

tile adhesive

sponge

mirror

flexible knife

abrasive paper

soft cloth

copper pipe

hacksaw

lamp fittings

plug

screwdriver

lampshade

1 Draw twice around the circular end of the cardboard tube on to the plywood. Cut around these circles using a jigsaw and cut the cardboard tube to the length required. Drill a hole through the centre of one of the plywood circles. Use a bradawl or awl to make a hole in the cardboard tube 2cm (¾in) in from one end and large enough to take the lamp power cord.

2 Use wood glue to stick the plywood circle without the drilled hole to the end of the tube near the cord hole. Leave to dry overnight, then paint the cardboard tube with shellac. Thread the cord in through the hole in the tube and then through the hollow metal rod. Stand the metal rod inside the tube with the screw thread at the top.

3 Mix some plaster of Paris with water and quickly pour it into the tube. Slip the second plywood circle over the metal rod and secure it with wood glue to the top of the cardboard tube. As soon as you have poured the plaster of Paris into the tube, you must work quickly to secure the top, as it is very important that the plaster dries with the rod in an upright position.

▶

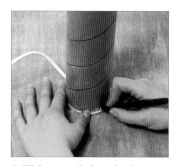

4 With a pencil, draw the design on to the tube, following the spiral lines already present on the cardboard tube. You can add variations and embellishments at this stage.

5 Cut the tiles for the outline colour into small pieces using tile nippers. Stick these to the lines of your design using tile adhesive. Use a sponge to wipe away any large blobs of adhesive that seep out from under the tesserae, then leave to dry overnight.

6 Select two colours of tile to fill the areas between the spiralling lines. Use the tile nippers to cut the tiles into various shapes and sizes, then cut the mirror into various shapes and sizes.

7 Spread tile adhesive on to the remaining cardboard area with a flexible knife, and apply the tesserae in separate bands of colour. Work on a small area at a time, so that the surface does not become too messy. Intersperse the coloured tesserae with pieces of mirror as you work. Cover the whole surface of the cardboard tube, then leave it to dry overnight.

8 Apply more tile adhesive over the whole area of the lamp stand, taking care to press it down between all the tesserae. Wipe off the excess adhesive with a damp sponge and leave the stand to dry overnight. Rub off any excess surface adhesive with abrasive paper, and polish with a dry, soft cloth.

9 Finish off by attaching all the fittings. Slip the copper pipe, cut to size, over the central rod, leaving the screw end exposed. Attach the lamp fittings, plug and lampshade.

Mosaic forms a very effective surround to a mirror: the undulating, fractured surface perfectly sets off the smooth, reflective plane of the glass, used here with china, delicate patterns and touches of gold.

Bathroom Mirror

you will need

2cm (¾in) thick plywood sheet, cut to size required

pencil

ruler

jigsaw (saber saw)

abrasive paper

PVA (white) glue

paintbrushes

wood primer

white undercoat paint

gloss paint

drill with rebate (rabbet) bit

mirror plate, with keyhole opening

2 x 2cm (¾in) screws

screwdriver

thick card (stock)

3mm (⅛in) thick foil-backed mirror

tile adhesive

flexible knife

masking tape

tracing paper (optional)

selection of china

tile nippers

tile grout

vinyl matt emulsion (flat latex) or acrylic paint (optional)

rubber spreader

nailbrush

soft cloth

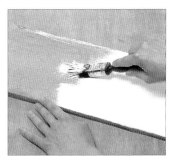

1 Using the template provided, draw the outer shape of the mirror frame on to the piece of plywood. Cut around this shape using a jigsaw, then sand down the rough edges. On to this panel, draw the shape of the mirror. Here, the shape of the mirror echoes the shape of the panel, but it could be a completely different shape if desired. Make sure it is a shape that the glass supplier will be able to reproduce.

2 Seal the sides and front of the base panel with diluted PVA glue, and paint the back, first with wood primer, then undercoat paint and finally gloss paint. Mark the position of the mirror plate on the back of the panel. Using a rebate (rabbet) bit, drill the area that will be under the keyhole-shaped opening so that it is large enough to take a screw head, then screw the mirror plate in position.

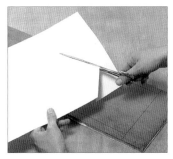

3 Make a card template in the exact dimensions of the mirror shape you have drawn on the base. Ask your supplier to cut a piece of 3mm (⅛in) foil-backed mirror using the template.

4 Stick the mirror in position using tile adhesive spread with a flexible knife. Leave to dry overnight.

▶

5 Trim 2mm (⅟₁₆in) from the card template all around the edge and cover the mirror with it, securing it in place with masking tape; this should prevent the mirror from being scratched or covered with adhesive. The mosaic will eventually overlap this 2mm (⅟₁₆in) of uncovered mirror.

6 Draw the design for the frame on the dry, sealed surface surrounding the mirror; use tracing paper and a soft pencil to copy and transfer your original plan, if you wish.

7 Using tile nippers, snip the smooth edges from the cups and plates you have collected. Use these to tile the outside edge of the base panel and to overlap the 2mm (⅟₁₆in) edges of the mirror, sticking them down with tile adhesive. Cut the remainder of the china into small pieces and stick these along the structural lines of your design.

8 Fill in the areas of detail between the outlining tesserae. When the mirror frame is completely tiled, leave to dry for 24 hours.

9 Mix tile grout with vinyl matt emulsion or acrylic paint, if colour is desired. Spread this over the surface of the tesserae using a rubber spreader, and rub it in by hand, making sure all the gaps are filled. Allow the surface to dry for 10 minutes, then brush off the excess grout with a stiff-bristled nailbrush. Wipe clean with a dry, soft cloth.

10 Leave the mirror overnight to dry thoroughly, then remove the protective card from the mirror. Finally, hang the mirror in position using the mirror plate on the back of the panel.

This abstract frame, with its glowing colours, was created using the semi-indirect method of mosaics. In this way, you can arrange the tesserae on paper first, before committing yourself to the final design.

Abstract Mirror

you will need

40cm (16in) diameter circle of wood

brown paper

pair of compasses

pencil

scissors

20cm (8in) diameter circle of mirror

black felt-tipped pen

masking tape

vitreous glass mosaic tiles

tile nippers

PVA (white) glue and brush

strip of plywood, 5mm (¼in) deeper than the circle of wood and 130cm (52in) long, painted black

hammer

tacks

craft (utility) knife

tile grout

sponge

tile adhesive

grout spreader

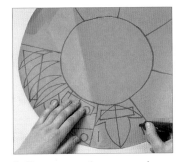

1 Using a pair of compasses, draw a circle on brown paper 2mm (⅟₁₆in) smaller than the wooden circle. Cut it out. Place the mirror in the centre and draw around it in black pen. Divide the border into eight equal sections. Draw a design clearly in each section.

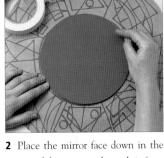

2 Place the mirror face down in the centre of the paper and attach it from underneath with masking tape.

3 Cut the tiles into tesserae of the right size with tile nippers. Stick them face down on the paper design, using PVA glue. Keep the gaps between them as even as possible.

4 When the design is complete, carefully lower the mosaic on to the board. Position the strip of plywood around the edge of the circle and attach it using a hammer and tacks to form a rim. Remove the mirror and cut away the brown paper underneath, using a craft knife.

▶

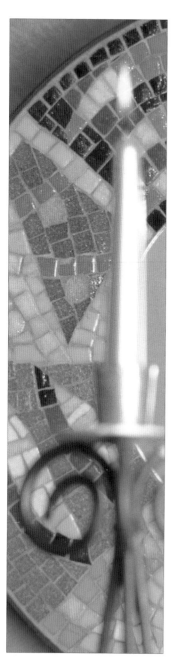

5 Rub a small amount of tile grout into the mosaic with your fingers, then wipe off the excess with a damp sponge. This will bind the tesserae together. Leave until almost dry.

6 Gently remove the mosaic from the board by turning it upside down. Using the fine-notched side of a grout spreader, spread the outer area of the board with tile adhesive. Lower the mosaic down into the adhesive, mosaic side down, and press firmly.

7 Coat the back of the mirror with tile adhesive and stick it in the centre. Leave to set for 20 minutes.

8 Dampen the paper with a wet sponge, wait for 10 minutes until the glue has dissolved, then gently peel it off the mosaic. Clean away any protruding lumps of adhesive with a damp sponge. Leave to dry, then re-grout, filling in any cracks, and sponge clean.

This delicate mosaic is made entirely from old cups and plates. The pretty trinket box is ideal for displaying on a dressing table, and can be used for storing jewellery, letters and other treasures.

Floral Trinket Box

you will need
wooden box
PVA (white) glue
paintbrush
bradawl or awl
soft dark pencil
selection of china: white and patterned
tile nippers
tile adhesive
admix
flexible knife
sponge
paint scraper
soft cloth

1 Prime the top and sides of the wooden box with diluted PVA glue. Leave to dry, then score at random with a bradawl or awl to provide a good key.

2 Enlarge the template provided to the required size and transfer it to the box, or using a soft pencil, draw a freehand grid on the box and a flower in each square.

3 Using tile nippers, cut white pieces of china into small squares. Mix the tile adhesive with admix following the manufacturer's instructions. Using a flexible knife, spread this along the grid lines, a small area at a time.

4 Press the white tesserae into the adhesive in neat, close-fitting rows. Cover all the grid lines on both the top and sides of the box. Leave to dry overnight.

▶

5 Using tile nippers, cut out small patterned pieces from the china and sort them into colours. Position the tesserae on the box and plan out the colour scheme for the mosaic before committing to the design.

6 Spread the tile adhesive and admix mixture over each square of the top and sides in turn. Press in the tesserae to make each flower and use a contrasting, plain colour in the background. Leave to dry.

7 Using your fingers, spread tile adhesive all over the surface of the mosaic, getting right into the crevices. Wipe off any excess adhesive with a damp cloth or sponge.

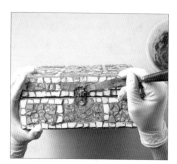

8 Using a flexible knife, smooth the tile adhesive around the hinges and clasp, if there is one. Remove any excess adhesive immediately with a sponge before it dries. Leave to dry.

9 Carefully scrape off any tile adhesive that may have dried on the surface of the mosaic with a paint scraper. Take care not to scratch the surface of the tiles.

10 When all the excess grout has been removed, polish the surface of the box with a dry, soft cloth, rubbing each tile fragment to a high shine.

This unusual garden urn is decorated with modern faces but has a look reminiscent of Byzantine icons. Many people shy away from attempting to draw the human form, but such a simple, naïve drawing is worth a try.

Garden Urn

you will need

large frost-resistant urn
yacht varnish and paintbrush (optional)
chalk
vitreous glass mosaic tiles in various colours
tile nippers
tile adhesive
flexible knife
sponge
abrasive paper
dilute hydrochloric acid, safety goggles and rubber gloves (optional)
soft cloth

1 If the urn is not glazed and it is to stand outdoors, paint the inside with yacht varnish to stop moisture seeping through from the inside and pushing the tesserae off. Leave to dry.

2 Divide the pot into quarters and draw your design on each quarter with chalk. The design used here depicts four different heads and shoulders. Keep the drawing very simple, sketching just the basic elements of the face.

3 Choose a dark colour from the range of vitreous glass tiles for the main outlines and details such as eyes and lips. Snip the tiles into eighths using tile nippers. Spread tile adhesive with a flexible knife and stick the tesserae to the lines of your drawing.

4 Select tiles in a range of colours for the flesh tones, and snip them into quarters.

▶

5 Working on a small area at a time, apply tile adhesive to one of the heads and shoulders and press the tesserae into it. Use a mixture of all the colours, but in areas of shade use more of the darker tesserae, and in highlighted areas use the lighter ones.

6 Repeat step 5 for the other heads, then choose colours for the area surrounding the heads. Spread these out on a clean table to see if they work together. A mixture of blues and whites with a little green was chosen here. Snip the pieces into quarters.

7 Working on a small area at a time, spread tile adhesive on to the surface and press the glass tesserae into it, making sure the colours are arranged randomly. Cover the entire outer surface of the urn, then leave to dry for 24 hours.

8 Mix up more tile adhesive and spread it over the surface of the mosaic with your fingers. Do this very thoroughly, making sure you fill all the gaps between the tesserae. This is especially important if the urn is going to be situated outside. Wipe off any excess adhesive with a sponge, then leave to dry for 24 hours.

9 Use abrasive paper to remove any adhesive that has dried on the surface of the mosaic. If the adhesive is proving hard to remove, dilute hydrochloric acid can be used, but you must wear goggles and rubber gloves and apply it outside or where there is good ventilation. Wash any acid residue from the surface with plenty of water. Leave to dry. Polish with a dry, soft cloth.

10 Finish by rubbing tile adhesive over the lip and down inside the pot. This prevents the mosaic from ending abruptly and gives the urn and mosaic a more unified and professional appearance.

In this piece, mosaic adds intense colour, and a contrasting effect, to a three-dimensional object. The colours and laying techniques convey an intensity of expression as well as a striking aesthetic effect.

Sculptural Head

you will need
plaster head
fine aluminium mesh
wire
tile adhesive
small plasterer's trowel
vitreous glass mosaic tiles in various colours
tile nippers
black tile grout
tiler's sponge
small screwdriver
fine wet-and-dry (silicon carbide) paper
soft cloth

1 In this example, the base has been made from an original plaster head. Press a fine aluminium mesh against the surface of a plaster head and fold and mould it carefully to create the contours of the face and head. Do this in two halves, from the front around the contours of the face, and from the back, then remove them and join them together with twists of wire.

2 Create the form by applying a 12mm (½in) thick layer of tile adhesive over the mesh head with a small plasterer's trowel. Apply a thin layer first and work into the surface of the mesh, followed immediately (that is before it dries out) with a thicker layer. Some further modelling can be done at this stage, using the build-up of adhesive to refine the contours.

3 Cover the head in quarter-cut vitreous glass tesserae, sticking them to the base with a thin layer of tile adhesive. Apply this to small areas at a time with a small plasterer's trowel. The eyebrows would be a good place to start, as their curving lines generate the undulating lines of the forehead.

4 The eyes are very important in giving the piece definition and character and need to be tackled early in the process, as they will generate the laying lines of the cheeks. To maintain the even flow of mosaic, try to use full-quarter tiles where possible and avoid resorting to very small pieces, which will look clumsy and can be difficult to fix firmly.

▶

5 Where you are forming a sudden change in plane, such as over the eyebrows, around the top of the crown and at the edge of the ears, try to fix the pieces so that one bevelled edge joins up to another. This will keep the joint width as narrow as possible. These pieces will slightly overhang the base, and it is important to use enough adhesive to bond them firmly.

6 The lines of mosaic around the circumference of the neck have been carefully merged with the lines across the cheeks. Junctions of smaller cut tiles can be made where the line created relates to the form, such as around the eye socket and abutting the ear, but where the form requires a more gradual transition a blending of the lines will be less distracting and neater.

7 Cover the neck and face in a series of three-colour mixes that blend into each other by carrying one colour over into the next mix and avoiding harsh dividing lines. Lay the hair, crown and dress in two-colour stripes; the more organized patterns help to suggest a different texture from the areas of "skin". Make a contrast between the uniform treatment of the dress and crown across the piece and the asymmetry of the face and hair.

8 When the piece is covered and the adhesive is dry, apply black tile grout. Work the grout into the joints, curves and awkward corners with your fingers. Black grout gives extra intensity to the colours.

9 While the grout is still wet, wipe it clean using a densely textured tiler's sponge. Rinse the sponge often and avoid passing a dirty side back over the mosaic, as this will spread the grout rather than remove it. In fiddly areas, you may need to scrape away excess grout with a small screwdriver. Rub down any sharp edges with fine wet-and-dry paper, then leave to dry. Polish the piece with a dry, soft cloth.

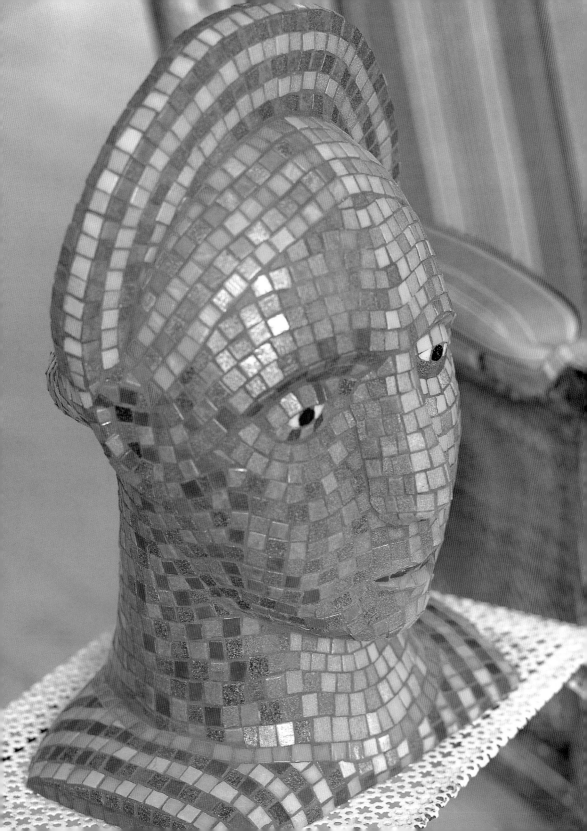

Complete with an ingenious thatched roof and pebbledash walls, this is a very desirable residence to attract nesting birds to your garden. Hang it out of reach of predators.

Thatched Bird House

1 Trace the templates from the back of the book, enlarging as necessary. Wearing a protective face mask, cut out the shapes from MDF using a saw.

2 Using a drill, cut an entrance hole in the top of the front wall. Drill a small hole in the top of the back wall, to hang the finished bird house.

3 Glue the base and walls together. Hold in position with masking tape until the glue is dry.

4 Using a craft knife and ruler and working on a cutting mat, cut a strip of roof flashing the length of the roof and 13cm (5in) wide.

5 Tape the roof sides together. Peel off the backing from the roof flashing, centre over the ridge and stick in place.

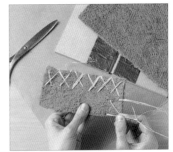

6 Wearing rubber gloves, spread tile adhesive over a small section of the front wall. Sprinkle aquarium gravel over the adhesive, placing darker stones around the entrance hole. Repeat until all the walls are covered with pebbledash.

7 Dilute PVA glue with water and brush over the hanging basket lining. Leave to dry. Cut a rectangle 28 x 14cm (11 x 5½in) for the thatched roof and a strip 15 x 7.5cm (6 x 3in) for the ridge.

8 Using raffia and a darning needle, make a row of large diagonal stitches along one long side of the ridge thatch. Work back in the opposite direction to make cross stitches. Make another row of cross stitches on the other side.

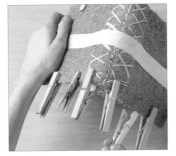

9 Glue the ridge thatch across the centre of the roof thatch. Leave to dry, then stitch down the middle in running stitch. Glue the MDF roof on top of the walls. Leave to dry, then glue the thatch on to the roof. Secure with tape and clothes pegs until dry.

10 Spread adhesive under the eaves and along the front edge of the roof. Stick small sticks along these edges and leave to dry. Dilute toning colours of watercolour paint with plenty of water and wash over the grout to blend it in. When dry, apply a liberal coat of varnish.

Furniture

In this chapter there are plenty of ideas for creating and redecorating pieces of furniture, old or new. Revamp an old chest of drawers, or give a new lease of life to an ageing bedhead. The designs here are just the beginning – every project will have a unique angle, and every room or garden is different, so your finished result will be completely original. Use mosaic to customize your furniture with colour and texture.

Almost every room in the house contains an item of furniture that could be personalized by mosaic: from storage chests and chests of drawers to bedheads, home office furniture and screens.

Chests, Beds and Screens

Bedheads, chests, cupboards and screens are just some of the pieces of furniture that can be transformed by mosaic. Just a quick look around your house will give you plenty of inspiration.

Chests

Mosaic can turn both kinds of chests into highly unusual objects. A chest with a lifting lid can have panels of mosaic applied to the lid and front, while chests of drawers (bureaux) can have small matching or related motifs on each drawer. It is vital with such items that the tesserae do not impede the movement of drawers or doors.

Above: Both end panels and a central panel on the door of this cupboard have been enlivened with mosaics using pieces of old china in a geometric design.

Left: The daisy-filled panels of this pine bedhead would look beautiful in a country-style bedroom.

Cupboards and dressers

Think about adding mosaic to the doors of cupboards or dressers. You do not have to cover the whole door; a small panel with perhaps a decorative border would suffice. Mosaic is an inventive way of reviving and personalizing mass-produced items of furniture or secondhand pieces.

Above: Each drawer of this miniature wooden storage chest has its own striking motif, with just five colours of tiles used in the whole piece.

Left: In this golden stained-glass mosaic screen, the stained glass was laid on top of clear glass so that the light can still shine through. Bands of colour flow freely across the panels, giving a sense of movement.

Mosaic can be heavy, so you need to be sure that the furniture joints and any hinges, as well as the floor, will carry the extra weight. A cupboard with rather weak hinges could have its doors hanging under the extra weight.

When working on wood, a compound called admix may be added to tile adhesive to make it more flexible.

Beds

Wooden bedheads and footboards provide the opportunity for a bedroom transformation. The decorative theme could be carried on to other pieces of furniture in the bedroom, such as a bedside cabinet or chest of drawers, for a matching set.

Instead of the folk art flowers used on the opposite page, you could draw a modern, abstract design and fill it in with bold colours. Consider other themes for different areas of the house: a young child's bed, for example, could have a snakes and ladders design.

Home office

Desks, computer tables, filing cabinets and other home office furniture could benefit from mosaic panels or inserts. Remember that such pieces must do the job for which they are intended: computer tables should form a wobble-free base for the equipment; filing cabinets must have drawers that open and close; and it has to be possible to write

and read easily at a desk. Adding personal touches in the form of mosaics – perhaps incorporating some symbol, logo or initials connected to the business – is a good way of making functional areas less intrusive in the rest of the living space.

Screens

A screen is the perfect solution for dividing a room into different areas, but a touch of lightness is needed to stop it becoming too slab-like. Mirror could be successful, as would gold, silver or other metallic materials in geometric and abstract designs. The play of light, natural or artificial, will add mystery, lightness and movement.

The humble table top is an ideal surface for a mosaicist, being flat and at a convenient height to be seen and admired. There are so many different kinds of table, that every room in the house can have one.

Tables

A chess or games table, side, hall or bedside table, perhaps even a dressing table, would be perfect for mosaic. Garden tables are also ideal.

Finding or making a table

Relatively inexpensive tables are available from second-hand shops, and mosaic is an imaginative and fulfilling way of personalizing them.

Alternatively, you could easily make your own table tops from MDF (medium-density fiberboard), plywood or other manufactured boards, creating different shapes and sizes to suit your mosaic design by cutting them out with a jigsaw (saber saw) or circular saw.

The edge of the table can be finished in mosaic or have a stainless-steel rim or similar edging. Any sharp mosaic edges should be sanded down. You can buy simple metal bases or frames to support the table tops from second-hand stores; alternatively, you could commission one from a blacksmith or craftsperson, or just make your own from blocks of wood.

Table surfaces

You need to make sure that the finished result is smooth and even: people must be able to put drinks and vases on them with no danger of them toppling over or wobbling precariously.

You could mosaic the entire table top or you may prefer to insert a decorative panel into a part of it, often the centre. A mosaic border around the edge would also look attractive. Such panels or borders must be flush or level

Above left: The strong rope design mosaic by Celia Gregory suits the square robustness of this coffee table.

Above: The robust nature of ceramic mosaic lends itself to garden furniture. Here the garden pots have been given a coat of paint to match the colour scheme.

with (not above or below) the rest of the table top, and this needs to be taken into account at the design stage.

If you want to insert a mosaic panel or border, you will need to calculate what depth the finished work will be, then remove that amount from the depth of the table top and sink the mosaic into the prepared area. You should also use pieces of tile throughout with the same thickness.

Non-porous materials, such as glazed clay, glass or a suitable stone, can be easily wiped dry without becoming stained. If the material you choose is porous, you could cover the entire surface of your design with a protective layer of glass. Ask a specialist to cut this to size.

Table-top designs

Your choice of design is, of course, personal, but it is worth noting that repeated patterns and continuous swirling or abstract designs work particularly well on circular tables. You could try a Celtic knot motif or an Islamic organic design. There are many pattern books available in craft shops to use for inspiration. The late Victorians were great pattern book makers, and in these you will find an abundance of choice for designs.

Above right: This table top by Elizabeth De'Ath is decorated with mosaic mirror, divided into sections and bands to create a distinct pattern.

Above far right: This Islamic-influenced table top and a roundel mosaic in similar patterns are by Elaine M. Goodwin.

Right: Celtic designs have a timeless quality that suits both modern and traditional furniture.

Mosaic works extremely well on furniture in the garden. A chair is perhaps not the first item that you might think of applying mosaic to, but would make a real focal point for any patio area.

Garden Furniture

Adding mosaic is a wonderful way to revive tired or battered pieces of garden furniture, and it will also make pieces more weather-resistant.

Tables

A garden table is an ideal subject for mosaic. Not only is it a flat, horizontal surface, and therefore easy to work on, but it, and its surrounding chairs, will often be the centre of attention on the patio or lawn, making it the perfect place to create a dramatic design.

Geometric designs can make an impact by contrasting with the flowing lines of flowers and trees that surround them, while designs inspired more directly by nature can complement their surroundings. Whatever the design or colours used, a mosaic can transform the most humble garden table of any size or shape.

Chairs and benches

White plastic garden furniture cannot be made into works of art, but a simple kitchen-style chair or a standardized garden bench are both ideal candidates for the mosaic treatment.

Right: An old chair is given a new lease of life by the addition of mosaic. A large, three-dimensional object such as this will require a deceptively large number of tesserae to cover it.

Almost any part of a chair or bench can take mosaic, though you must always remember that they are for sitting on and leaning against, so the mosaic must be flush, smooth and even.

Preparation

Think carefully about the amount of mosaic materials required: covering a large table top or an entire chair (or even a set of chairs) will take a large number of tesserae.

The element of unity is also important. There should be continuity of pattern or colour to avoid the end result looking disjointed. Pieces do not need to be identical, but they must have some strong visual factor linking them, such as colour or pattern.

Below: A quirky sea urchin seat stands invitingly on the lawn. Vitreous glass tiles are suitable for outdoor use.

Above: This outstanding table is encrusted with scallop, cockle, cowrie, snail, mussel and limpet shells, plus a sea urchin.

Below: Ceramic floor tiles were used to create the star design on this table, and tiny gold tesserae were placed in the large gaps.

Never throw away your favourite china when it gets chipped or broken. Instead, give it another chance to shine as one of the patterns in a table-top mosaic. Unlike in a jigsaw, the pieces don't have to fit.

Mosaic Table Top

you will need

2cm (¾in) thick chipboard (particle board)

saw

5 x 2.5cm (2 x 1in) wood for frame

mitre saw

wood glue

panel pins (brads)

hammer

hardboard or thick card (stock)

metal ruler

craft (utility) knife

self-healing cutting mat

PVA (white) glue

paintbrushes

old china and clay pots

old towels

tile adhesive

grout spreader

tile grout

sponge

soft cloth

paint

polyurethane varnish (optional)

1 Cut the chipboard to make a base of the required size for a table. Mitre the length of wood to make a frame to surround the base. Glue and pin the frame. There must be a recess of about 5cm (2in) depending on the depth of the material you are using for the mosaic.

2 Cut a matching piece of thick card or hardboard to use for planning the design. Use a metal rule and a craft knife, being careful to press down on to a cut-resistant surface like a cutting mat.

3 Paint the chipboard with diluted PVA glue, to seal the base.

4 Place large pieces of china and pieces of clay pot between two old towels.

▶

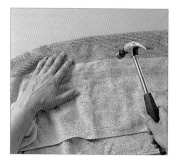

5 Smash the china and clay pot with a hammer. This can be done in a controlled way to get the shapes you need and to protect your eyes.

6 Plan the layout of your design on the hardboard or card. The design can be whatever you want: random, geometric or representational.

7 Using the notched side of a grout spreader coat the board with a layer of tile adhesive 5mm (¼in) deep. This spreader was made out of thick card.

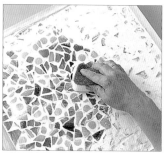

8 Transfer all the pieces, bedding them down in the adhesive to hide the different thicknesses and to make the surface as level as you can.

9 Leave to dry overnight, then apply the tile grout with a grout spreader. Ensure the grout is evenly distributed between the mosaic pieces.

10 When the grout begins to dry, wipe off the excess with a damp sponge.

11 When the grout is dry, use a dry, soft cloth to buff up the shiny ceramic surface, so revealing all the colours.

12 Paint the frame, using a colour that complements the mosaic, and apply two coats of polyurethane varnish if it is for outdoor use.

The bold design of this table top and the simplicity of its metal frame combine to create a table that would look good in the conservatory or garden. Tiny chips of gold-leaf smalti create glinting highlights.

Star Garden Table

you will need
2cm (¾in) thick plywood
pencil
string
drawing pin (thumb tack)
jigsaw (saber saw)
abrasive paper
PVA (white) glue
paintbrush
tape measure (optional)
selection of ceramic floor tiles
tile nippers
tile adhesive
flexible knife
sponge
piece of sacking (heavy cloth)
hammer
gold-leaf tiles
soft brush
plant mister
dilute hydrochloric acid, goggles and rubber gloves (optional)
metal table frame
screws
screwdriver
soft cloth

1 Follow the instructions for the Shades of Blue Garden Table on page 192 to cut a circle from the plywood. Then prime with diluted PVA glue, paying special attention to the edges.

2 Using the template provided, draw a simple design on the table top. You may need to use a tape measure to get the proportions right, but don't be too rigid about the geometry, as a freehand approach suits this method of working.

3 Cut the floor tiles that are in your outlining colour into small pieces using tile nippers. Try to cut them into a variety of shapes, as uniform shapes would jar with the crazy-paving effect of the smashed tesserae used for the rest of the table.

4 Using a flexible knife, spread tile adhesive around the edge of the table top. Firmly press the outlining tesserae into the adhesive, making sure they do not overlap the edges.

▶

5 Apply tile adhesive to the lines of your drawing and press in the outlining tesserae. Use a sponge to wipe away any large bits of adhesive that have squashed out from under the edges of the tesserae, and leave to dry overnight.

6 Cover the remaining tiles with a piece of sacking and smash them with a hammer. Apply tile adhesive to small areas at a time and press in the tile fragments between the outlines of the table top. Do this carefully, as the finished surface must be as flat as possible. Leave to dry overnight or while working on another area.

7 Using a flexible knife, smooth tile adhesive on to the edges of the table. Cut gold-leaf tiles into tiny, irregular tesserae using tile nippers. Place these in the larger gaps between the broken tiles on the table top. If necessary, first insert a blob of tile adhesive to ensure that the gold is at the same level as the tiles as the surface should be flat and smooth. Leave to dry overnight.

8 Spoon tile adhesive powder on to the surface of the table and smooth it into all the gaps with a soft brush. Spray water over the table. When the powder has absorbed enough water, wipe away any excess with a cloth. If the adhesive sinks when wetted, repeat this process. Leave to dry for 24 hours.

9 Turn the table top over and rub tile adhesive into the plywood on the underside with your fingers. Leave to dry overnight. Clean off excess adhesive with abrasive paper. Alternatively, use dilute hydrochloric acid, wearing goggles and rubber gloves, and apply it outside or where there is good ventilation. Wash any acid residue from the surface.

10 When clean, turn the table top face down on a protected surface and screw the metal frame in place using screws that are no longer than the thickness of the plywood. Finally, polish the table top with a dry, soft cloth.

This simple bought chest with drawers has been transformed by mosaic motifs into an individual, playful piece of furniture. The many white tesserae and the white adhesive give the shelf a fresh, clean look.

Storage Chest

you will need
chest with drawers
acrylic white undercoat paint
paintbrush
pencil
thin ceramic household tiles in
five colours, plus white
tile nippers
tile adhesive
flexible knife
sponge
abrasive paper
paint scraper
soft cloth

1 Paint the chest and drawers inside and out with watered-down white undercoat paint. Leave to dry.

2 Draw a simple motif on the front of each drawer. Choose motifs that have a bold outline and are easily recognizable when executed in one colour, like a red heart, star, flower, spiral or fish.

3 Cut the tiles into unevenly shaped tesserae using tile nippers. Using a flexible knife, spread some tile adhesive within the outline of one of the motifs, then firmly press single-coloured tesserae into it.

4 Spread tile adhesive on the rest of the drawer front, one area at a time, then surround the motif with tesserae of a different colour. Take care not to overlap the edges of the drawer. Cover the remaining drawer fronts using a different combination of two colours each time.

5 Cut tiny slivers of white tile. Stick these to the narrow front edges of the chest with tile adhesive. Do this very carefully so that none of the tesserae overlaps the edge.

6 Cut more white tiles into various shapes and sizes, then stick these to the large, flat outside surfaces of the chest. When all four surfaces are covered, leave the chest and the drawers to dry overnight.

7 Spread tile adhesive over the surface of the chest and drawers with a flexible knife. Take special care when smoothing the adhesive into the thin edges of the chest and the edges of the drawer fronts, making sure it is flush with the edges. When all the gaps between the tesserae are filled, wipe off most of the excess adhesive with a damp sponge. Leave to dry for 24 hours.

8 Sand off any remaining surface adhesive from the chest and drawers. Then use an implement with a sharp, flat edge, such as a paintscraper, to scrape along the inside edge of the chest and the sides of the drawers. Do this carefully to ensure there are no overlapping tesserae and that the action of the drawers is not impeded. Polish with a dry, soft cloth.

There is something immensely pleasing about the simple regularity of black-and-white patterns, whether the tiles are set chequerboard style or as diamonds. The border could be thicker or set in one colour only.

Black-and-white Tiled Table

1 Remove the table top and seal with a coat of diluted PVA glue. When the wood has dried, score the surface using a craft knife.

2 To help you to centre the tiles and work out how wide the borders will be, use a pencil and ruler to draw dividing lines (as shown) on the table top.

3 Cut four lengths of wooden batten to fit around the edges of the table. Attach with wood glue and panel pins, leaving a lip around the top edge of exactly the depth of the tiles.

4 Cut a few tiles diagonally to make triangles. Lay these out as a border on the table top and fill in with whole tiles to see how many will fit. Draw border lines around the edges.

5 Spread tile adhesive over the surface of the table top, inside the border lines, using a notched spreader. Starting with the triangular border tiles, set out the pattern, butting the tiles together and leaving only very small gaps for the grouting.

6 Cut strips of tile to fit around the borders, then fix in place as before. Once the tiles have dried, grout the surface, removing any excess with a damp sponge. When dry, polish the tiles with a dry, soft cloth. Attach the table top to the legs and seal and paint the table frame and legs if desired.

The daisy-filled panels of this pine bedhead, with matching footboard, would look beautiful in a country bedroom containing distressed wood furniture. The same design could be used on other panelled pieces.

Mosaic Bedhead

you will need
unvarnished pine bedhead and
footboard
PVA (white) glue
paintbrush
craft (utility) knife
tile adhesive
admix
flexible knife
soft pencil
plain glazed ceramic tiles: white,
orange, green and honey-coloured
piece of sacking (heavy cloth)
hammer
tile nippers
rubber spreader or cloth pad
sponge
abrasive paper
soft cloth

1 Seal the surface of the wood with diluted PVA glue, then score the surface with a craft knife. Mix the tile adhesive with admix according to the instructions.

2 Using a flexible knife, fill any recesses in the areas to be decorated with the adhesive mixture. Leave for 24 hours to allow the adhesive to set.

3 Using the template provided, draw a daisy design on the panels with a soft pencil.

4 Wrap each white and orange tile separately in a piece of sacking and break them with a hammer. Trim the white tile pieces into petal shapes with mosaic nippers. Trim the orange tile pieces into round centres for the daisies.

5 Spread the tile adhesive mixture over the daisy shapes on the panels. Press the white and orange tesserae in place to make the flowers.

6 Smash the green tiles as before. Shape the pieces with tile nippers to make stems and leaves.

7 Spread the tile adhesive mixture over the appropriate areas of the design, then press the green tesserae into position to make leaves and stems. Leave to dry for 24 hours.

8 Finally, smash the honey-coloured tiles as before. Spread the tile adhesive mixture around the daisies and fill in the background, cutting the tesserae as necessary to fit.

9 Using a rubber spreader or cloth pad, spread more adhesive over the mosaic. Push the adhesive well down into the spaces and make sure that all the sharp corners are covered. Remove any excess adhesive with a damp sponge, then leave to dry for 24 hours.

10 Lightly smooth the surface of the mosaic with abrasive paper. Polish with a dry, soft cloth.

A panelled piece of furniture is ideal for mosaic because it gives you a ready-made frame in which to work. This simple, geometric design is made with pieces of old china and is particularly effective.

Decorative Panel

you will need

piece of wooden furniture with a
framed panel or panels
white spirit (paint thinner)
PVA (white) glue
paintbrushes
bradawl or awl
soft dark pencil
masking tape
old china
tile nippers
tile adhesive
admix
flexible knife
cloths
abrasive paper
paint scraper

1 Remove any varnish from the areas of wood you wish to mosaic with white spirit. Prime with diluted PVA glue and leave to dry. Score the surface with a bradawl or awl.

2 Draw a simple design on to the wood for the first panel. In this project we started with the cupboard door.

3 Stick masking tape around the raised edges of the panel(s) to protect the surrounding wood.

4 Using tile nippers, cut the old china into small, random shapes. Sort the pieces into colours or shades of particular colours. Test out the colour scheme by positioning the pieces on the design until you are satisfied.

5 Mix the tile adhesive with admix according to the manufacturer's instructions. Working on a small area at a time, spread the mixture over each area of the pencil design with a flexible knife and press on the tesserae. Leave to dry.

▶

6 Grout the mosaic with more tile adhesive and admix mixture. The china pieces will make an uneven surface, so use a piece of cloth to reach into all the gaps. Wipe off the excess then leave to dry overnight.

7 Carefully sand off any residual tile adhesive that may have dried on the surface of the mosaic, using fine abrasive paper. Use a paint-scraper to reach stubborn or awkward areas, such as those next to the wood.

8 Once the residual adhesive is removed, carefully pull off the masking tape from around the edges of the mosaic panels.

9 Finally, remove any remaining dried adhesive from the mosaic panels and polish the surface with a dry, soft cloth.

Sea urchins are found clinging to wild, rocky shorelines or nestling in rock pools. Their simple, pleasing shapes bring a taste of the ocean to your garden. They come in many colours, including these soft blues.

Sea Urchin Garden Seat

you will need

4 whole breezeblocks (cinderblocks) and 1 small cut piece

sand

cement

hammer

cold chisel

charcoal

vitreous glass mosaic tiles

tile adhesive

black cement stain

notched trowel

tile nippers

slate

piece of sacking (heavy cloth)

glass baubles, silver and

glass circles or stones

1 Mix 3 parts sand to 1 part cement with some water. Use this mortar to join the breezeblocks into a cube formed from two L shapes, with a cut block in the centre.

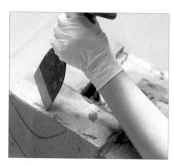

2 When the mortar is dry, knock off the corners of the blocks with a hammer and cold chisel. Continue to shape the blocks into a flat dome, with the cut block at the top.

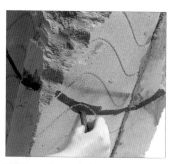

3 Using charcoal, draw a curved line on each side of the cube to give the impression of a rounded sea urchin. Draw lines radiating out from the centre. Keep your choice of colours simple and bold. Lay out the design before you start and apply the tiles to check the spacing. Vitreous glass tiles were chosen because of their suitability for outdoor work. Cut them into strips for easy lines or soak them off the mesh.

4 Add a small amount of black cement stain to the tile adhesive and trowel it directly on to the surface of the block, no more than 5mm (¼in) thick. Place each tile on the surface of the adhesive and tap it down sharply, once only, with the tile nippers. Do not adjust the tiles too much or they will lose their adhesion. Wrap the slate in a piece of sacking and break into pieces with a hammer.

5 Avoid making any sharp edges, as these will have to be filed down afterwards. Use just one dark shade of tiles for the curved line marked in step 3 to give the design visual clarity. Place the broken slate pieces on the adhesive around the square base of the seat and tap them down with the tile nippers.

6 In between the gaps on the square base of the seat, place glass baubles, silver and glass circles, blue and white cut tiles or stones in the pattern of running water. Leave to dry completely. Grout the seat with sand, cement and black stain mixed with water. Allow to dry slowly but thoroughly. To secure the seat in position, dig out a shallow base for two breezeblocks, and then mortar the seat to them.

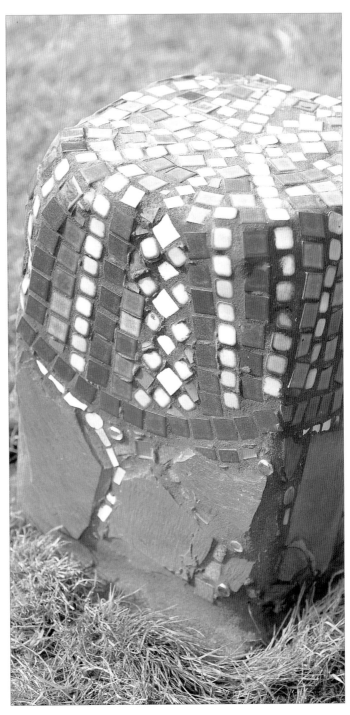

This striking table has been decorated with only bits of broken china and ceramic mosaic tiles, yet with clever colour coordination and a very simple design, it makes an attractive piece of garden furniture.

Shades of Blue Garden Table

you will need

2.5cm (1in) thick plywood
string
drawing pin (thumb tack)
pencil
jigsaw (saber saw)
abrasive paper
wood primer
paintbrush
broken china in various colours
and patterns
tile nippers
tile adhesive
flexible knife
tile grout
cement stain (optional)
sponge
soft cloth

1 To mark a circle on the plywood, tie one end of a length of string, cut to the desired radius of the table top, to a drawing pin, and tie a pencil to the other end. Push the pin into the centre of the plywood, then draw the circle. Cut it out using a jigsaw and sand the edges. Draw your design, adjusting the string to draw concentric circles. Use the template provided.

2 Prime the plywood circle with wood primer on the front, back and around the edge. Apply a thick and even coat, and allow each side to dry before proceeding with the next. Allow the primer to dry thoroughly according to the manufacturer's instructions before proceeding further.

3 Using tile nippers, snip pieces of the china to fit your chosen design and arrange them on the table top. Also snip some more regularly shaped pieces, which will decorate the rim of the table.

4 Spread tile adhesive on to the back of each piece of china with a flexible knife before fixing it in position. Cover the whole table with the design, then mosaic the rim.

5 Mix up the grout, adding a stain if desired, then rub it into all the gaps with your fingers. Do not forget the rim. Clean off any excess with a damp sponge, then leave to dry. Polish with a dry, soft cloth.

This traditional design uses the colours seen in ancient Roman mosaics to create a table top suitable for a simple metal base. Unglazed tiles are much easier than glazed tiles to cut and shape for this precise design.

Star Table

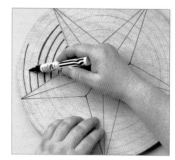

1 Follow the instructions for the Shades of Blue Garden Table (on page 192) to cut a circle from the plywood. Prime one side of the plywood with diluted PVA glue and leave to dry. Score with a bradawl or awl. Using a pair of compasses, draw circles 12mm (½in) apart, working out from the centre, then draw a large star on top. If you wish, go over the design in felt-tipped pen.

2 Using tile nippers, cut the white tiles into neat quarters. Apply PVA glue to the base in small sections, using a fine paintbrush. Stick the tesserae on to alternate sections of the star. Keep the rows straight and the gaps between the tesserae even and to a minimum. Trim the tesserae as necessary to fit. Continue laying the tesserae until all the white sections are complete.

3 Cut up the beige tiles into neat quarters and fill in the other sections of the star in the same way as the white tiles in step 2.

4 Cut the black tiles into neat quarters and glue around the edge of the plywood. Leave until it is completely dry.

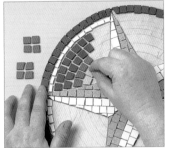

5 Glue a row of black quarter tiles around the outer edge of the table top. Cut some white quarter tiles in half and glue these inside the black circle, keeping the gaps to a minimum. Cut the terracotta tiles into quarters.

6 Using your drawn lines as a guide, fill in the rest of the background with alternating bands of colour. Lay out the tesserae before you glue them in place. Leave to dry overnight. Grout with tile adhesive, then clean the surface with a damp sponge. Leave to dry, then sand off any remaining adhesive and polish with a dry, soft cloth.

The combination of colours and the simple design of this mosaic table create a striking piece of furniture. The table can be used outdoors in good weather, but is not completely weatherproof.

Flower Garden Table

you will need

2.5cm (1in) thick plywood sheet

string

drawing pin (thumb tack)

soft dark pencil

jigsaw (saber saw)

abrasive paper

paper

masking tape

large sheet of tracing paper

PVA (white) glue

paintbrush

vitreous glass mosaic tiles: off-white, light verdigris, dark verdigris, moss, gold-veined verdigris, gold-veined green

tile nippers

tile adhesive

flexible knife

soft cloth

tile grout

grout spreader

sponge

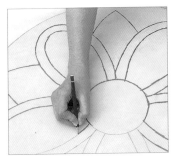

1 Follow the instructions for the project on page 192 to cut a circle from the plywood. Using the template as a guide, draw a large, rounded petal, with half a pointed petal on each side, on paper. Enlarge it until it is the right size for the table top. Then make four copies and stick them all together, so that you have five rounded and five pointed petals. Now trace the design on to tracing paper.

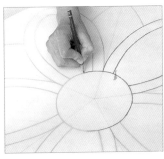

2 Turn the tracing paper over so that the pencil lines are facing down. Place the paper on top of the piece of plywood, and draw over the lines of the design with the pencil to transfer the marks to the plywood.

3 Seal the board with diluted PVA glue, making sure you seal the edge of the plywood as well.

4 Using the tile nippers, cut the glass tiles into halves and thirds so you have a variety of widths. Make a small pile of each colour and save some whole tiles to cut into wedges later. ▶

5 Using a flexible knife, spread tile adhesive over one area at a time, approximately 3mm (⅛in) deep. Select off-white, light verdigris, dark verdigris and moss-coloured tesserae, and press them into the tile adhesive, leaving a tiny gap between each piece for the grout to be applied later. Wipe away any adhesive spillages immediately with a cloth.

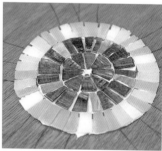

6 Fill in the area inside the ring with the gold-veined verdigris and gold-veined green tesserae. In order to achieve a neat finish in the centre of the design, nibble the tesserae into wedge shapes.

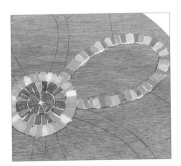

7 Stick down the outside rim of one of the rounded petals, using the light verdigris, dark verdigris and gold-veined verdigris tesserae.

8 Fill in the rounded petal with the light verdigris, dark verdigris, gold-veined verdigris and gold-veined green tesserae, nibbling them to fit neatly within the rim of the petals. Repeat for the other rounded petals.

9 Fill in the pointed petals with the gold-veined verdigris, gold-veined green, light verdigris and dark verdigris tesserae.

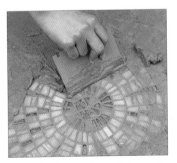

10 Fill in the area between the flower design and the edge of the plywood with the off-white, light verdigris and moss tesserae. Leave to dry for a day.

11 Push tile grout into all the cracks between the tesserae using a grout-spreader. Wipe any excess grout off the table top and edge with a damp sponge, then leave to dry.

12 When the table top is dry, turn it over on to a protected surface and spread the base evenly with some tile adhesive in order to seal it. When it is dry, turn the table back again and polish the surface with a dry, soft cloth.

This wonderful table is literally strewn with daisies – green stems twine around the legs and a carpet of pretty white flowers spreads over the top. If the table has a rim, saw it off first to make the shape easier to mosaic.

Daisy-covered Table

you will need
small table
white spirit (paint thinner)
abrasive paper (sandpaper)
PVA (white) glue
paintbrush
bradawl or awl
soft dark pencil
thin-glazed ceramic household tiles:
yellow, white, green, pale pink
tile nippers
tile adhesive
admix
flexible knife
hammer
piece of sacking (heavy cloth)
rubber spreader
sponge
soft cloth

1 Remove any old wax, dirt, paint or varnish from the table using white spirit, then sand and prime with diluted PVA glue. Leave to dry, then score all the surfaces with a bradawl or awl.

2 Draw flowers and stems twisting around the legs and spreading over the table top. Take care with your design where the legs join the table top.

3 Using tile nippers, cut the yellow tiles into small squares, then nip off the corners to make circles for the centres of the flowers.

4 Cut the white tiles into small, equal size oblongs. Make these into petal shapes by nipping off the corners of each oblong.

▶

5 Mix the tile adhesive and admix together. Using a flexible knife, spread the mixture over a pencilled flower outline. Press in a yellow flower centre and the white petals – you may need to cut some petals on the legs in half. Complete all the flowers in this way.

6 Spread a thin coat of the adhesive mixture along the pencil outlines of the stems and leaves. Cut the green tiles into appropriate stem and leaf shapes and press them in place. Leave to dry overnight.

7 Using a hammer, break up the pale pink tiles. It is advisable to wrap each tile in a piece of sacking to prevent splintering and shattering.

8 Working on a small area at a time, spread the adhesive mixture over the background areas. Press in the pale pink tile pieces to fit. Leave to dry overnight.

9 Grout the mosaic with tile adhesive, using a rubber spreader for the large flat areas and your fingers for the smaller areas. Wipe off the excess adhesive with a damp sponge and leave to dry overnight.

10 Carefully sand the surface of the table top and legs to remove any lumps of dried adhesive still remaining. Wipe with a damp sponge, if necessary, and polish with a dry, soft cloth.

In this project, the mosaics are laid in shapes inset on a surface, rather than over the entire area, and the intervening veneer forms are equally important. The lines give the table a sensual and dynamic feeling.

Stained-glass Table

you will need

110 x 70cm (43 x 28in) MDF (medium-density fiberboard) 18mm (¾in) thick

soft pencil

tracing paper

scissors

iron

3mm (⅛in) thick oak veneer

craft (utility) knife

3mm (⅛in) thick stained-glass tiles: red, iridescent pink and rippled clear glass

red chestnut wood stain

paintbrushes

clear polyurethane varnish

PVA (white) glue

contact adhesive

G-clamps

softwood blocks

tile grout

red cement stain

sponge

glass cleaner

21mm (⅞in) thick stainless-steel edging to cover edge of MDF and tiles

1 On the piece of MDF draw six wavy lines with a soft pencil down the length of the board. These define the three bands that will be filled with the stained-glass and the four bands for the wooden veneer.

2 Trace the lines on to tracing paper. Then cut out templates of the four bands for the veneer. The wooden veneer should be 3mm (⅛in) thick, or the same thickness as the glass tiles to be used for the mosaic, so that they create a flat surface.

3 Iron the cut-out templates flat, using a warm, not hot, heat, as the tracing paper tends to crinkle and fold.

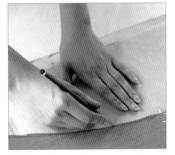

4 Place the templates on to the oak veneer. Using a soft pencil, carefully draw a line around the edge of each template. Placing any straight lines along the straight edge of the veneer makes it easier for cutting.

▶

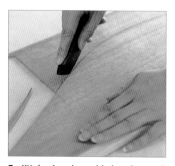

5 With the sharp blade of a craft knife, and working on a protected surface, score a strong line along the pencil marks. Work the curved lines in sections, removing excess veneer as you go.

6 Place the four cut-out sections of veneer in their correct positions on the table. Using tile nippers, snip the stained-glass tiles into small pieces, laying them in position until the desired effect is achieved. In the planning, be aware of the balance of different coloured and rippled glass.

7 Lay the pieces of veneer on a protected surface and apply two thin coats of red chestnut wood stain. Allow to dry. Apply several coats of clear varnish to each piece, allowing each coat to dry before applying the next.

8 Place the veneer panels back in position on the table. Cover the back of the stained-glass tesserae evenly with PVA glue, using a small paintbrush. Arrange the pieces in a random arrangement on the table in a ratio of four red tiles to every two pink and one clear.

9 To stick the veneer down, use contact adhesive, following the manufacturer's instructions carefully. Apply a thin film of this glue on to both the back of the veneer and the surface of the table. After about 10 minutes, or when the glue is tacky, bring the two surfaces together and press down hard, clamp (using softwood blocks to protect the veneer) and leave to dry. Note that once the two surfaces have made contact, no repositioning is possible.

10 Carefully grout the mosaic bands with a grey tile grout mixed with red cement stain. Clean off the excess trying not to get any grout on the veneer. When it is nearly dry, go over the mosaic areas with a sponge dipped in glass cleaner to remove excess grout. When the grout is completely dry, glue the stainless-steel edging in position around the table using contact adhesive.

In this project, the coloured glass tesserae are laid on top of pieces of clear glass. Placing the screen in front of a window by day or a glowing fire at night means that light can shine through it.

Stained-glass Screen

you will need

mitre block
tape measure
hacksaw
3 pieces of 2.5 x 4cm (1 x 1½in)
wood, each 206cm (81in) long, with
a 12mm (½in) rebate (rabbet)
wood glue
hammer
12 corner staples
dark pencil
drill
4 small hinges and screws
screwdriver
large sheet of paper
black felt-tipped pen
3 pieces of clear glass, each
70 x 25cm (28 x 10in)
permanent felt-tipped pen
glass cutter
7 pieces of coloured glass,
27cm (10½in) square
clear all-purpose adhesive
tile grout
black cement stain
toothbrush
paint scraper
soft cloth
3 pieces of rectangular moulding,
each 186cm (74in) long
panel pins (brads)
12 metal corner plates and screws

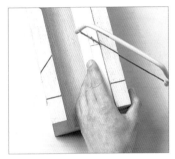

1 Using a mitre block and a hacksaw, cut each piece of rebated wood into two 74cm (29in) long pieces and two 29cm (11½in) long pieces. These will form the wooden frame for the screen.

2 Lay the pieces of wood out on a flat surface to make three oblong frames. Glue the mitred ends together with wood glue, checking they are at right angles. Leave to dry, then hammer in a corner staple at each corner.

3 Place one frame on top of another, with the rebates facing outwards. With a dark pencil, mark the position of two hinges and their screw holes, as shown. Using a drill, make a shallow guidehole for each screw, then screw in the hinges. Attach the third wooden frame in the same way to form a three-piece screen.

▶

4 Place the three frames face down on a large sheet of paper. Using a black felt-tipped pen, draw around the inner edge of each frame. Then draw a simple design that flows in bands of colour from one frame to the next.

5 Place the pieces of clear glass over the paper drawings – the glass will be slightly larger. Using a permanent felt-tipped pen, trace your design on to the pieces of glass, taking care not to press too hard against them.

6 Using a glass cutter, cut 12 right-angled triangles of coloured glass for the corners of the screen. Reserve them on one side. Cut the rest of the coloured glass into random shaped pieces of roughly similar size.

7 Using clear adhesive, glue the coloured pieces on to the clear glass panels. Work on a section of your design at a time, following each band across to the other panels. Leave to dry for 2 hours.

8 Mix the tile grout with the black cement stain and rub it over the surface of the mosaic. Use a toothbrush to make sure all the gaps are filled. Leave to dry for 1 hour.

9 When completely dry, clean off any smaller areas of excess grout with a soft cloth. Residual, stubborn grout can be carefully removed with a paint scraper.

10 Glue one of the reserved right-angled triangles of coloured glass over the corner of the frames, at the front. Repeat with the other triangles, on each corner of the frame.

11 Cut each length of moulding into two 70cm (28in) lengths and two 23cm (9in) lengths. Place the glass panels within their frames, ensuring that they are the right way up, and slot the beading behind them. Fix them in place with panel pins, being very careful as you use the hammer.

12 Make shallow guideholes with a drill, then screw the corner plates to the back of each corner of the frame. Finally, polish the surface of each of the mosaic panels with a dry, soft cloth.

With a little work and imagination, this battered old chair has been transformed into an unusual, exciting piece of furniture. This example shows the extremes to which mosaic can successfully be taken.

Crazy Paving Chair

you will need

wooden chair

2cm (¾in) thick plywood sheet and jigsaw (saber saw) (optional)

white spirit (paint thinner)

abrasive paper

PVA (white) glue

paintbrush

wood glue

tile adhesive

admix

flexible knife

pencil or chalk

large selection of china

tile nippers

dilute hydrochloric acid, goggles and rubber gloves (optional)

soft cloth

1 If the chair you have chosen has a padded seat, remove it. There may be a wooden pallet beneath the padding that you can use as a base for the mosaic. If not, cut a piece of plywood to fit in its place.

2 Strip the chair of any paint or varnish with white spirit and sand down with coarse-grade abrasive paper. Then paint the whole chair with diluted PVA glue to seal it.

3 When the surface is dry, stick the seat in place with a strong wood glue. Use tile adhesive and admix (mixed to the manufacturer's instructions) to fill any gaps around the edge. This will give extra strength and flexibility.

4 Draw a design or motifs on any large flat surfaces of the chair with a pencil or chalk. Use simple shapes that are easy to work with.

5 Select china that has colours and patterns to suit the motifs you have drawn. Using tile nippers, cut the china into the appropriate shapes and sizes for your design.

▶

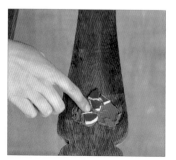

6 Spread the adhesive mixture within the areas of your design and press the cut china firmly into it. Select china to cover the rest of the chair. As you are unlikely to have enough of the same pattern to cover the whole chair, choose two or three patterns that look good together.

7 Cut the china into small, varied shapes. Working on small areas at a time, begin to tile the rest of the chair. Start with the back of the chair first, moving on to the legs, and finally the seat.

8 Where one section of wood meets another, change the pattern of the china you are using.

9 Cut appropriately patterned china into thin slivers and use these to tile the edges of any thin sections of wood. Here, the edges of the back rest are covered. Leave for at least 24 hours to dry completely.

10 Mix up some more tile adhesive and admix. Using a flexible knife, smooth this into the four corners of every piece of wood. Use your fingers to rub it over the flat surfaces. Work on a small area at a time and try to clean off most of the excess as you go. Leave overnight to dry.

11 Sand off the excess adhesive. This can be quite a difficult job, as there are many awkward angles. Alternatively, dilute hydrochloric acid can be used, but you must wear goggles and rubber gloves and apply it either outside or where there is good ventilation. Wash any residue from the surface with plenty of water and, when dry, polish with a dry, soft cloth.

This simple table top has been transformed with a shell mosaic to make a piece of furniture that would be perfect for a patio or conservatory. The symmetrical arrangement of the shells makes an eye-catching design.

Shell Table

1 Using a ruler, pencil, protractor and a pair of compasses, draw a geometric pattern on the table top, following the one shown here or using a design of your own.

2 Using PVA glue and a fine paintbrush, stick a scallop shell to the centre of the table. Glue pink shell pieces from an old necklace inside the starfish shape and surround the starfish with a circle of small snail shells.

3 Break up a sea urchin into tesserae using tile nippers, and glue them in a circle outside the snail shells.

4 Glue ten scallop shells around the edge of the table top, spacing them evenly. Fill in the gaps between the them with mussel shells. Glue cowrie shells in arches between the scallops.

5 Glue a limpet shell in the middle of each space in the inner circle. Fill in the spaces around the limpet shells in between the legs of the starfish with small cockle shells.

6 Fill in the remaining spaces on the table top with an assortment of small shells arranged in a regular pattern.

7 Starting in the centre and working on only a small area at a time, spread tile grout over the surface of the mosaic. Use a grout spreader or small palette knife to press the grout into the gaps.

8 Use a paintbrush to work the grout into the gaps and smooth the surface with a little water. Press firmly with a damp flannel to impact the grout around the shells. Rub the flannel over the shells in an outward direction to remove any grout from the surface of the shells.

9 Repeat steps 7–8 until you have grouted the whole mosaic. Leave to dry for several hours, then polish with a mop attachment on your drill or with a soft cloth.

10 Paint the grouting with diluted emulsion or watercolour paints: pale blue-green for the inner circle and outer edge, and pale ochre for the mid-way band. Finally, apply several coats of pale blue-green colourwash to the edge of the table top.

This lovely mosaic table provides a stunning focal point for any room in the home. With its swirling pattern, the mosaic evokes fresh sea breezes sweeping in off the water.

Mosaic Table

you will need

piece of plywood

jigsaw (saber saw)

sharp knife

PVA (white) glue

paintbrushes

pencil

tile nippers

vitreous glass tesserae, in various colours

cement-based tile adhesive powder

soft brush

plastic spray bottle

cloths

fine abrasive paper

1 Cut the plywood to the desired shape for your table. Score it with a sharp knife and prime it with a coat of diluted PVA glue. Leave to dry.

2 For the table design pictured here, use a pencil to draw a series of swirls radiating from the centre of the table. If you prefer, create your own design.

3 Use tile nippers to cut white glass tiles into quarters, and use different densities of white to add interest to the finished design.

4 Brush PVA glue along the pencil line swirls, then position the white glass tiles on top of the layer of glue, smooth side up.

5 Select your colours for the areas between the white lines. Here, browns and sand colours form the edge while blues, greens and whites are used for the central areas. Spread out your selected colours to see whether the combinations work.

6 Using the tile nippers, cut all of the coloured squares you have chosen into quarters.

7 Glue the central pieces to the table-top with PVA glue. To finish off the edge, glue pieces around the border of the table to match the design of the top surface. Leave the glue to dry thoroughly overnight.

8 Sprinkle dry cement-based tile adhesive over the mosaic and spread it with a brush, filling all the spaces. Spray with water wetting all of the cement. Wipe away any excess.

9 Mix up some tile adhesive with water and rub it into the edges of the table with your fingers. Leave it to dry overnight.

10 Rub off any excess cement with fine abrasive paper and finish the table by polishing the mosaic thoroughly with a soft cloth.

In Situ

Some objects are freestanding, but some are bound to be affected by their position in a room or garden. Even loose tiles are often designed with a particular situation in mind, and this will influence the shape, colour and texture of the chosen design. Mosaics for use as a floor in a minimalist bathroom will have different criteria than a purely decorative feature. Projects that are destined for the outdoors will need particular consideration.

Walls in the home are perfect as settings for mosaic. It can cover a whole wall or be used in the form of insets or panels. Mosaic is ideal in hardworking areas such as the hall, utility room, kitchen or bathroom.

Interior Walls

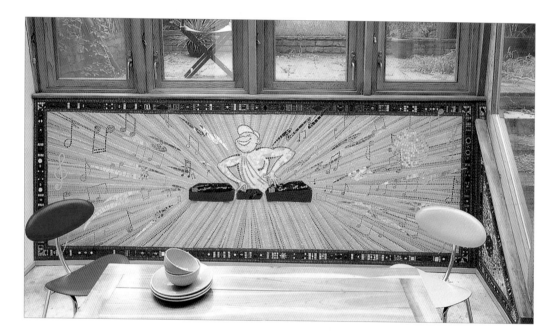

Entire walls of mosaic can look stunning, though they are ambitious projects that should not be undertaken by the inexperienced mosaicist. When planning such a feature, the elements of the design should be kept in scale with their setting: on the wall pictured opposite, the design as an entirety is composed of smaller patterns that can be absorbed by the eye at close quarters – there is no need to step back to try and see the whole. Different decorative schemes can be achieved with mosaic inside the home, from restful and intimate to bold and striking.

Practicalities

If you want to apply mosaic directly to an interior wall, you need to check first that the wall is strong enough to take the size and weight of mosaic and grout that you have in mind. Second, the wall's surface must be even. A strong torch beam shone across the wall will show up areas of unevenness.

Mirror

In some houses or apartments space is at a premium, especially in the bathroom. Using mirror is a good way to create the illusion of a room being

much larger than it really is, and while a whole mirrored wall might be a little daunting, a fragmented wall of mirror mosaic is less revealing yet achieves the same illusion of space.

Above: This wall piece by Celia Gregory appears to be exploding with sound and transforms the conservatory in which it has been built.

Opposite: The Sublime Wall, created by Robert Grace from various sizes of mosaic sheets, has a large overall pattern along with detail to hold interest close up.

More manageable in size than complete murals, and more realistic projects for someone new to mosaic, decorative splashbacks, wall panels and shelves will brighten any room in the house.

Splashbacks, Panels and Shelves

Since the great strength of mosaic is its impact, an entire wall covered in it may be more than you want. In such cases, the ideal solution is a small area, such as a splashback or decorative panel, or even a shelf, specifically designed to suit its surroundings or its owner, or both.

Splashbacks

Mosaic makes perfect splashbacks for cookers (stoves), kitchen sinks and bathroom basins, transforming such items into something unique to you. The design must be practical, as it will receive much wear and tear. A splashback can be formed of a single panel or tiles grouped together.

In a kitchen, simple checks or plain colours with borders work well, while in a bathroom you might like to suggest the movement of waves and water. If you are aiming for something more personal, here is the opportunity to devise an image that picks up on the room's colour scheme but also incorporates elements that are individual to you and your family, such as your initials, a favourite flower or a family crest.

Friezes

Somewhere between splashbacks and wall panels come friezes. There are occasions when a minimal amount of decoration is all that is needed to

transform an area of the house. A frieze, or similar narrow band or border, may be more effective than a larger element in small spaces such as a downstairs cloakroom or a shower room, or in busy areas such as a porch or hallway, where too much elaboration tends to be overlooked amid the bustle of people coming and going.

A small mosaic could also outline a window (perfect to highlight a porthole-style opening), a fire surround or mantelpiece to great effect.

Above: Watery themes suit mosaic panel splashbacks in kitchens and bathrooms.

Wall panels

A hanging wall panel makes a wonderful picture with depth and impact, and a plainly decorated room can be transformed by a well-executed mosaic panel. Including a border into its design finishes off any mosaic, but if you want to heighten the impression of a work of art, the mosaic panel could be framed before it is hung in position.

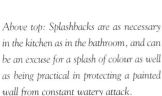

Above top: Splashbacks are as necessary in the kitchen as in the bathroom, and can be an excuse for a splash of colour as well as being practical in protecting a painted wall from constant watery attack.

Above: A mosaiced wall around the side of a garden pond. The broken china with the odd sea shell is set into a waterproof combined adhesive and grout, which was rubbed with a mixture of garden soil and pond water to age the mosaic and so successfully blends the new with the old.

Wall panels can come in all shapes and sizes. A large panel could cover almost an entire wall, dominating the room, while a small one could demand attention by its bold colouring or eye-catching design.

Shelves

A further method of adding mosaic to walls is by way of a shelf or decorated rail. A shelf is an ideal project for a beginner, especially if a simple, all-over design is chosen rather than anything

Above: Gates of the Living – maximum impact with minimum elaboration in this elegant panel by Elaine M. Goodwin.

too complicated. Whether the mosaic is bright and colourful, made from pieces of old china, or calm and restful, made from broken slate, the result is still the introduction of a stunning design element into a room in a functional, yet decorative way. The same applies to a mosaiced rack or rail – adding a unique touch of colour.

Hallways, garden rooms, kitchens, utility rooms and bathrooms are obvious choices for mosaic, but it can also furnish living rooms without seeming too cold or hard to walk on.

Interior Flooring

Mosaic is a practical flooring choice for most areas, being versatile and durable – several examples around 2,000 years old are still in very good condition. Most mosaic materials are tough: they resist marks, spills, scuffs and stains, and are not inclined to fade over time. With the right preparation, they will stick to most surfaces and be comfortable underfoot. Any floor finish must be able to withstand feet, shoes, paws, claws and perhaps wheels as well.

A mosaic, whether covering the whole floor or just part of it, may be all the decoration a floor needs. Ornamentation does not always need to be at eye level to be effective, and treating your room scheme in this way can make a refreshing change.

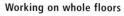

Above: Mosaic flooring is practical and hard-wearing in a bathroom but must be smooth to protect bare feet.

Left: Children can actually play on this fun and practical mosaic patio floor. Climb the ladders, but if you land on a snake, you slip back down.

Working on whole floors

There is no reason at all why you should not mosaic a whole floor, but this is a major undertaking, requiring many hours of patient and skilled work. Alternatively, an inset is an effective way of achieving almost the same result with a fraction of the work.

Choose good, hard-wearing materials that are proof against the risk of damage. Stone and suitably glazed clay are ideal; glass is less so but can be used with care. The floor must be level and even before you lay the mosaic, otherwise it never will be.

Right: Classic black and white tiles are enlivened by a floor inset with mosaic in a stylized reptile and ivy leaf design by Elaine M. Goodwin.

Below: Diamonds of stone and rough-textured pebbles would be perfect in a cottage or farmhouse.

It is important to remember scale when designing for floors. The eye will not want so much detail at this distance, either in the design itself or in the size of stone or tesserae: ensure they are not too small, or the overall result will appear too fussy. Large sections of colour with bold elements such as central motifs and borders work well.

Above: This simple mosaic border is inserted into marble stone flooring. Designed by Celia Gregory, the pattern follows the edge of the pool, enhancing the shape without competing with the main tiles of the floor design.

Above right: Sea-inspired designs, such as sailing boats, shells or fish, are naturally at home in the bathroom as long as they are waterproof enough to withstand wear.

Opposite: The colours are allowed to speak for themselves in this unfussy, but boldly decorated bathroom with its dramatic stained-glass window.

Creative effects

Mosaic can be used on a large scale in a domestic setting. In the bathroom, whole floors and walls can be covered, or you can be less dramatic and cover just the floor. You could also cover the skirting (base) board to link the floor to the walls, or create a contrast.

The colour palette available is vast, especially if you use vitreous glass mosaic sheets. You could choose to echo interior details, such as stained glass in a window, or to co-ordinate the mosaic with other features in the room, such as the colour of the curtains or the bathroom suite.

For hallways, you might choose to work within a more muted colour palette, such as a soft green to balance a rich terracotta mosaic floor. On a porch, a warm shade also creates a welcoming feel.

Dividing a large floor area into sub-sections with the use of decorative borders helps to lead the eye through from the door along the corridors to the foot of the stairs.

Mosaic has a natural affinity with bathrooms. Soft, creamy colours and an elegant border will create a restful decorative scheme and a room to relax in. Marine life and nautical themes fit well into a bathroom scheme.

Living areas are suitable for mosaics, too. A small mosaic, such as a hearth, can be laid to give a sophisticated, smooth surface and create a focal point in a room. Black and white is a classic colour combination for tiled kitchen floors and can be livened up with a smart mosaic inset. If you have a quarry tile floor, a warm, terracotta mosaic would suit best.

Water features, such as fountains and ponds, or outdoor wall panels, are ideal ways of giving mosaic a more prominent role in the garden. The reflective qualities of many tiles make them highly suited to water.

Garden Installations

With the natural affinity between mosaic and water, fountains and other water features are ideal opportunities for the mosaicist to display their skill and imagination. The robustness and strength of colour of mosaic proves an effective counterbalance to the clear, fleeting nature of water.

Mosaic is ideally suited to gardens: it can be varied to suit any setting, its resistance to water means that rain or fountains cannot harm it or dim its vibrancy, and the play of ever-changing outdoor light adds constant interest.

It is best to keep any water feature in proportion. In a small courtyard, it can be tucked into a corner, mounted on a wall or even set in a container.

For a natural look, a mosaic of shells, stone or pebble can form a subtle framework for a pool or fountain, which darkens and gleams where the

water moistens the stones. In a formal garden, you might choose to line the floor or the edge of a pool or pond with a suitable motif, while in an urban garden, a square or rectangular feature with geometric decoration looks good. In a cool, green or white garden, you could install a fountain to create delicate dappled reflections.

Above: Circles of oblong mosaics in blues and sea greens grow darker towards the centre of this pond by Trevor Caley, creating an illusion of depth, while random gold splashes add intriguing glitter.

Left: An elegant mirrored fountain by Rebecca Newnham.

Opposite: For richness, nothing beats gold, whether on its own or as part of a design for a bowl. A collection of water features by Elaine M. Goodwin.

In this panel, the tiles have been laid very close together to avoid the need for grout. This allows the range of tones used here to relate to one another as directly as possible, giving a luminous, glowing appearance.

Abstract Colour Panel

you will need

vitreous glass mosaic tiles in various colours

coloured pencils to match the tiles

paper

tracing paper

tile nippers

MDF (medium-density fiberboard) 50 x 50cm (20 x 20in) with frame

different coloured felt-tipped pens

wood stain

paintbrushes

PVA (white) glue

soft cloth

1 Match the proposed tile colours to the pencils to enable you to produce an accurate coloured drawing. As this scheme is fairly complex, involving boxes within boxes, and tonal colour changes, a line drawing was produced as a plan for the coloured sketch.

2 Draw an accurate coloured sketch. To get a good idea of how the different blocks of tones and shading will work, put a layer of tracing paper over the line drawing and fill in the coloured areas. Use the tile nippers to cut the mosaic tiles in your chosen colours.

3 Draw the fundamentals of the design on to the board using felt-tipped pens. It is not necessary to mark up any more detail than you see here. The segmented pattern is sketched in black, and the ladder lines in different colours. Stain the frame of the board before starting to stick down the tiles.

4 Sort your tiles into tones of greater or lesser intensity. Paint each area of the board that you are working on with a good layer of PVA glue. If the layer is too thin, the tiles will fail to adhere; if it is too thick, the glue will squeeze between the joints on to the tile face. Start by laying the coloured ladder shapes.

5 Continue working around the board, filling in the different coloured areas as you go. Wipe off any blobs of glue as you work, then wipe over the whole thing with a cloth when you have finished to remove any residual adhesive. Finally, polish with a dry, soft cloth.

Norma Vondee has decorated the door of this bathroom cabinet with a witty mosaic. The shadows and highlights give the bottle, glass and pot a three-dimensional appearance.

Bathroom Cabinet

you will need

wall-mounted cabinet with door

3mm (⅛in) thick plywood sheet

saw

bradawl or awl

pencil

ceramic mosaic tiles

tile nippers

PVA (white) glue

paintbrush

masking tape

sand

cement

red cement stain

grout spreader

sponge

soft cloth

1 Remove the wooden or glass panel in the door of the bathroom cabinet. Cut a piece of plywood to the same size and score the surface with a bradawl or awl. Using the template provided, draw your design on the plywood. Mark in the ellipses and areas of shadow.

2 Cut the ceramic mosaic tiles into precise shapes using the tile nippers. Apply these tesserae to the main outlines of the shapes, fixing them in place with PVA glue applied with a fine paintbrush. Take extra care when tiling curved areas, snipping the tiles into wedge shapes to ensure they fit.

3 Fill the areas inside the outlines in contrasting colours. Here, reflections and highlights are depicted using different shades of tesserae to create the illusion of a three-dimensional scene.

4 Outline the shapes with a row of tesserae in the background colour. If making a larger design, you could use a double row of tesserae to outline the subjects of the mosaic.

5 Fill in the background colour with tesserae arranged in straight lines, and leave overnight to dry. Secure the panel in position on the cabinet door and mask the frame with tape. Mix 3 parts sand and 1 part cement with water and a little red cement stain. Grout the mosaic with this mixture using a grout spreader. Clean the surface carefully with a damp sponge and leave to dry as slowly as possible, then polish with a dry, soft cloth.

Create an outdoor "fireside rug" from pebbles, broken garden pots and old china ginger-jar tops. The simple design is not difficult to achieve and makes an appealing, witty motif in a paved patio.

Pretty Pebble Rug

you will need
spade
fine aggregate to fill the area to a depth of 10cm (4in)
cement
watering can
water for mixing
selection of pebbles, pieces of slate, terracotta pots, china-pot lid tops
tile nippers
sharp sand
mortar colour
straightedge
hammer
soft brush
board to cover rug area
4 bricks
plastic sheeting

Preparation

For the flat bed, dig a pit 15cm (6in) deep and to the dimensions of the panel. The "rug" illustrated here measures 60 x 90cm (2 x 3ft). Mix equal parts of fine aggregate and cement. Using a watering can, dribble in a little water at a time until you have a dry, crumbly mix. Use this to fill the area, leaving a 5cm (2in) clearance. Allow the mix to dry. Gather together plenty of materials for the design and lay them out for size on the dry bed before you begin. Using tile nippers, cut off the bottoms of at least six terracotta pots and snip off the rims in sections. Choose pebbles and slates that are long enough to bed in at least 2.5cm (1in) below the surface of the rug.

1 Prepare the mortar bedding by mixing equal quantities of sharp sand and cement. Add the mortar colour and mix in well. The design is worked while the mortar mix is dry. However, the rug has to be completed in a day because moisture from the atmosphere will begin to set the mortar.

2 Pour the dry mix on to the flat bed and, using a straightedge, smooth it out until it is level with the rest of the paving. Then remove a small quantity from the centre so the mix does not overflow as you work.

3 Starting from the outside and using the hammer, tap in pebbles, slates and the rim sections from the terracotta pots to make a level, decorative border. Brush the mortar over the worked areas to make sure any gaps are filled.

4 To build up the border design, continue working towards the centre, carefully hammering in the pebbles, slates and terracotta as you go. Use the china pot lid tops to add a splash of colour to the four corners.

5 Work out a central design to provide a contrast with the border. Cut the pieces as necessary and hammer into position. Brush mortar evenly over the surface. Using a watering can with a fine rose, dampen the surface.

Aftercare

The damp rug will set hard as it absorbs the moisture from the watering can. Once complete, protect the rug for three days by covering it with a board raised on bricks then overlaid by plastic sheeting. Avoid walking on the rug for a month to allow the mortar to set thoroughly.

In this simple yet striking wheel design, the areas between the spokes can be planted with alpines or herbs, which could be surrounded by pebbles. It also looks effective with no plants, just pebbles.

Miniature Pebble Circle

you will need
for a wheel about 2.5m (8ft)
in diameter:
2 x 15cm (6in) lengths of wood
string
spade
62 bricks
5kg (11lb) bag of sand and cement mix
mortar trowel
pots, slates, broken terracotta

1 Make a simple pair of compasses using the two pieces of wood linked by a piece of string the length of the radius of the wheel. Dig out the approximate area of the wheel. Using the compasses, mark out the circle and central area. Place bricks around the edge of the circle and inside it to form spokes, like a wheel.

2 Walk over the surface of the circle to flatten the earth and ensure it is level. Add sufficient water to the sand and cement mix to achieve a crumbly consistency. Using a mortar trowel, smooth the cement into the centre of the circle.

3 Working quickly before the cement sets, press in a border of slates.

4 Working in concentric rings, add a circle of terracotta and another of slates, then a wheel of pebbles and terracotta. Fill the spokes of the circle with small pebbles.

These large-scale pebble mosaics are very hardwearing and can be repeated as many times as necessary to make a path or patio. This slab measures 36cm (14in) square – anything larger becomes too heavy.

Mosaic Slabs

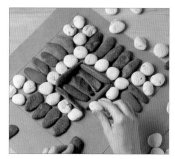

1 Arrange the pebbles that make up the design on a piece of paper the same size as the finished slab.

2 Nail together the four pieces of wood to make a square frame. Cover the floor with a plastic sheet. Wearing rubber gloves, mix the cement in a bucket and fill the frame.

3 Press the cement down well, especially into the corners. Smooth the surface just below the top of the frame.

4 Transfer the pebbles from the paper on to the cement, pressing each pebble firmly in place. Leave for several days for the cement to set.

5 Remove the slab from the frame by banging the edge of the frame firmly on the ground. Repeat to make other designs.

This dramatic mosaic creates the invigorating effect of rocks sparkling with drops of water in a mountain stream. This project is quick to complete, as it does not need to be grouted.

Slate Shelf

you will need

2cm (¾in) thick plywood sheet

saw

bradawl or awl

PVA (white) glue

paintbrush

hammer

slate

piece of sacking (heavy cloth)

tile adhesive

black cement stain

flexible knife

pebbles

glass globules: blue, grey, white

silver smalti

tile nippers

1 Cut the piece of thick plywood to the desired size with a saw. Lightly score one side with a bradawl or awl, then prime with diluted PVA glue.

2 Using a hammer, break the slate into large chunks. It is advisable to wrap the slate in a piece of sacking to prevent injury.

3 Mix the tile adhesive with half a teaspoon of black cement stain. Mix to a thick paste with cold water.

4 Using a flexible knife, spread the tile adhesive in a thick, even layer over the scored side of the plywood. Smooth it over the front to conceal the edge.

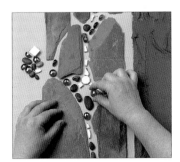

5 Arrange the broken slate, pebbles, glass globules and silver smalti on a flat surface next to the board in your chosen design, making any adjustments until you are satisfied.

6 Transfer the design, piece by piece, to the board. Tap the slate with the side of the tile nippers to settle it, but do not move any pieces once firmly positioned. Leave to dry overnight.

This useful and colourful kitchen rail is made out of old patterned china. The kitchen theme can be carried through by drawing around cups, plates and jars to create the circular designs.

China Rail

you will need

12mm (½in) thick MDF (medium-density fiberboard), cut to 60 x 25cm (24 x 10in)

jigsaw (saber saw)

abrasive paper

PVA (white) glue

paintbrush

dark pencil

60cm (24in) long metal rail, with struts

screws

screwdriver

plates, cups and jars, in different sizes

hammer

old patterned china

piece of sacking (heavy cloth)

tile nippers

soft cloths

tile grout

rubber spreader

paint scraper

S-shaped metal hooks

2 protruding mirror plates

1 Using a jigsaw cut the MDF so that it is 15cm (6in) high on each side, rising to a smooth curve in the centre. Sand the edges with abrasive paper until smooth. Prime both sides of the board with diluted PVA glue.

2 Using a dark pencil, mark the position of the rail fittings and screw holes clearly on the front of the board, one at each end.

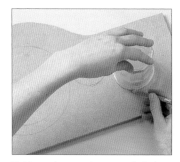

3 Using the template provided, draw around upturned plates, cups and jars to create a design of circles in different sizes.

4 Using a hammer, break up the old patterned china. It is advisable to wrap each piece in sacking first to prevent injuries.

▶

5 Using tile nippers, trim the pieces of china into neat squares, making the best use of the existing patterns on the china. Cut up all the china in this way. Try to arrange to have a mixture of patterned and colourful plain china to create contrast in the finished design. The patterned pieces might have a theme such as being black and white or having a recurring colour throughout the tesserae.

6 Working from the outside top layer first, stick the tesserae to the board with PVA glue, following the lines of your pencil design. Build up the pattern, leaving a slight space in between each tile for the grout to fill. You may find it easier to work from the outside pattern inwards. Avoid laying tesserae over the marked screwholes. Remove any excess glue with a cloth as you work, and when the design is complete, leave to dry thoroughly, preferably overnight.

7 Rub your hands over the surface of the mosaic to check for any loose tesserae. If any pieces have worked their way loose, glue these down again and leave to dry. Then, using a rubber spreader, spread tile grout over the surface of the mosaic, filling all the gaps between the tesserae. Leave to dry for one hour.

8 Polish the mosaic with a soft cloth, removing any grout that may have dried on the surface. Scrape off any stubborn grout with a paint scraper if necessary. Turn the board over and screw a protruding mirror plate in the centre of each side edge.

9 Smooth tile grout along all the edges of the board for a smooth finish. Leave to dry overnight, then sand smooth.

10 Screw the rail and struts to the front of the board, then screw the board firmly to the wall, using the mirror plates. Hang the S-shaped hooks on the rail.

The top of this kitchen shelf is exuberantly decorated in random colours, reminiscent of Antoni Gaudí's garden mosaics in Barcelona. You can achieve a quite different effect by using shades of one colour.

Crazy Paving Shelf

you will need

ready-made wooden shelf, with brackets

tape measure

2cm (¾in) thick MDF (medium-density fiberboard) or pine

saw

metal cup hooks

pencil

clamps

drill

wood glue

screwdriver

screws

plain glazed ceramic household tiles: oranges, reds, pinks, blues

piece of sacking (heavy cloth)

hammer

tile nippers

tile adhesive

notched trowel

tile grout

cement stain

rubber spreader

sponge

soft cloth

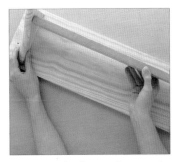

1 Measure the distance between the shelf brackets. Cut a backing strip of MDF or pine to fit, allowing a border all the way around the edges wide enough to accommodate your design.

2 Space the cup hooks at equal distances on the backing strip and draw around them. Clamp the backing strip, then drill screw holes for the cup hooks. Drill a hole at either end as extra fixing for the finished shelf.

3 Mark the position of the backing strip between the shelf brackets. Using clamps, drill a hole in each bracket, then drill a hole at either end of the backing strip to match. Glue the backing strip in place with wood glue, then screw firmly together.

▶

4 Wrap each tile separately in a piece of sacking and break it with a hammer. Trim the pieces into triangles with tile nippers, keeping some edge pieces to one side.

5 Using a notched trowel, spread a thick layer of tile adhesive over one-third of the shelf top, then press different coloured tesserae into the adhesive.

6 Cut square and rectangular pieces from the original edges of the dark blue tiles. Remove any sharp pieces. Apply the tile pieces to the shelf edges as before, to give them a smooth, safe finish. Complete the rest of the shelf top with the brightly coloured tiles.

7 Apply adhesive to the backing strip as before, leaving spaces for the cup hooks and avoiding the end screw holes. Break the dark blue tiles and cut into triangles as before, then cover the backing strip and brackets with blue mosaic. Leave to dry thoroughly.

8 Mix the tile grout with some cement stain, following the manufacturer's instructions. Add water and mix thoroughly to a firm consistency.

9 Spread the grout over the shelf with a rubber spreader, pushing it well down into the spaces between the tesserae and making sure that any sharp edges are covered. Remove excess grout with a damp sponge. Leave to dry completely, then polish the surface with a dry, soft cloth. Screw the shelf to the wall, using the shelf fixings and the holes drilled through the backing strip.

Mosaic is an ideal surface for decorating bathrooms and kitchens since it is waterproof and easy to wipe clean. This simple design is made of tiles in two colours, alternated to give a chequerboard effect.

Splashback Squares

you will need

12mm (½in) thick plywood sheet, cut to fit along the top of your basin or sink and half as deep

PVA (white) glue

paintbrushes

bradawl or awl

soft dark pencil

thin-glazed ceramic household tiles in two contrasting colours

tile nippers

flexible knife

tile adhesive

damp sponge

grout spreader or cloth pad

abrasive paper

yacht varnish

4 domed mirror screws

screwdriver

1 Prime both sides of the plywood with diluted PVA glue. Leave to dry, then score across one side with a bradawl or awl to create a key for the tile to adhere to.

2 Divide the scored side of the plywood into eight squares. Using the template provided, draw a simple and easily recognizable motif of your choice into each square.

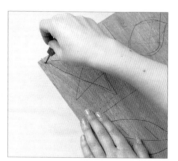

3 Make a hole in each corner of the plywood, using a bradawl or awl. These will form the holes for the screws to fix the splashback to the wall in its final position behind the sink.

4 Using tile nippers, cut the tiles into random shapes. Following your drawn designs, and using a flexible knife, stick the tiles in place with PVA glue over the pencil markings on each square. Position the tiles carefully around the holes made for hanging. Wipe off any excess glue with a damp sponge before it dries. Leave until completely dry, preferably overnight.

5 Spread tile adhesive over the surface of the mosaic with a grout spreader or cloth pad, smoothing around the edges with your fingers. Wipe off any excess adhesive and re-open the hanging holes. Leave to dry overnight.

6 Carefully sand off any remaining dried adhesive on the surface of the mosaic. Paint the back of the plywood with yacht varnish to seal it and make it waterproof, and leave to dry for 1–2 hours. Fasten the splashback to the wall with domed mirror screws inserted through the holes at each corner.

A skirting board or step riser is an unusual and discreet way of introducing mosaic into your home. You can use a repeated design (such as this daisy), a succession of motifs, or a combination of the two.

Daisy Skirting Board

you will need

skirting (base) board to fit the room

abrasive paper

PVA (white) glue

paintbrush

dark pencil

ruler

piece of sacking (heavy cloth)

selection of marble tiles

hammer

tile adhesive

flexible knife

sponge

soft cloth

1 Roughen the surface of the skirting board with coarse-grade abrasive paper, then prime with diluted PVA glue. Leave to dry.

2 Mark the skirting board into small, equally spaced sections. Using a dark pencil, draw a simple motif in each section. Here, the motif is a daisy.

3 Smash the marble tiles for the daisies into small pieces with a hammer. It is advisable to wrap the tiles in a piece of sacking.

4 Using a flexible knife and working on a small area at a time, spread tile adhesive along the lines of your drawing. Press the broken pieces of marble firmly into the adhesive. Choose tesserae in shapes that echo those of the design. The marble can be roughly shaped by tapping the edges of larger tesserae with a hammer. When each motif is tiled, wipe off any excess adhesive with a sponge and leave to dry overnight.

5 Break up the tiles in the background colour with a hammer. Working on a small area at a time, spread adhesive on to the untiled sections of skirting board and press the tesserae into it. When the surface is covered, use small pieces of the background colour to tile along the top edge of the skirting, ensuring that the tesserae do not overlap the edge. Leave to dry for 24 hours.

6 Rub more tile adhesive into the surface of the mosaic with your fingers, filling all the gaps between the tesserae. Use a flexible knife to spread the adhesive into the edge. Wipe off any excess with a damp sponge and leave overnight to dry.

7 Sand off any adhesive that has dried on the surface of the mosaic and polish the surface with a dry, soft cloth. Fix the skirting board in position.

Give your bathroom a new lease of life with this colourful and original fish splashback. Beads clustered together make an effective addition to mosaics, and are perfect for creating intricate shapes.

Beaded Fish Splashback

1 Sketch the design to fit the splashback on a large sheet of paper, keeping the shapes simple and bold. Use a sheet of carbon paper to transfer the design to the plywood by drawing firmly over all the lines using a pencil.

2 Apply the mosaic border. Lay out all the tiles first, alternating the colours. Then apply wood glue to the border, a small section at a time, positioning the tiles carefully on top of the glue as you work along.

4 Spread green filler thickly over the seaweed fronds, then carefully press in metallic green bugle beads. Fill in the fish fins using green filler and metallic green square beads. Make sure all the beads are on their sides so that the holes do not show.

5 Mix up another small amount of interior filler, this time colouring it with the orange acrylic paint. Spread filler thickly over the starfish and press in orange square frosted beads. Use some darker beads for shading.

3 Following the manufacturer's instructions, mix up a small amount of interior filler, then add some green acrylic paint to colour it.

6 Glue on a large bead for the fish eye using wood glue. Mix up some white filler and spread it thickly on to a 5cm-(2in)-square section of the fish body and press in mixed beads. Repeat, working in small sections, until the fish is complete.

7 Glue on large beads for bubbles. For the background design and the rocks at the bottom of the splashback, use mosaic tile nippers to cut the mosaic tiles into 1cm (½in) squares.

8 Fill in the background, varying the shades and sticking the tiles down with wood glue. Clip the edges of the tiles to fit any curves. Mix up some tile grout following the manufacturer's instructions and spread over the design. Spread lightly and carefully over the beaded areas. Wipe off with a damp cloth and leave to dry.

Mosaic is an ideal decorative surface or wall cladding for areas in which water is present, such as this splashback for a bathroom basin. It is made from roughly broken tiles, with chips of mirror to catch the light.

Fish Mosaic Splashback

you will need

tape measure

4mm (⅛in) thick plywood sheet

saw

PVA (white) glue

paintbrush

soft dark pencil

bradawl or awl

ceramic household tiles: light grey, dark grey, soft pink, cream, and soft blue

hammer

piece of sacking (heavy cloth)

tile nippers

tile adhesive

flexible knife

thin edging tiles

mirror

soft brush

plant mister

drinking straw

scissors

abrasive paper

soft cloth

drill

wall plugs (plastic anchors)

4 domed mirror screws

screwdriver

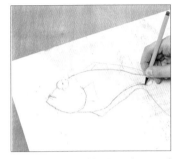

1 Measure the width of your basin and cut the plywood to size. Prime the surface with diluted PVA glue. When it is dry, using the template provided, draw a fish design on the plywood.

2 Using a bradawl or awl, make a hole through the plywood in each corner.

3 Select the colours of the tiles to be used for tesserae; here, two similar greys are used for the fish and a muted pink for the starfish. Smash the tiles into a variety of shapes using the hammer. It is advisable to wrap the tiles in a piece of sacking for this procedure.

4 Select a suitable tile that has a soft base with a thin glaze, such as a Mexican tile. Using the tile nippers, nibble two circles for the eyes of the fish. Then use a bradawl or awl to carefully make a hole in the centre of each.

▶

5 Spread some tile adhesive on to the base within the outlines of your drawing. Fix the tesserae within the drawn lines, using a lighter grey for the fins and tail and a darker grey for the body of the fish. Try to find tesserae in shapes that will fit within the drawing and suggest the movement of the fish. Use the pinkish tiles to fill in the starfish outline.

6 When the fish and starfish are complete, smash tiles of the background colour, in this case a soft blue. Spread some tile adhesive on to the base, a small area at a time. Press the background tesserae firmly into the adhesive. Be careful not to tile over the hanging holes in the corners.

7 Cut thin edging tiles into short segments and fix them around the edge of the mosaic. Using tile nippers, cut the mirror into small pieces. Press these tesserae into the larger gaps in the design, on top of a blob of adhesive to keep them level with the other tesserae. Leave to dry for 24 hours.

8 Spoon dry tile adhesive on to the surface of the splashback and brush it into the cracks using a soft brush. Avoid the area around the hanging holes. Spray the surface with plenty of water using a plant mister.

9 Cut a drinking straw into four pieces and stand one over the hole in each corner. Use some tile adhesive to grout around the straws. Leave to dry for 12 hours.

10 Remove the straws and sand off any adhesive remaining on the surface of the splashback, then polish with a dry, soft cloth. Place the splashback against the wall and mark the positions of the screw holes. Drill the holes and insert wall plugs. Use mirror screws with domed heads to screw the splashback in position.

Storage of coats is always a problem, but if they have to be hung in a hall or room, a coat rack made of brightly coloured vitreous glass tiles will make this an interesting feature rather than a necessary evil.

Coat Rack

you will need

12mm (½in) thick MDF (medium-density fiberboard) or plywood sheet, cut to desired size

pencil

ruler

jigsaw (saber saw)

abrasive paper

2 mirror plates

2 x 12mm (½in) screws

screwdriver

3 coat hooks

sharp knife

PVA (white) glue

paintbrushes

vitreous glass mosaic tiles: blue, yellow, green, red

tile nippers

tile grout

rubber spreader

soft cloths

nailbrush

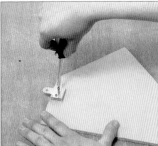

1 Using the template provided, draw the outline of the top on to the MDF or plywood, using a pencil and ruler to make sure the proportions of the three triangles are correct. Cut around the outline using a jigsaw. Sand down any rough edges.

2 Attach two mirror plates to the back of the base, one at each end. Make sure the hanging screw holes stick out far enough from the sides of the base, so that when the sides are tiled with the tesserae the holes will remain uncovered. ▶

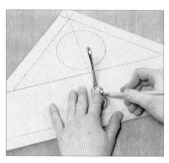

3 Draw the mosaic design on the surface of the base. Place the coat hooks in position and draw around them.

4 Score the base with a sharp knife and prime the front, back and sides with diluted PVA glue.

5 Cut some blue vitreous glass tiles in half with tile nippers. Fix these half tiles alternated with whole tiles all around the edge of the base with PVA glue applied carefully with a fine paintbrush.

6 Stick tesserae to the areas between the main outlines in the other colours. Cover the entire surface, except for the areas where the hooks will be screwed in. Cut more blue tiles in half and carefully stick them along the sides of the base. Leave to dry for 24 hours.

7 Using a rubber spreader, spread tile grout over the surface of the mosaic, pushing it into the gaps between the tesserae. Wipe off the excess grout with a damp cloth and leave for about 10 minutes, so that the surface dries. Then use a nailbrush to scrub off any grout that has dried on the surface of the mosaic. Leave to dry for 24 hours.

8 Sand off any remaining grout on the surface of the mosaic, then polish with a dry, soft cloth. Screw the coat hooks into position, and hang in place.

A mosaic splashback makes a very practical surface above a sink, as it is strong and durable as well as waterproof. This jaunty boat design is made entirely from broken tile mosaic.

Boat Splashback

you will need

1.5cm (½in) plywood, cut to the desired size

PVA (white) glue

paintbrush

craft (utility) knife

pencil

work bench and clamps

bradawl or awl

plain, glazed ceramic tiles: red, pale blue, dark blue and white

piece of heavy sacking

hammer

tile nippers

old knife or flexible spreader

cement-based tile adhesive

white, glazed ceramic tile border strip

mirror tiles

sponge

scissors

plastic drinking straw

sanding block

lint-free cloth

yacht varnish and brush

1 Seal the front and back of the cut plywood with diluted PVA glue. Leave it to dry, then score the front of the board with a craft knife.

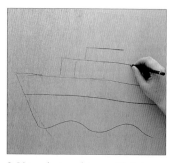

2 Using the template provided, draw a boat on the front of the board. Put the board on a work bench, then clamp in position and use a bradawl or awl to make a screw hole in each corner.

3 Wrap each tile separately in heavy sacking and break with a hammer. Trim the pieces with tile nippers if necessary. Using a knife or flexible spreader, spread tile adhesive within the lines of the drawing, then stick down the tesserae, as shown.

4 Build up the shape, leaving the portholes and windows blank. Fill in the background sea and sky with pale blue tile pieces. Continue to within 1cm (½in) of the edge of the board, avoiding the screw holes.

5 Cut up the white border strip into short lengths with tile nippers. Fill in the border around the edge of the design, working as before, and leaving a gap between each border piece for grouting.

6 Add pieces of mirror tile to make the portholes and windows. Remove excess adhesive from the surface of the splashback with a damp sponge. Leave to dry for 24 hours. Push a length of drinking straw into each hole.

7 Spread more tile adhesive over the surface, covering any sharp edges. Smooth the adhesive around the straws. Remove excess adhesive with a damp sponge, then leave the splashback to dry for 24 hours. Smooth the tile surface lightly with a sanding block, then polish with a dry, lint-free cloth. Seal the back of the board with two coats of yacht varnish, allowing it to dry between coats.

This hearth mosaic has a simple, contemporary feel with a strong use of colour, bringing a new lease of life to this old fireplace. It has been laid using a semi-indirect technique to ensure a smooth finish.

Mosaic Hearth

you will need

chisel

hammer

brown paper

craft (utility) knife

scissors

PVA (white) glue

sponge

wooden board

adhesive tape

pencil

ruler

vitreous glass mosaic tiles: dark purple, light purple, and contrasting colours for the border infill

tile nippers

matt (flat) cream porcelain tiles

paintbrush

tile adhesive

notched trowel and bucket

wire (steel) wool

screwdriver

tile grout

abrasive paper

soft cloth

1 Using a chisel and hammer, remove any old tiles from the fireplace. Chisel away any remaining tile adhesive. It is essential to have a very smooth surface on which to lay the mosaic if you are to get a good result.

2 To make a template, take a piece of brown paper, larger than the area to be mosaiced, and fold over the edges to fit the space exactly. It can be tricky around the more detailed areas. Using a craft knife and scissors, cut out the shape accurately. Check it by placing it back into the hearth.

3 Brush away any loose debris from the fireplace. Seal the concrete by sponging some diluted PVA glue all over it. Allow to dry.

4 This technique works in reverse, so turn the template upside down. Place the template on a piece of wooden board and stick it down with adhesive tape to ensure that the paper does not move around.

5 Mark the base line of the border edging at 2mm (¹⁄₁₆in) in from the edge (this allows a margin of error when fitting). Measuring from this line, mark three more lines: one at 2cm (¾in), the second at 7cm (2¾in) and the third at 9cm (3½in). Stick strips of dark purple border tiles with PVA glue along the two narrow bands, paper side down, leaving a 5cm (2in) gap for the detail (see step 6). The bulk of the design is made up of sheets of pale purple vitreous glass, cut with a craft knife and laid in position, paper side down. Fill as much of the space as possible with whole tiles. Clip tiles to fit any gaps left at the back and sides of the mosaic, and stick them in place later.

6 The detail of the border is made from matt cream porcelain tiles clipped into quarters with the tile nippers. Position these in a central line that runs between and parallel to the two strips of dark purple vitreous glass. Take care that the lines meet neatly at their corners. Then, starting in one corner, make a grid with cut quarters of cream tile at 2.5cm (1in) intervals inside the two dark purple bands. Fill in the gaps with a variety of colours from the vitreous glass range, clipped into quarters. To ensure the correct spacing, lay the tiles down before you stick them in position. Adjust the spacing so that the uniformed design works, taking particular care in the corners.

7 Using a small paintbrush, apply PVA glue to the front of the small tiles, and stick them on to the paper.

8 Apply PVA glue to the paper backing on the light purple tiles and stick them in position on the brown paper, filling in the gaps with the clipped tiles. Leave to dry for several hours.

9 Cut up the mosaic into manageable pieces. Lift them up, shaking gently to remove tile fragments and any loose tiles. Stick these back in place.

▶

10 Back on-site, lay the sections of the mosaic, tile-side down. It should fit, and all you will see is brown paper. Put the sheets carefully to one side, so that the order in which they need to be placed is obvious.

11 Apply some grey tile adhesive to the concrete surface with a notched trowel, ensuring you lay a good even bed. Carefully lay down the sheets, tile-side down. Once you are happy with the positioning of the sheets, press them into the adhesive and rub over the surface with a damp sponge. Leave to dry for 24 hours.

12 Fill a bucket with warm water and dampen the brown paper with a wet sponge. Leave for 5 minutes, then dampen again.

13 When the paper is ready it should peel off easily. Some bits will stick, but these can be cleaned off with wire wool. Wash the mosaic and glue back any pieces that have come loose.

14 There is a tendency with this technique for adhesive to squeeze up between the gaps, and it tends to be a different colour from the grout. Clear this excess away with a screwdriver.

15 Grout the mosaic with a grey tile grout. Remove any excess grout with a damp sponge, then leave it to dry. Sand off any dried-on grout, then polish with a dry, soft cloth.

This decorative work is made with handpainted Mexican tiles, which are widely available. The blue-and-white patterned tesserae make a lively background, and the tree trunk is simply the back of the tiles.

Tree of Life Wall Panel

you will need

2cm (¾in) thick plywood sheet, cut to the size required (adjust your measurements to fit a row of whole border tiles in each direction)

pencil

drill and rebate (rabbet) bit

mirror plate, with keyhole opening

screwdriver

2 x 12mm (½in) screws

PVA (white) glue

paintbrush

bradawl or awl

small handpainted glazed ceramic tiles, for the border

tape measure

soft dark pencil

blue-and-white handpainted glazed ceramic tiles

plain glazed ceramic household tiles: green, brown and beige

tile nippers

tile adhesive

soft brush

plant mister

sponge

soft cloth

1 On the back of the plywood, mark a point halfway across the width and a third from the top. Drill a rebate to fit under the keyhole of the mirror plate. Screw the plate in place and prime both sides and the edge of the board with diluted PVA glue. Leave to dry, then score the front with a bradawl or awl.

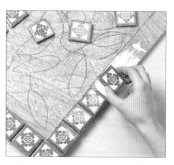

2 Measure the border tiles and draw a frame to match this size on the front of the board. Using the template provided, draw a tree in the centre. Cover the border of the board with PVA glue and stick the border tiles in position, placing them closely together and following the frame line.

3 Use tile nippers to cut the blue-and-white tiles into small, irregular shapes. Glue into place for the sky. Cut brown tiles for the trunk; glue them face down on the board and prime with diluted glue. Cut and glue tiles for the leaves and earth. Leave to dry overnight.

4 Brush dry tile adhesive over the panel, filling all the gaps. Spray with water until saturated. When dry, repeat if necessary, then rub adhesive into the crevices, wiping off the excess with a damp sponge. Dry overnight, then polish with a dry, soft cloth.

This lovely design is inspired by the cool tiled floors in Mediterranean countries. The finished mosaic is covered with a sheet of sticky-back plastic and lowered on to the floor in sections.

Lemon Tree Floor

you will need

pencil

coloured paper

scissors

large sheet of white paper

black felt-tipped pen

glazed ceramic household tiles:

various shades of yellow, green and

grey, and white

tile cutter

tile nippers

old plain and patterned china

black ceramic mosaic tiles

white glazed ceramic tiles

large sheet of sticky-back plastic

(contact paper)

craft (utility) knife

tile adhesive

notched and rubber spreaders

sponge

soft cloth

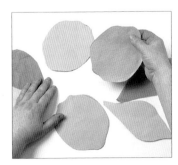

1 Draw sufficient lemon and leaf shapes on sheets of different coloured papers to cover the area of floor you wish to mosaic.

2 Cut the leaves and lemons out and arrange them on the large sheet of white paper. When you are happy with the design, draw in details such as stems and a decorative border around the edge of the design, using a felt-tipped pen.

3 Using a tile cutter, score all the coloured ceramic household tiles down the centre. You may need to practise on some spares to get a straight line. Break each tile into neat halves by applying equal pressure on either side of the scored line with the tile cutter. This will result in a clean break.

4 Using tile nippers, cut these tile pieces into small, equal-size tesserae. Cut up the china in the same way. Also cut up some of the black mosaic tiles, enough to outline each lemon, again into equal-size pieces.

▶

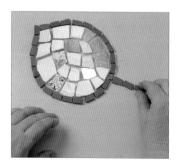

5 Following your paper design, arrange the pieces on a flat surface. To make the lemons appear three-dimensional, place the darker shades on one side. Outline each shape with black mosaic tiles and extend to make a stem.

6 Using tile nippers, cut the white glazed tiles into random shapes. Fill in the background with a mosaic of large and small pieces. When a section is complete, hold the pieces together with a sheet of sticky-back plastic.

7 Finish with a border. This undulating border is made of square, yellow-toned tesserae, outlined with rectangular black tiles.

8 Peel the backing paper off the sticky back plastic and lay it carefully over the loose mosaic. You may have to work in sections.

9 Smooth your hands over the plastic to make sure it has adhered to all the tesserae and that any air bubbles are eliminated.

10 Using a craft knife, cut through the plastic to separate the mosaic into manageable sections.

11 Spread tile adhesive over the floor area, using a notched spreader. Lower the mosaic carefully into the tile adhesive, section by section. Press down and leave to dry overnight. Peel off the plastic then grout the mosaic with more tile adhesive. Wipe off any excess adhesive with a damp sponge, leave to to dry, then polish with a dry, soft cloth.

Gardens offer mosaic artists the opportunity to experiment with more playful wall mosaics. This rather tongue-in-cheek princess design uses tesserae of vitreous glass in vibrant colours that will not fade.

Princess Wall Mosaic

you will need

brown paper

pencil

tracing paper

scissors

vitreous glass mosaic tiles in various
colours: pink, gold, blue and red

tile nippers

PVA (white) glue

mirror

large wooden board

tile adhesive

notched trowel

grout spreader

sponge

abrasive paper

dilute hydrochloric acid, goggles and
rubber gloves (optional)

soft cloth

1 Using the template provided, draw a design for a princess on brown paper. This reverse method means that your mosaic will be worked in reverse, so plan your picture accordingly.

2 Make a tracing of the outline of your drawing and cut this out. You will use this later as a template to mark the area of the wall to be covered with tile adhesive.

3 Using tile nippers, cut vitreous glass mosaic tiles in the chosen outlining colour into eighths.

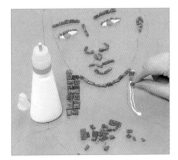

4 Stick these tesserae face down on to the main lines of your drawing using PVA glue. Stick down any key features, such as the eyes and lips, in contrasting colours.

▶

5 Cut pink vitreous glass tiles into quarters. Glue these face down to fill in the areas of skin between the outlines.

6 Cut the mirror into small pieces about the same size as the quartered vitreous glass tesserae.

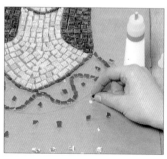

7 Stick the pieces of mirror face down on to the dress and in the crown.

8 Cut the tiles for the dress and the crown into quarters and glue them face down between the pieces of mirror. Leave the paper-backed mosaic to dry securely in position.

9 Transfer the mosaic to its final location, carrying it on a large wooden board to prevent any tesserae coming loose. Draw around the tracing paper template on the wall or floor. Spread tile adhesive over this area using a notched trowel, then press the mosaic into it, paper side up. Leave to dry for about 2 hours, then dampen the paper with a sponge and gently peel it away. Leave to dry overnight.

10 Grout the mosaic with more tile adhesive, using a grout spreader. Clean off any excess adhesive with a damp sponge and leave the mosaic to dry overnight. Remove any remaining cement with abrasive paper. Alternatively, dilute hydrochloric acid can be used, but you must wear goggles and rubber gloves and apply it outside or where there is good ventilation. Wash any acid residue from the surface with plenty of water. Finish by polishing the mosaic with a dry, soft cloth.

This richly textured panel is composed of tesserae cut from a variety of patterned china. Motifs are cut out and used as focal points for the patterns; some are raised to give them extra emphasis.

Mosaic Panel

you will need

2cm (¾in) thick plywood sheet
pencil
thick card (stock) (optional)
jigsaw (saber saw)
abrasive paper
PVA (white) glue
paintbrushes
wood primer
white undercoat paint
gloss paint
mirror plate, with keyhole opening
drill and rebate (rabbet) bit
2 x 2cm (¾in) screws
screwdriver
tracing paper (optional)
ruler, set square (triangle) and
pair of compasses (optional)
selection of china
tile nippers
tile adhesive
tile grout
cement stain, vinyl matt emulsion (flat latex) or acrylic paint (optional)
grout spreader
nailbrush
soft cloth

1 Draw the outer shape of the panel on to the sheet of plywood. (If you are unsure about drawing directly on to the surface, make a stencil from thick card.) Cut out around this shape using a jigsaw and sand down the rough edges. Seal one side and the edges with diluted PVA glue. Paint the unsealed side with wood primer, undercoat paint and then gloss paint, allowing each coat to dry before applying the next.

2 Mark the position of the mirror plate on the unsealed back of the panel. Using a drill, rebate the area that will be under the keyhole-shaped opening so that it is large enough to take a screw head. Screw the mirror plate in position.

3 Draw your design on the sealed top surface. If necessary, trace and transfer your original design. Tools such as a ruler, set square and pair of compasses are helpful if your design has geometric elements.

▶

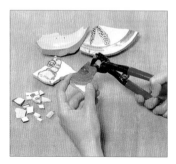

4 Sort the china into groups according to colour and pattern, and select interesting motifs that could be used to form the centrepieces of designs. Using the tile nippers, cut the china into the desired shapes.

5 Using smooth edges cut from cups and plates, press the pieces into the tile adhesive first, then use them to tile the edges of the panel. Use small, regular-shaped tesserae to tile the structural lines of the design.

6 Raise small areas of the mosaic to give greater emphasis to sections of the design by setting the tesserae on a larger mound of tile adhesive. Cut more china and use it to form the patterns between the structural lines. Leave the panel to dry for 24 hours.

7 If you want the tile grout to be coloured, add cement stain, vinyl matt emulsion or acrylic paint to it. (If this is to be used indoors, cement stain is not essential.) Spread the grout over the surface using a grout spreader. Rub it into the gaps with your fingers.

8 Allow the surface to dry for a few minutes, then scrub off any excess grout using a stiff nailbrush.

9 Leave to dry for 24 hours, then polish the surface with a dry, soft cloth.

This stunning pond is perfect for a small town garden, especially if it is sited near to a patio so that you can admire it while entertaining or dining alfresco on long summer evenings.

Mosaic Pond

1 Mark out the design on a piece of paper. This does not have to be to scale, but it will give you some idea of the pattern and colour arrangement.

2 Smash the tiles using a hammer and some sacking. Smash each colour of tile separately and keep the pieces in separate piles.

3 Dig a hole in the ground to accommodate the pond. Bed the pond in with a layer of sand. You will probably have to try the pond in the hole a few times until you get a good fit. Check that it is level with a spirit level. Using a piece of chalk, mark out the design on the bottom of the pond.

4 Construct the decking by nailing the wooden planks to two cross supports to create a rectangular shape, and then cut out the oval shape with a jigsaw. (The picture shows the decking viewed from below.) Lay the oval-shaped piece of decking over the pond, and check that it is level using a spirit level.

▶

5 Spread a layer of tile adhesive over the first part of the design using an adhesive spreader.

6 Stick the broken pieces of tile along the edge, but within the chalk line. Fill in the inside area. Use tile nippers to get the perfect shape. Finish this colour band.

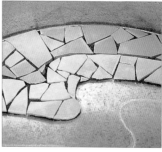

7 Start on the next colour, sticking down the tiles around the edge inside the chalk line as before. Finish this colour band.

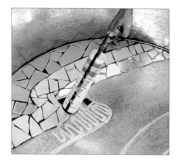

8 Cut up the mirror using the tile nippers. Cover the area for the pieces of mirror with glue from a glue gun, and stick down the mirror pieces as for the tile pieces. Finally, stick down the last colour of tile.

9 Allow the mosaic work to dry for three days. Grout the bottom of the pond with the tile grout, using a flat trowel.

10 Clean with a damp sponge, then fill the pond with water.

This striking water feature is perfect for use outdoors on a patio or indoors in a conservatory. Being portable, it can be brought in and out of the garden and would make a perfect centrepiece.

Fountain Bowl

you will need

circular wooden panel, slightly smaller than the reservoir

small dustbin (trash can) to act as a reservoir, about 60cm (24in) in diameter and 75cm (30in) deep

screws

screwdriver

4 wheeled feet

4 wooden blocks

drill

5cm (2in) length of copper pipe, 2cm (¾in) in diameter

hammer

white plastic container

small pump (4 litres/ 1 gallon per minute)

selection of vitreous glass mosaic tiles in a range of rich tropical colours

paper

tile nippers

fibreglass bowl with a 2cm (¾in) hole drilled in the centre

copper spraypaint (optional)

glue and glue gun

tile grout

grout spreader

sponge

1 Fix the wooden panel inside the reservoir by screwing through from the outside of the dustbin. Attach the wheeled feet to the blocks of wood and screw them to the underside of the wooden panel. Drill a hole near the base of the reservoir for the pump cable.

2 Using a hammer, flatten the piece of copper pipe at one end in order to create a narrow jet of water. Using the tip of a screwdriver, open up the flattened end of the copper pipe slightly to ensure that the water will flow freely.

3 Position the white container in the centre of the reservoir, resting on the wooden panel. Add the pump, threading the cable through the hole drilled near the base of the reservoir in step 1.

4 Select the glass tiles in a range of colours to achieve a bold, brightly coloured effect.

▶

5 It is a good idea to test out the mosaic design on a piece of paper first. Arrange the tiles in concentric circles to achieve a pleasing blend of colours.

6 If necessary, cut the tiles into halves using the tile nippers.

7 Spray the outside of the fibreglass bowl with copper paint if desired. Starting at the rim of the bowl, apply two lines of glue from a glue gun, keeping a small gap between the lines.

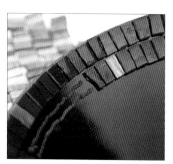

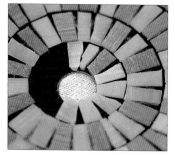

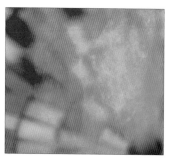

8 Press each tile firmly on to the adhesive. When the first row of tiles is in place, follow the same procedure for the second row, and continue with each row until you reach the centre.

9 Finish by laying the final circle of tiles around the hole in the centre of the dish. You may have to cut the tiles to fit the final row. Allow to dry. Spread tile grout between the tiles using the grout spreader. Allow to dry, then wipe clean with a damp sponge. Fill the white container with water and place the bowl over the copper pipe.

10 Plug in the pump, then adjust its flow rate to create a range of different sounds, from gushing fountain to gentle trickle, depending on your mood.

No artistic skills are required for this stunning mosaic, as the picture is simply an old etching enlarged on a photocopier. The tesserae are glued on to fibreglass mesh, then lowered into position on the floor.

Black-and-white Floor

you will need

black-and-white image

clear film (plastic wrap)

masking tape

fibreglass mesh

unglazed ceramic mosaic tiles:

black and white

tile nippers

PVA (white) glue

paintbrush

craft (utility) knife

tile adhesive

notched spreader

flat wooden board

hammer

grout spreader

sponge

soft cloth

1 Decide on the image you wish to use, or you may wish to build up a picture from various elements. Or, using the template provided, enlarge on a photocopier to the required size.

2 Working on a large work surface, cover the photocopy with clear film and secure the edges with masking tape. If your picture is built up from more than one image, repeat this process for all the sections.

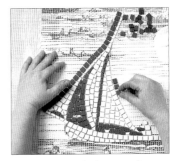

3 Position a piece of fibreglass mesh over the clear film, and tape it down to the work surface with masking tape. Using tile nippers, cut the tiles into quarters.

4 Beginning with the main features, such as the boat, glue the tesserae to the fibreglass mesh using PVA glue and a fine paintbrush. Build up the picture, using the light and shade of the photocopy as a guide.

▶

5 Outline the panel with a geometric border in black and white, cutting some of the tesserae in half to make triangular shapes.

6 Fill in the background of the design, simplifying and accentuating the black and white areas, until the photocopy is completely covered. Leave to dry.

7 Using a craft knife, cut through the mesh and clear film, chopping the mosaic into manageable sections. You may find it helpful to cut around the boat shape, as shown.

8 Turn the sections over and peel off the clear film. Using the craft knife, pierce any holes in the mesh that are clogged with glue.

9 Spread tile adhesive over the bathroom floor, using a notched spreader. Work from the part of the floor furthest away from the door.

10 Carefully lay each section of the mosaic on the tile adhesive, mesh side down.

11 Place a flat wooden board over each part of the mosaic and tap with a hammer to make sure the tesserae are firmly embedded into the adhesive. Leave to dry overnight, then grout with more tile adhesive, using a grout spreader. Wipe away any excess with a damp sponge, then leave to dry. Finally, polish with a dry, soft cloth.

The ancient tradition of games, paths and puzzles in mosaic gives this simple, strong design an ageless appeal. The background is quick and easy to do, and the swirling design of the snakes uses vibrant colours.

Snakes and Ladders Floor

you will need

paper

felt-tipped pens

tape measure

scissors

clear film (plastic wrap)

fibreglass mesh

vitreous glass mosaic tiles in various

colours and matt (flat) black

tile nippers

PVA (white) glue

paintbrush

patio cleaner

black cement stain

tile adhesive

notched trowel

sand

cement

sponge

1 Draw up a plan for the whole board. Play a game on it to make sure that it works. Measure out one of the outside paving slabs to be covered. Cut out 25 pieces of paper to fit the slab.

2 Fold them into quarters and mark out the sections. These are the 100 squares needed for your game. Copy out your design on to the 25 squares of paper using a thick felt-tipped pen.

3 Cover the front of each of the 25 squares with clear film and then a piece of mesh, cut to size.

4 Outline each of the 100 squares with matt black tiles, cut in half. Use PVA glue and a fine paintbrush to stick them to the mesh. Outline the numbers with quarter tiles and the snakes with both half and quarter tiles. Fill in the snakes and ladders with glossy, brightly coloured glass tiles.

5 Fill in the background squares with different colours for even and odd squares. Leave the squares to dry overnight, then turn them over, peel off the paper and the plastic film (used to prevent the tiles and mesh sticking to the paper) and leave until totally dry. Make sure all the tiles are stuck on to the fibreglass mesh, and restick any that fall off.

6 Clean all the paving slabs with patio cleaner and rinse well. Add a black cement stain to the tile adhesive, following the manufacturer's instructions, and apply a thin, even layer to each square with a notched trowel.

7 Lay on the design, one section at a time, allowing for gaps between the slabs. Mark all the pieces clearly and refer to the plan often as you work. Tamp down the squares gently and evenly. Leave to dry completely.

8 Grout the mosaic, using a mixture of sand, cement and water, with an added black stain. Wipe off the excess with a damp sponge and allow to dry slowly.

CERAMICS, TILES & GLASS

Hand-painting china and glassware is an increasingly popular craft,
as the results can be so rewarding. Simple designs are often the most
effective, so a confident hand and a good sense of colour are really all
you need to create lovely, unique pieces. Modern ceramic paints are very
durable, and some can even be heat-set to make them dishwasher-proof,
so you can create tableware as well as beautiful ornamental pieces. You
can also transform plain ceramic tiles, to make fabulous details and borders
for tiled walls or even complete murals.

Painting
Ceramics

You do not need to be an expert artist or have trained drawing skills to paint beautiful designs on ceramics. All you need is the enthusiasm to have a go, and a design or a colour palette that will inspire you to follow through your idea. And if you don't have the confidence to create your own designs to begin with, there are templates provided to help you get started and make it really easy to achieve great results.

The production of pottery is one of the most ancient creative and practical arts, and potters have always decorated their wares using a large number of different techniques.

The History of Painted Ceramics

Until recently, the addition of surface decoration to ceramics was restricted to those with access to a kiln, as painted designs had either to be protected by a glaze or applied using enamels, which needed to be fired to make them permanent.

The origins of glazing techniques are unknown, though they must have begun in a simple attempt to make pots watertight. However, because the glaze transformed the appearance of pottery, it inevitably became a means of ornamentation in addition to its practical purpose. Chinese potters developed coloured glazes and were

Below: Stamped pots in bold colours make a strong statement.

producing monochromatic coloured wares over a thousand years ago. Their early brush-painted patterns were in black or brown, applied directly to the bare clay and covered with a clear glaze, but under the Ming dynasty the characteristic blue-and-white style emerged, with figures painted in cobalt blue under the glaze. The artists of the Ming period also employed overglaze decoration, which demanded great skill in the preparation of the enamels and in achieving the correct firing temperature to weld them to the surface of the clay.

Below: Simple motifs, minimal and bright blocks of colours add interest to a plain ceramic.

The artistry of oriental porcelain was imitated in Europe in the production of earthenware, such as Italian majolica in the 15th century and English and Dutch Delftware in the 17th century. In these wares coloured pigments were applied over an opaque white glaze and then fixed by firing. When European factories eventually succeeded in making true porcelain in the 18th century they continued to imitate oriental styles, protecting brush-painted decorations with clear lead glaze. In an attempt to make this highly skilled process less costly, some 18th-century porcelain

Below: Almost any design can be stencilled and stamped on to crockery.

Right: An elegant star adds colour to a plain ceramic cup.

Below: Classical scrolls lend a traditional look to a large bowl.

was painted with unfired pigments after glazing, but the paint did not adhere well so the technique was largely abandoned.

However, in the last twenty years, special ceramic paints have been developed that can be applied over a glaze and then fixed in an ordinary domestic oven. The results are both durable and washable, so that anyone can now create beautifully decorated china at home for practical use as well as for display.

Sources of inspiration

Ideas for decorative designs can spring from anywhere. You may be inspired simply by the colours of the paints or the shapes of the pieces you are decorating. You may be following a particular stylistic theme in a room: a rich red dining room with an antique table, for example, might suggest china decorated with an elaborate red and gold Indian paisley pattern, while pots for a conservatory might call for motifs based on natural plant forms.

Colour and pattern ideas can come from historical styles, such as the tendrils and arabesques of Art Nouveau or the angular, dramatic shapes of Art Deco. Or they may come from other countries and cultures. Hot regions, where bright sunlight complements high-key colour schemes, might inspire designs for the kitchen or garden. Although delicate detailing is achievable in ceramic painting, a plainer, freer style is easier to master and better suited to modern interiors, and Mediterranean, African and South American cultures can provide strong but simple ideas.

Looking at designs in different media can often be fruitful: study old wallpapers, wrapping papers, printed fabrics or oriental rugs to find graphic motifs on which to base your painting. Art of the 20th century is a rich source: Matisse's bold, intense paper cut-outs, Gauguin's tropical landscapes, Mondrian's geometry or Klee's pattern-making all explore the interaction of colour and form in ways that are relevant.

Above all, you can go directly to nature, both for form and colour. Leaves, flowers, berries, animals, shells, rocks, soft and mountainous landscapes and calm seascapes all offer an abundance of subjects and motifs, and the natural geometry of seedheads or snowflakes can become the basis for symmetrical designs.

A variety of materials is needed for painting on ceramics, all of which are available from craft stores. Many items can be improvised, but some materials, such as paints, have to be specially purchased.

Materials

surfaces that may come in contact with foodstuffs or the mouth such as serving plates, bowls and cups.

Solvent-based ceramic paints
These come in a huge range of colours and lend themselves well to varied painting styles such as wash effects. White spirit (paint thinner) can be used to dilute the paint and to clean paintbrushes after use. Solvent-based paints take approximately 24 hours to dry. They can then be varnished to protect the finish.

Water-based ceramic paints
Sold under various trade names and specially made for painting glazed ceramics, these paints are available in a range of colours. They produce a strong, opaque, flat colour and can be diluted with water. Wash paintbrushes in warm water immediately after painting. Water-based paints dry in around 3 hours; do not attempt to bake them until they are completely dry or the colour may bubble. Baking the painted item will make the colour durable enough for a dishwasher. Put the item in a cold oven and do not remove it after baking until it has completely cooled. Always follow the paint manufacturer's instructions for the temperature and baking time, and do a test first as over-firing can turn the colour slightly brown.

Enamel paints
These paints are not made exclusively for china and ceramics. They are available in a range of colours and dry to a hard and durable finish. They contain lead and should only ever be used for decorative purposes and not on items that will contain food.

Masking fluid
Watercolour art masking fluid is used to mask off areas of the design while colour is applied to the surrounding area. Apply to a clean, dry surface. Always allow the masking fluid to dry before filling in the design with paint.

Polyurethane varnish and glazes
Apply varnish evenly, using a large, flat brush and stroking in one direction over the ceramic. The more coats you apply, the more durable and washable the surface, but keep each of the coats thin, allowing a minimum of 4 hours' drying time between coats. Polyurethane varnish is unsuitable for

No expensive specialist equipment is required for painting ceramics. In fact, you probably already have much of the equipment needed among your normal household supplies.

Equipment

Paintbrushes
Use a fine brush for details, and a wide soft brush for covering larger areas.

Paint palette
Use to mix and hold paints.

Pencils and pens
A hard pencil is good for transferring designs; a soft for direct marking.

Printing blocks
Use for printing repeated patterns.

Ruler or straightedge
Plastic rules measure adequately. For cutting, metal ones are better.

Scissors
Use to cut paper patterns.

Self-healing cutting mat
This protects the work surface when cutting paper with a craft knife.

Stencil cardboard
This is manila card (cardboard) water-proofed with linseed oil.

Tracing paper
Use with carbon paper to transfer designs on to the object to be painted.

White spirit (paint thinner)
Use to clean brushes, to remove paint mistakes and to thin paint.

Carbon paper
Use to transfer designs on to ceramic. Place it carbon side down, on the object. Stick the image drawn on tracing paper on top. Draw over the image to transfer it to the ceramic.

Clear adhesive tape
Use for sticking designs to ceramic.

Craft knife
Use with a metal ruler and cutting mat for cutting papers and cardboard.

Masking film (frisket paper)
This self-adhesive transparent paper has a waxed paper backing, which peels away. Use it to mask out areas you want to keep blank.

Masking tape
Use to hold stencils in place and to mask off areas of ceramic.

Natural and synthetic sponges
Use to create paint effects for anything from an even to a textured finish.

The projects in this chapter do not require any specialist skills but it is worth practising a few painting techniques before you start. The tips suggested below will prove useful as you work through the ideas.

Techniques

Cleaning china

Before painting any white china, always clean it thoroughly to remove any invisible traces of dirt or grease. Effective cleaning agents are cleaning fluid, turpentine, methylated spirit (methyl alcohol), lighter fuel or white spirit (paint thinner). Keep these materials away from naked flames.

Safe drinking vessels

To ensure that there is no possibility of any paint being swallowed when drinking from a mug or glass, adapt designs so that any colour you paint is at least 3cm/1¼in below the rim of drinking vessels. Otherwise the piece should be fired in a kiln.

Working with paints

Paints suitable for applying to china are available in water or oil-based types. When mixing up a shade of your own, remember that the two types of paint cannot be intermixed. Always thoroughly clean brushes as directed by the paint manufacturer.

Using paintbrushes

Always use an appropriate size paintbrush for the task in hand. Larger areas should always be painted with a wide brush using bold strokes, while fine brushes are best for all detailed work.

Watery effects

You can achieve a watery effect in oil-based colours by diluting paints with white spirit (paint thinner). Water-based paints can be diluted by adding water.

Creating white lines

If you want to leave thin lines of china showing through areas of colour, paint them first with masking fluid. This can be gently peeled off when the paint is dry to reveal the white china beneath. Use an instrument with a sharp point such as a craft knife or compass to lift off the dried masking fluid.

Using masking fluid

Add a drop of water-based paint to masking fluid before use when you are working on plain white china. This will help you to see where the masking fluid has been applied, enabling you to wipe it off easily when you are ready to do so.

Preparing a sponge

Use a craft knife to cut cubes of sponge for sponging paint. Hold the sponge taut as you slice down into it to make cutting easier and the lines straight. Keep several sponge cubes to hand when sponging as you may need to change them frequently.

Testing a sponge

Before sponging on to your china after loading the sponge with paint, test the print on a scrap piece of paper. The first print or two will be too saturated with paint to achieve a pleasing effect.

Sponging variations

A stencilled design can be made more interesting by varying the density of the sponging within the image or by adding more than one colour. Allow the first coat of paint to dry partially before the application of the second.

Printing blocks

Test the print on scrap paper before you print on the china. When using printing blocks, roll the block lightly on to the surface to ensure you get a good, even print.

Straight lines

Masking tape is useful for painting straight edges, stripes and even checks and squares. Just stick it down to mark out areas you do not want painted and apply the paint. Remove the tape before the paint is completely dry; straight lines of paint will be left.

Removing masking tape or film

When using masking tape or film (frisket paper), it is better to remove it before the paint is completely dry as this will give a cleaner edge to the pattern beneath.

Tracing

Use tracing paper and a soft pencil to transfer designs directly on to china. First trace the template or the design you wish to use, then fix the tracing paper to the china with pieces of masking tape. Rub over the traced design with a soft pencil to transfer.

Removing guide markings

Pencil or pen guide marks on the china are easy to wipe off once the paint is completely dry or has been baked. Use a damp paper towel or cloth and take care not to rub the paint too hard.

Testing new techniques

Always test out a technique that you have not tried before. Apply the new technique to a spare piece of china, which can be cleaned up easily, rather than to a piece you are already in the process of decorating.

Removing unwanted paint

Use a pencil eraser or cotton buds (swabs) to tidy up a design or to wipe off small areas of unwanted paint. For larger areas use a damp paper towel or cloth. Allow the cleaned area to dry before repainting.

Preparing a stencil A stencil is a thin sheet with a decorative pattern cut out, through which paint is applied. This can be used to repeat the pattern on a chosen surface. Try designing and making your own.

1 To transfer a template on to a piece of stencil cardboard, place a piece of tracing paper over the design, and draw over it with a hard pencil.

2 Turn over the tracing paper, and on the back of the design rub over the lines you have drawn with a pencil.

3 Turn the tracing paper back to the right side and place on top of a sheet of stencil cardboard. Draw over the original lines with a hard pencil.

4 To cut out the stencil, place the stencil on to a cutting mat or piece of thick cardboard and tape in place. Use a craft knife for cutting.

5 To transfer a detailed design using carbon paper, place the stencil over a piece of carbon paper, carbon side down. Attach the carbon paper to the china piece with masking tape. Use a soft pencil to trace the shape lightly on to the china.

This design works best with a salt and pepper set that is shaped with six flat sides. If your pots are not multi-faceted, divide them into six sections lengthways using a pencil.

Funky Condiment Set

you will need
plain salt and pepper pots (shakers)
cleaning fluid
cloth
soft pencil
masking fluid
water-based ceramic paints: turquoise
dark pink and white
craft (utility) knife or pair
of compasses
fine artist's paintbrush
paint palette

1 Thoroughly clean the pots, using cleaning fluid and a cloth. Draw small oval shapes on alternate sections of one of the pots. Fill each oval with masking fluid. This needs to be quite thick, so it is best to apply two coats, allowing the first to dry before applying the second.

2 Apply circles of masking fluid around the holes in the top of one of the pots. Leave the masking fluid to dry completely.

3 Apply the first colour of paint over the alternate sections marked with the oval shapes: here turqoise has been used. Use single strokes, taking care not to pull off the masking fluid.

4 Paint the base of the pot in a contrasting colour: here dark pink has been used. Next, lighten the colour used for the base with a little white paint and paint the top of the pot. Leave to dry.

5 Paint the bottom rim of each pot with the same light pink as for the top. Leave the paint to dry. Using a craft knife or compass point, pierce the masking fluid in the centre of each oval shape and carefully peel it away. Repeat for the second pot.

Plain white china tea sets are ubiquitous, so you should have no trouble finding a design you like. Paint with pastel colours and summer motifs for a truly desirable tea service.

Summer Tea Service

you will need

plain china tea cup, saucer and teapot

cleaning fluid and cloth

tracing paper

pencil

plain paper

spray adhesive

carbon paper

scissors

clear adhesive tape

fine felt-tipped pen

water-based enamel paints: lime

light green, pale lilac, pink

and dark blue

paint palette

very fine, medium and wide,

artist's paintbrushes

1 Thoroughly clean the china, using cleaning fluid and a cloth to remove all traces of dust and dirt. Trace the templates provided, enlarging them if necessary, and transfer them on to a piece of plain paper. Coat the back of the paper with spray adhesive and place this on top of a sheet of carbon paper, with the carbon side down. Cut out the uneven row of squares for the teapot, leaving a narrow margin.

2 Wrap the cut-out row of squares around the teapot, holding it in position with adhesive tape. Go over the drawn outline of the squares with a fine felt-tipped pen to transfer the outlines on to the teapot. Remove the carbon paper cut-outs.

3 Cut out the designs for the teacup and saucer. Use adhesive tape to hold the cut-outs in position on the china, and trace over the design with a felt-tipped pen. Remove the carbon paper.

4 Paint the background of the teapot, lid and saucer with lime and light green paints. Allow the paint to dry. Paint the background of the teacup pale lilac. Allow to dry.

5 Fill the squares on the teacup with colour. Here they are lime, green and pink. Leave to dry.

6 Cut around the leaf and spirals. Tape some of these over the coloured squares around the cup, saucer and teapot, and go over the designs with a felt-tipped pen to transfer.

7 Using a very fine paintbrush, paint over the leaf and spiral designs on the teapot, cup and saucer in dark blue paint. Allow to dry.

The fresh checkerboard scheme shown here is typical of the kitsch designs popular in the 1950s. The style can be extended to other white ceramics to create an entire tableware set.

1950s Jug and Butter Dish

you will need

plain china jug (pitcher) and butter dish

white spirit (paint thinner) or cleaning fluid and cloth

fine felt-tipped pen

ruler

coloured masking film (frisket paper)

scissors

tape measure

tracing paper

soft pencil

sponge

water-based ceramic paints: yellow, blue, red and white

paint palette

fine artist's paintbrush

1 Clean the crockery, using white spirit or cleaning fluid and a cloth. Mark 1cm (½in) squares on the paper backing of the masking film and cut out. Peel away the backing from each square and stick each one 1cm (½in) apart along the top edge of the jug and butter dish. Stick a second row beneath the first. Make three rows on the jug and four on the dish.

2 Draw a freehand rose on the tracing paper and enlarge if necessary. Transfer the rose to the paper backing of the masking film and cut out, using scissors. Make four rose cut-outs for the butter dish and two for the jug. Peel away the paper backing and to each side of the dish stick a rose lengthways. Stick one rose to each side of the jug.

3 Cut a 2cm- (¾in)-wide strip of masking film the same length as the rim of the dish, and cut another one to the rim of the jug. Peel away the backing paper and stick the film along the bottom edge of the bottom row of squares.

4 Cut a 1.5cm (⅝in) cube of sponge. Load the sponge cube with yellow paint and apply the paint all over the checkerboard. Leave to dry. Peel the masking film shapes off the jug and butter dish to reveal the pattern.

5 Mix some blue paint into the yellow to make green. In the blank spaces left by the rose templates, paint in the stems and leaves freehand. Leave paint to dry.

6 Mix a darker green colour, and use this to paint details on to the stems and leaves. Leave to dry.

7 Mix two shades of pink, using red and white paint. Paint the flowerhead area with the paler shade of pink and leave to dry. Add details for the petals with the darker shade of pink.

Stencilling offers a quick and easy method of decorating china. The simple shapes of these limes look terrific adorning a fruit bowl. Choose just two or three bold colours for maximum effect.

Citrus Fruit Bowl

you will need

soft pencil
tracing paper
masking tape
stencil cardboard
self-healing cutting mat
craft (utility) knife
plain fruit bowl
cleaning fluid
cloth
yellow chinagraph pencil
water-based ceramic paints: citrus
green, mid-green, dark green
and yellow
paint palette
fine and medium artist's paintbrushes
acrylic varnish (optional)

1 Using the template provided draw a lime on to tracing paper. Use masking tape to hold the tracing paper in place, transfer the lime outline to a piece of stencil cardboard. Working on a self-healing cutting mat, carefully cut all around the shape of the lime using a craft knife with a sharp blade.

2 Clean a plain fruit bowl. Attach the stencil to the bowl using masking tape. Draw inside the stencil outline on to the bowl using a yellow chinagraph pencil. Repeat to draw several limes all over the bowl.

3 Fill in all the lime shapes with citrus green paint using an artist's paintbrush. Allow the paint to dry completely. Add highlights to each of the fruits using the mid-green paint and allow the paint to dry thoroughly as before.

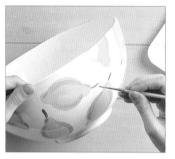

4 Paint a stalk at the end of each lime shape in the dark green paint. Allow to dry. Paint the background all over the outside of the bowl yellow, leaving a thin white outline around each of the lime shapes to help them stand out.

5 To complete the bowl, either use a clean brush to apply a coat of acrylic varnish over the painted section, or bake the bowl in the oven, following the paint manufacturer's instructions.

Add colour to a plain white dinner service by embellishing it with ceramic paints. Vary the motifs, or use just one per item, so that each place setting is different.

Seashore-style China

you will need

tracing paper

pencil

scissors

china plates and soup bowls

cloth

cleaning fluid

ruler

carbon paper

masking tape

blue solvent-based ceramic paint

fine artist's paintbrush

cloth

1 Copy the templates from the back of the book on to tracing paper. Cut out the shapes with scissors. Clean the plate and bowl thoroughly with a cloth and cleaning fluid.

2 To decorate a plate, find and mark the middle with a ruler and pencil. Divide the plate into eight equal parts and lightly mark up the eight sections in pencil.

3 If you make plenty of copies of each design, you can use your templates to experiment with various design options.

4 Cut a piece of carbon paper into small pieces to fit your templates.

5 Place the carbon paper under the template designs on the plate and stick them down firmly with masking tape to secure.

6 Trace around the template outlines with a sharp pencil, then remove the masking tape, templates and carbon paper to reveal the design.

7 Paint in the shapes carefully using blue solvent-based ceramic paint. Leave to dry thoroughly.

8 Mark, trace and paint the design in the centre of the soup bowl. Add small dots on the handles of the bowl. Leave to dry. Remove the pencil lines.

Ceramics with low-relief decorative motifs are ideal for painting. Like children's colouring books, the shapes are all set out ready to colour in and, as there are no clearly defined outlines, mistakes will go unnoticed.

Low-relief Ceramic

you will need

clean, white glazed pitcher with a low-relief fruit motif

solvent-based ceramic paints: acid yellow, golden yellow, light green, medium green and dark green

fine and medium artist's paintbrushes

polyurethane varnish or glaze

1 Paint some of the lemons on the pitcher acid yellow. Vary them so that one group has two acid yellow lemons, the next group one, and so on. Leave a narrow white line around each lemon, and leave the seed cases and the small circles at the base of the fruit white. Allow to dry.

2 Work your way around the relief pattern at the top of the pitcher, painting the remaining fruit a rich golden yellow. Using two yellows for the fruit creates a sense of depth and variety. Once again, leave a narrow white line around each fruit, and leave the paint to dry.

3 Starting with light green, paint roughly a third of the leaves, evenly spaced apart if possible, but don't worry about being too exact. Leave the central midrib of each leaf and a narrow line around each leaf white. Allow to dry. Paint the small circles.

4 Paint a third of the leaves medium green, spacing them evenly. Paint a narrow green line around the base of the pitcher and leave to dry. Paint the remaining leaves dark green and leave to dry.

5 Paint the rim (or the handle) of the pitcher in acid yellow, leaving a narrow white line at the lower edge. Once the paint is dry, varnish the pitcher with polyurethane varnish or the glaze provided specially by the ceramic paint manufacturer for this purpose.

Imagine the effect produced by a whole set of this delightful sponge-ware design, set out on your kitchen shelves. Painting your own mugs in this lovely decorative style is an easy way of transforming plain china.

Stamped Spongeware

you will need
ballpoint pen
cellulose kitchen sponge
scissors
all-purpose glue
corrugated cardboard
ceramic paints: dark blue and dark green
paint palette
kitchen paper
clean, white china mugs
masking tape
craft (utility) knife
fine black felt-tipped pen
stencil brush or small cosmetic sponge

1 Draw a crab on the sponge. Cut out and glue to the corrugated cardboard. Trim as close as possible. Press the sponge into the blue paint and blot any excess on kitchen paper. Stamp the crab evenly on to the mugs.

2 Allow to dry. Stick the masking tape around the bottom edge of the mug. Draw the border freehand on the tape with a black felt-tipped pen. Carefully cut away the bottom edge of the masking tape using a craft knife.

3 Use the cosmetic sponge to decorate the border. Use both the blue and green paints, to add depth. Sponge the handles and stamp more mugs with related motifs. Peel off the masking tape. Set the paints.

A set of delicately frosted plates would look terrific for winter dinner settings and this snowflake design is child's play to achieve. Make up as many differently designed snowflakes as you like.

Sponged Snowflake Plate

you will need
plain china plate
cleaning fluid
cloth
pencil
cup
masking film (frisket paper)
scissors
craft (utility) knife
self-healing cutting mat
sponge
paint dish
water-based ceramic paints: ice blue,
dark blue and gold

2 Draw a partial snowflake design on to one triangle and shade the areas that will be cut away. Ensure that parts of the folded edges remain intact. Cut out the design using a craft knife and self-healing cutting mat. Repeat to make seven more snowflake shapes. Unfold them, peel away the backing paper and position them on the plate.

3 Load a sponge cube with ice blue paint and dab it all over the plate. When dry, sponge darker blue around the outer and inner rims. Allow to dry, then dab a sponge loaded with gold paint around the edge of the plate, the inner rim and dark areas to highlight them. Remove the film snowflakes and then set the paint following the manufacturer's instructions.

1 Clean the plate thoroughly. Draw round an upturned cup on to the backing paper of masking film to make eight circles. Cut out the circles with scissors. Fold each circle in half. Crease each semi-circle twice to make three equal sections. Fold these sections over each other to make a triangle with a curved edge.

Jazz up herb containers to match your kitchen decor. Each of these jars bears a coloured panel which can be used to display the name of the herb contained within.

Kitchen Herb Jars

you will need

tracing paper
soft pencil
carbon paper
masking tape
6 plain china herb jars
cleaning fluid
cloth
blue chinagraph pencil
water-based enamel paints: blue, lime green, dark green and turquoise
artist's paintbrush
paint palette
dried-out felt-tipped pen

1 Using the templates provided, draw one large and one small leaf design, each on a separate piece of tracing paper. Attach the tracing paper to carbon paper, carbon side down, with masking tape.

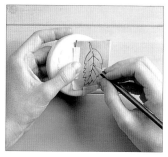

2 Clean the jars. Attach the tracing of the larger leaf on to the lid of a jar, to one side, and trace the outline with a pencil to transfer the design. Replace the tracing in another position on the lid and repeat.

3 Attach the smaller tracing to the side of a jar and trace the leaf outline on to the jar. Repeat the process to transfer the outline several times in different places around the jar, leaving a large space in the centre of one side for the "lozenge".

4 Using a blue chinagraph pencil, draw a freehand oval shape in the large space you have left. Fill in the oval with blue paint.

5 Before the paint dries, draw a design, pattern or a word on the oval shape, using an old dried-out felt-tipped pen. The felt tip will remove the blue paint to reveal the white china beneath.

6 Paint the herb leaves lime green. Allow the paint to dry completely. Add detail to the leaves in a darker green paint. Allow to dry.

7 Fill in the background in turquoise, leaving a thin white outline around each image. Paint the background of the lid in the same way. Leave paint to dry. Paint the remaining jars in complementary colours.

The colour scheme of this decorative wall plate is inspired by the rich colours of medieval tapestries. Solvent-based paints are used as they are available in metallic colours which can be diluted.

Heraldic Wall Plate

you will need
large, shallow, white-glazed plate
self-sticking dots
scissors
solvent-based ceramic paint: yellow, red, gold, black and green
fine and medium artist's paintbrushes
turpentine or clear rubbing alcohol
craft (utility) knife
hard pencil
tracing paper
pair of compasses
carbon paper
masking tape
polyurethane varnish or glaze

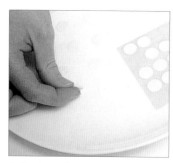

1 Stick small, sticky-backed dots at random over the middle of the plate. Cut some more of the dots in half, and stick them around the natural edge of the centre, where it meets the rim section of the plate. Press them down firmly.

2 Paint a small area of the centre with a thick coat of yellow solvent-based ceramic paint. Dip the paintbrush in turpentine or rubbing alcohol and spread the paint for a colourwashed effect. Work outwards to the edge of the centre section. Leave to dry.

3 Carefully remove the sticky-backed dots using the edge of a craft knife. If any of the yellow paint has bled under the dots, use a fine paintbrush dipped in solvent to remove it, so that you are left with a clean outline around all the white circles.

4 Using the same colourwashing technique, paint the rim of the plate red. Paint up to the yellow; do not worry if you go slightly over it. Leave the red paint to dry. Draw around the rim of the plate on to tracing paper. Measure and draw the central circle of the plate on to the tracing paper with a pair of compasses.

5 Cut out the outer ring of tracing paper and fold into eighths. The folds mark the top of each fleur-de-lis. Cut a carbon paper ring the same size. Place it face down on the rim and fix with masking tape. Open out the tracing paper and tape on top. Mark the points on the plate. Remove the carbon and tracing paper.

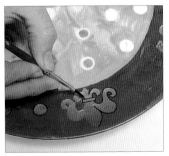

6 Using the template provided, draw a fleur-de-lis, slightly smaller than the rim depth, on to tracing paper. Cut a square of carbon paper the same size. Align the motif with a mark. Securing with masking tape, slip the carbon paper underneath. Transfer to the plate. Repeat around the rim.

7 Using gold paint, paint the fleur-de-lis motifs, the centres of the white dots, and dots between the fleur-de-lis. The gold ceramic paint will be quite translucent, and you may have to paint two coats, especially over the red, to achieve a rich tone. Allow the paint to dry between coats.

8 Using a fine paintbrush and black paint, carefully work around the fleur-de-lis motifs and the white dots to create a crisp outline. Leave the paint to dry.

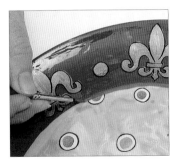

9 Using a medium paintbrush, paint a green line all around the edge of the yellow circle. Try to keep the line as even as possible. You may find it easier with a fine paintbrush, going round two or three times. Cover the paint with varnish or glaze.

Brighten up a plain china lampbase with a series of quirky patterns in bright turquoise, pink, lime and lilac. You will need to dismantle the base before painting it.

Patterned Lampbase

you will need
ceramic lampbase
cleaning fluid
cloth
soft pencil
tracing paper
plain paper
scissors
carbon paper
clear adhesive tape
solvent-based ceramic paints: lilac,
turquoise, pink, lime and black
fine and medium artist's paintbrushes
lampshade

1 Clean the lampbase and remove the electrical components. Trace the background template from the back of the book and transfer to a piece of paper. Using the paper as a guide, transfer the background design on to the lampbase with a soft pencil.

2 Trace the pattern templates at the back of the book on to tracing paper and transfer on to a sheet of plain paper. Cut out the designs, and attach them to carbon paper using clear adhesive tape.

3 Paint the background of the lampbase using a medium paintbrush. First paint in the lilac sections, then add the turquoise, pink and lime. Leave the paint to dry.

4 Arrange the designs around the painted lampbase, then fix them in place with clear adhesive tape. Use a soft pencil to transfer the design through the carbon paper on to the lampbase. Press lightly on the plain paper to leave a clear print.

5 Using the black ceramic paint and a fine paintbrush, work carefully over the outlines made by the carbon paper. When the paint is completely dry, refit the electrics to the lampbase and attach a lampshade in a complementary colour.

Coffee cups handpainted with broad brush strokes and lots of little raised dots of paint are simpler to create than you would think…with the help of a little self-adhesive vinyl.

Leaf Motif Cup and Saucer

you will need

white ceramic cup and saucer
cleaning fluid
cloth
cotton buds (swabs)
pencil
paper
scissors
self-adhesive vinyl
green water-based ceramic paint
medium artist's paintbrush
hair dryer (optional)
craft (utility) knife
pewter acrylic paint with nozzle-tipped tube

1 Clean any grease from the china to be painted using cleaning fluid and a cloth or cotton bud. Using the templates provided, draw leaves and circles on to paper. Cut them out and draw around them on the backing of the self-adhesive vinyl. Cut out. Peel away the backing paper and stick the pieces on the china.

2 Paint around the leaf and circle shapes with green water-based ceramic paint, applying several coats of paint in order to achieve a solid colour. Leave the centre circle of the saucer white. Leave each coat to air-dry before applying the next, or use a hair dryer for speed.

3 To ensure that the design has a tidy edge, cut around each sticky shape carefully with a craft knife, then peel off the sticky-backed plastic.

4 Clean up any smudges with a cotton bud dipped in acetone or water. Paint fine green lines out from the centre of each circle.

5 Using pewter paint and the nozzle-tipped paint tube, mark the outlines and details of the leaves with rows of small dots. Leave for 36 hours, then bake, following the manufacturer's instructions. The paint will withstand everyday use, but not the dishwasher.

Sunflowers seem to be perennially popular as decorating motifs. They certainly make a wonderfully cheerful design. Be adventurous and try your hand at this freehand decoration.

Sunflower Vase

you will need
plain white ceramic vase
cleaning fluid
cloth
tracing paper
soft pencil
masking tape
chinagraph pencils: yellow and blue
water-based enamel paints: yellow,
pale green, light brown, dark green,
very pale brown and sky blue
fine and medium artist's paintbrushes
paint palette

1 Clean the vase thoroughly. Enlarge the template provided and transfer to tracing paper. Fix the tracing to the vase using masking tape, and rub with a soft pencil to transfer the image.

2 Reposition the tracing paper to transfer the sunflower design all around the vase. Highlight the outline of each design with a yellow chinagraph pencil.

3 Fill in the petals with yellow paint and the stalks and leaves with pale green. Allow to dry. Paint the flowerhead centres light brown. Include a circle of short lines around the edge of each flower centre. Allow to dry.

4 Add detail to the leaves using a darker shade of green. Add dabs of very pale brown to the centre of each flowerhead. Allow to dry. Fill in the background with sky blue paint, leaving a white edge showing around the flower. Allow to dry.

5 Finally, draw around the outline and central detail of each flower with a blue chinagraph pencil.

A set of plain-glazed earthenware mugs can be made more interesting by adding some contrasting decoration. If the set is made of different coloured mugs, use paint colours that are harmonious.

Hand-painted Mugs

you will need
4 plain colour-glazed earthenware
mugs
cleaning fluid
cloth
pencils, one with eraser tip
water-based ceramic paints in
contrasting colours plus white
fine artist's paintbrushes
paint palette

1 Thoroughly clean the mugs. Draw several differetly sized circles all around one of the mugs with a pencil, leaving the top 5cm (2in) clear. Draw the circles freehand so that they are not perfectly formed.

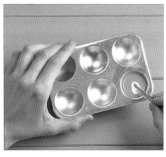

2 Mix up your first contrast colour, adding some white to make it opaque.

3 Fill in a circle on one of the mugs in a contrasting colour.

4 Before the paint dries, starting in the middle of the circle and using the eraser tip of a pencil, draw the spiral out to the edge. Try to do this in one movement, for a neater design.

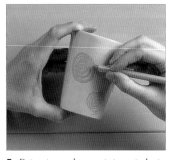

5 Paint in each remaining circle in turn, drawing out a spiral before the paint dries.

6 Using a fine paintbrush, paint radiating lines around the spirals. Leave to dry.

7 Using a fine paintbrush, paint a line detail down the outside of the handle.

8 Repeat the design on each mug, using contrasting colours, if liked.

Imaginative seaside designs applied to a plain ceramic soap dish and toothbrush holder will transform the look of your bathroom, giving it an underwater theme.

Seashore Bathroom Set

you will need

plain china soap dish and
toothbrush holder or mug

cleaning fluid

cloth

tracing paper

soft and hard pencils

plain paper

adhesive spray

carbon paper

scissors or craft (utility) knife

masking tape

water-based ceramic paints: mid-blue,
ivory, turquoise, lemon, pink,
white and dark blue

fine and medium artist's paintbrushes

paint palette

1 Clean the china well. Trace the templates at the back of the book, enlarging if necessary. Transfer the designs on to plain paper. Spray the back of the paper with adhesive and stick to the back of a sheet of carbon paper. Cut out the designs, leaving a margin all round. Tape on to the china; transfer the lines with a hard pencil. Remove the carbon.

2 Using a medium paintbrush, paint a border around the soap dish, and then paint the background in mid-blue. When it is dry, paint the fish and shells, using the ivory, turquoise, lemon and pink paints. Paint the toothbrush holder in the same way.

3 When the paint is completely dry, add the final touches to the soap dish and toothbrush holder. Paint on white dots and fine squiggles to create the effect of water. Using a fine paintbrush and the dark blue paint, carefully sketch in any detailing on the fish and shells. Allow to dry.

This cheerful sun design would be particularly welcome on the breakfast table for milk, orange juice or a simple posy of flowers. The colours could be adapted to suit your other china.

Morning Sun Face

you will need
white ceramic jug (pitcher)
cleaning fluid
cloth
tracing paper
hard and soft pencils
scissors
masking tape
acrylic china paints: black, bright yellow, ochre, blue, red and white
fine artist's paintbrushes
paint palette
hair dryer (optional)

2 Go over the sun's outlines with black paint and allow to dry; a hair dryer can speed up the process. Paint the main face and inner rays in bright yellow and then paint the cheeks and other parts of the rays in ochre.

3 Paint the background blue, then add fine details to the sun's face. Highlight each eye with a white dot. Set, following the manufacturer's instructions. The paint will withstand everyday use, but not the dishwasher.

1 Clean the china to remove any grease. Trace the template at the back of the book, try it for size and enlarge it if necessary. Cut it out roughly then rub over the back with a soft pencil. Make several cuts around the edge of the circle, so that the template will lie flat, and tape it in place. Draw over the outlines with a hard pencil to transfer the design.

The bright yellow stars on this coffee cup and saucer set shine out from the strong background, making this a stunning design. A complete set would be a glorious addition to the dinner table.

Espresso Cups and Saucers

you will need

4 plain espresso cups and saucers

white spirit (paint thinner) or cleaning fluid

cloth

pen

coloured masking film (frisket paper)

scissors

sponge

water-based enamel paints: mid-blue, darker blue and yellow

kitchen paper

fine artist's paintbrush

cotton buds

1 Thoroughly clean the china pieces with white spirit or cleaning fluid and a cloth. Allow to dry.

2 Using the template provided, draw several stars on to masking film. Cut each out accurately.

3 Remove the backing paper from the stars and stick them on to the first cup and saucer in a pleasing pattern.

4 Load a sponge cube with mid-blue paint and dab the china all over with it. Leave the paint to dry completely.

5 Load another sponge cube with a darker shade of blue and lightly sponge over the light blue. Leave to dry.

6 Peel off the plastic stars and clean away any paint that has leaked beneath them, using kitchen paper.

7 Using a fine paintbrush, fill in the stars with yellow paint. Use cotton buds (swabs) to tidy the edges of the design, if necessary.

8 Clean the rims of the cup and saucer, carefully removing any excess paint. If you intend to use the set, fire it first in a pottery kiln, following the paint manufacturer's instructions.

The painted images in this design are applied to the bowls in a way that leaves them interestingly textured. You could vary the colours you use according to the paints you have available and the room decor.

Decorated Pasta Bowls

1 Clean the bowls with the cleaning fluid and a cloth. Paint a rough background on the outside of the bowls, using water to weaken the consistency of the paint. A mix of mid- and dark blue, deep violet, green and white is used here. Leave to dry.

2 Enlarge the template provided and transfer the image on to tracing paper. Transfer the image on to acetate. Do the same with any other images you are including.

3 On the other side of the acetate, thickly paint one of the dove images in white.

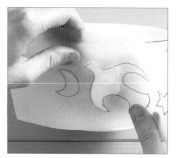

4 Before the paint dries, quickly press the shape on to the bowl. Peel off the acetate and wipe it clean. When the image on the bowl is dry, paint the other dove in white and firmly press the shape on to the bowl again.

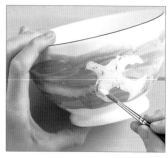

5 The texture of the dove outline will probably be very rough. Tidy it up using the mid-blue and white paint, until you get a shape you like.

6 When the painted dove is dry, print the star using the same method as for the dove, pressing the paint on to the china with your thumb. The paint mix used here is white, yellow and red.

7 Repeat the procedure to print the moon, using yellow paint.

8 Paint the heart in the centre of the dove on the acetate and transfer it to the bowl in the same way as above. Use a mix of yellow, red and white. Leave to dry.

9 Tidy the shape, using the mixed painted colours, until you are happy with the result. Leave to dry.

10 Paint in the dove's eye, using dark blue paint. When all the paint is thoroughly dry, varnish the image area with matt acrylic varnish.

Blue and whie are a classic combination that always appear fresh and appealing. Draw this design freehand using a felt-tipped pen and erase the lines until you are happy with them.

Oriental Bowl

you will need
white glazed bowl
tape measure
fine felt-tipped pen
light blue, medium blue and dark blue
craft (utility) knife
damp cloth
solvent-based ceramic paints
fine and medium artist's paintbrushes
polyurethane varnish or glaze

1 Mark a line 6cm (2⅜in) from the rim of the bowl, using a tape measure and a felt-tipped pen. Using the template provided, draw the decorative scrolls on the bowl above the 6cm (2⅜in) line. Combine horizontal undulating lines with curling "C" shapes.

2 Using a medium paint brush, paint the scrolls light blue. Keep the tone evenly flat and dense. Allow to dry.

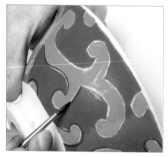

3 Paint medium blue over all of the remaining area above the horizontal line. Paint up to the edges of the scrolls first, then fill in the remaining white areas. Leave to dry.

4 Using a craft knife, scratch around the edges of the light blue scrolls to reveal the white beneath. This technique gives an uneven, broken edge; use a damp cloth to wipe away the paint chips.

5 Using a fine paintbrush, paint a dark blue line around each scroll, to add depth and contrast to the pattern. Leave visible as much of the white as possible. Leave to dry. Using the same dark blue and a brush, paint the base of the bowl as far as its natural rim, which is left white. Leave to dry. Varnish or glaze for extra durability.

The application of a few blocks of gold colour, highlighted by sketched leaf outlines which are positioned like falling leaves, quickly turns a plain white coffee pot into an elegant piece of ceramic ware.

Autumn Leaf Coffee Pot

you will need

hard and soft pencils
stencil cardboard
craft (utility) knife
metal ruler
self-healing cutting mat
carbon paper
fine felt-tipped pen
plain ceramic coffee pot
cleaning fluid
cloth
masking tape
sponge
water-based ceramic paints:
gold and black
fine artist's paintbrush
paint dish

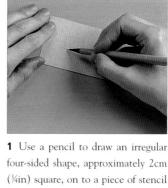

1 Use a pencil to draw an irregular four-sided shape, approximately 2cm (¾in) square, on to a piece of stencil cardboard. Using a sharp craft knife, a metal ruler and self-healing cutting mat, cut the shape away, leaving the cardboard border intact.

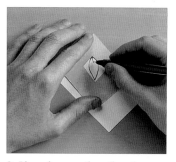

2 Place the stencil cardboard over a piece of carbon paper, carbon side down. Using the template provided, draw the outline of a leaf with a centre vein through the stencil hole on to the piece of carbon paper, using a fine felt-tipped pen.

3 Clean the china using cleaning fluid and a cloth. Attach the stencil to the pot with masking tape. Load a small sponge cube with gold paint. Lightly dab it over the stencil, without going over the outside edge of the cardboard. Leave to dry. Remove the stencil.

4 Replace the stencil in a new position on the coffee pot, rotating it slightly. Avoid sticking the masking tape over the previously painted shape. Dab the stencil with gold paint as before. Repeat the process to create a random pattern over the entire coffee pot, including the spout and lid.

5 Using masking tape, carefully attach the carbon paper with the leaf drawing over a stencilled gold shape so that the leaf outline overlaps the edge of colour. With a sharp soft pencil, lightly transfer the leaf shape on to the coffee pot.

6 Remove the carbon paper and trace the shape over the remaining blocks of gold colour. Position the leaves at slightly different angles each time.

7 Darken the leaf outlines with black paint, using a fine paintbrush. Leave to dry. Fill in the leaf veins with black paint. Leave to dry.

8 Finish off the design by painting the knob of the coffee pot lid with gold paint. Allow to dry.

Stylized holly leaves and berries decorate the rim of this festive oval platter, while the gold outlines and gold-spattered centre add seasonal glamour. Display this painted plate heaped high with mince pies.

Holly Christmas Platter

you will need

masking film (frisket paper)

white glazed oval plate

scissors

craft (utility) knife

hard and soft pencils

watercolour paper or

flexible cardboard

fine felt-tipped pen (optional)

solvent-based ceramic paints: rich dark green, bright red, maroon, gold

fine and medium artist's paintbrushes

white spirit (paint thinner)

toothbrush

paint palette

polyurethane varnish

1 Cut out a rectangle of masking film, roughly the size of the plate. Take the backing off and stick on to the plate, pressing it outwards from the centre. Using a craft knife, cut around the inner oval edge of the rim to mask out the plate centre. Remove the excess.

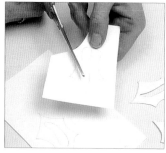

2 Using the template provided, draw two or three holly leaves with an elongated oval for the midrib on to watercolour paper or flexible cardboard. Give the leaves different curving shapes to add interest. Cut out the leaves and centres using a craft knife or small sharp scissors.

3 Arrange the leaves around the rim, leaving room for stems and a line at the top and bottom of the rim. Mark with a pencil where the first leaf starts. Fill in any space with extra berries. Draw around the leaves using a fine felt-tipped pen or pencil.

4 Add the stems, some straight, others curved, some single, others joining to form sprigs. To fill the gaps, draw berries singly or in pairs.

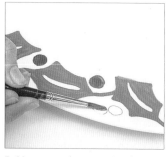

5 Using a medium paintbrush, paint the holly leaves and stems green, leaving the midrib white. Allow to dry, then add touches of green to highlight. Allow to dry, then paint the berries red and leave to dry.

6 Paint the maroon background. Use a fine paintbrush to go round the leaves, stems and berries first, leaving a narrow white outline, as shown. Infill the awkward background spaces with a fine paintbrush, then switch to a medium paintbrush for the rest. Allow to dry.

7 Using a medium paintbrush, paint a gold outline around the leaves and berries, and along one side of the stems. Try to leave as much white outline as possible exposed. Leave to dry. Using the edge of a craft knife, lift the masking paper off the middle of the plate.

8 To spatter the platter gold, mix two parts paint to one part white spirit. Pour a little paint into a saucer, and then spatter the platter with gold by rubbing your thumb over a toothbrush dipped in paint. Leave to dry. Paint a narrow red band around the rim. When dry, coat with varnish.

This wildly painted vase is a celebration in itself. The colours and patterns used here are merely suggestions. You can use the ideas to create your own joyful sequence of colours and shapes.

Carnival Vase

you will need
plain white vase
cleaning fluid
cloth
fine felt-tipped pen or soft pencil
enamel paints: pale green, dark green, red, orange and black
very fine artist's paintbrush
paint palette
tissue

1 Clean the vase with cleaning fluid and a soft cloth. Draw irregular bands horizontally around the vase, dividing it into eight. Do this quite feely, using a felt-tipped pen or soft pencil.

2 Divide three of the bands vertically into an even number of sections. The bands do not need to be regular.

3 Select a sectioned band and draw a rolling wave in each section of that band around the vase.

4 In another sectioned band, draw vertical zigzags to divide the sections into triangles. Divide another band into small squares, ensuring there is an even number around the vase

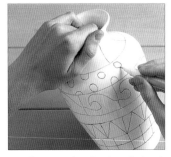

5 Fill in another band with hand-drawn circles, some of them nudging the edges of the band.

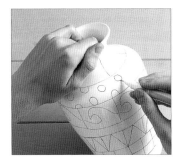

6 Paint alternate squares of the double row pale green. Then paint the band around the small circles pale green as well. Leave to dry before painting the next section

7 Paint alternate sections of a third sectioned horizontal band dark green. Paint the downward pointing triangles dark green. Leave to dry.

8 Paint the small circles red, leaving a small band of original vase showing through between the red and the surrounding pale green. Then paint the wave red. Leave to dry.

9 Paint the three remaining bands, including some around the neck, in orange, leaving some of the white showing through if desired. Paint inside the neck too. Leave to dry.

10 Wipe off any pen marks with a damp tissue. Using a fine paintbrush, paint black outlines to emphasize colour transitions. Leave to dry.

Imagine the delight this painted tea set featuring playful rabbits will bring to a child you know. This fun design is easy to accomplish using the templates provided; they can be enlarged as necessary.

Fun Bunnies Tea Set

you will need

plain china mug, plate and bowl

cleaning fluid

cloth

tracing paper

soft pencil

plain paper

adhesive spray

carbon paper

scissors

clear adhesive tape

fine felt-tipped pen

cotton bud (swab)

water-based enamel paints: yellow, turquoise, red, green and blue

fine and medium artist's paintbrushes

paint palette

1 Thoroughly clean the china mug, plate and bowl with cleaning fluid and a cloth. Trace the templates for the rabbits and flower at the back of the book and transfer them to a piece of plain paper. Spray the back of the paper with glue and place it on top of a sheet of carbon paper, carbon side down. Cut out around the drawings, leaving a narrow margin.

2 Arrange the cut-out drawings around the china mug, plate and bowl, securing them in place with clear adhesive tape. Go over the designs with a felt-tipped pen to transfer the designs to the china pieces. Remove the cut-outs and clean any smudges carefully with a cotton bud.

3 Paint the background areas of the centre of the bowl in yellow.

4 Paint the remaining background areas, around the rim of the bowl, in turquoise. Leave to dry.

5 Begin to paint in the details. Here the flowers are painted red, turquoise and green.

◀ **6** Using a fine paintbrush, paint over the outlines of the large rabbits and flowers with blue paint. Paint over the outlines of the smaller rabbits on the rim of the plate with blue paint.

▶ **7** Paint the mug handle turquoise. Allow to dry. The pieces should be fired in a kiln to make them foodsafe.

This is a freehand project and the loosely drawn oranges, leaves and flowers do not demand sophisticated artistic skill. The black outlines and the red ground colour help define the shapes.

Contemporary Fruit Bowl

you will need
large, round white-glazed bowl
fine felt-tipped pen
orange-yellow, lilac, lime green,
dark green, rich burgundy, black,
solvent-based ceramic paint
fine and medium artist's paintbrushes
polyurethane varnish or glaze, for
solvent-based ceramic paint

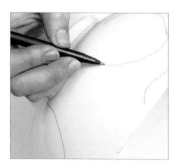

1 Using a felt-tipped pen, draw four or five roughly circular, whole oranges on to the bowl, leaving space between them for leaves and flowers. Draw four or five cut-off oranges along the top rim and base, of the bowl as if the design extended indefinitely.

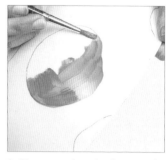

2 Using a medium brush, paint the oranges, spreading the paint thinly to give a water-washed tone. Allow to dry completely.

3 Draw stylized flowers peeping out from behind the oranges. Draw one flower behind every whole orange, with a cut-off circle representing the centre of the flower.

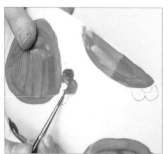

4 Paint the flowers lilac, using a small brush and spreading the paint thinly. Leave the centres white.

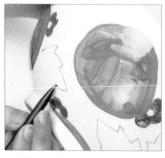

5 Using a felt-tipped pen, draw the leaves, one large and one small, for each orange. Space them to fill the background area evenly. Draw part or half leaves attached to oranges along the rim and base of the bowl, to balance the design.

6 Paint all the small leaves lime green, spreading the paint thinly. Leave to dry.

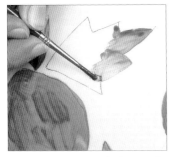

7 Using the same method, paint the large leaves dark green and leave to dry thoroughly.

8 Paint the ground rich burgundy. Starting with a fine brush, paint round the fruit shapes, leaving a narrow white outline. Use a larger brush for infill. Spread the paint thinly, so the brushstrokes remain visible, for textural variety. Paint the rim and base for a tidy finish.

9 Using a medium brush and black paint, paint loosely around the images. Vary the pressure on the brush so that the line is sometimes thick, and at other times thin. Paint the midribs in the leaves and add the circular centres in the flowers.

10 Using dark green, paint the rim at the base. Spread the paint thinly, so the brush marks show and emphasize the hand-painted quality of the design. Coat the paint with varnish or glaze when dry.

This project is inspired by rich paisley shawls and spicy Indian colours. Paisley is the classic decorative motif on clothing and upholstery fabrics and is perfect for a traditionally decorated home.

Paisley Teapot

1 Using a cloth tape measure and felt-tipped pen, mark 8mm (⅓in) down from the rim, all the way around the teapot, and join the dots together to form a band.

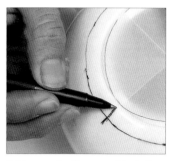

2 Measure the diameter of the hole in the top. Draw a circle, the same size, on to tracing paper. Cut out, fold in quarters, unfold, then rest flat on the hole, lining the folds up with the handle and spout. Mark the points where the folds touch the teapot. Do the same on the base.

3 Place the tape measure over the body of the pot, along the contours, joining the upper and lower points. Draw a line along the tape measure. Repeat on the other side. This gives the centre line. Measure the height of the pot, from the centre line to the spout, and along the circumference.

4 Enlarge the paisley template provided, slightly less than the pot's height and half the measured width, and transfer it to tracing paper. Cut out larger than the tracing. Cut a piece of carbon paper the same size. Stick the tracing on the carbon and stick to the centre line of the teapot. Trace.

5 Remove the tracing paper and repeat the opposite image on the other side of the centre line. Repeat on the other side of the pot. Draw a diamond within a diamond between the motifs. Draw freehand reverse curls, then a lozenge by the curls. At the top draw four scallops on each side of the pot.

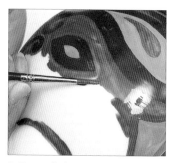

6 Gently rub out the centre line, then paint all the red areas. Leave to dry. Paint the lid red and leave to dry.

7 Paint the yellow ochre areas on the pot, including the scallops. paisley motifs, diamonds and ovals. Paint the knob on the lid. Leave to dry.

8 Paint all the remaining areas dark orange. If you intend to make practical use of the teapot, leave the area above the scallops white.

9 Place bright orange paint in a container. Dip a small piece of sponge into the paint, dab the excess on to scrap paper, then dab on to the pot and lid. If you intend to use the pot, mask out any white areas first. Leave to dry.

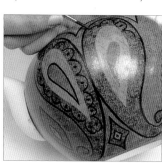

10 Using a fine brush and black paint, outline the shapes. Decorate the lid with elongated black dots. Leave to dry and varnish to finish.

Kitchen storage jars are always useful, and when adorned with bold designs such as these colourful vegetables they add quirky visual detail to your kitchen and will become a strong focal point of a shelf.

Vegetable Storage Jars

you will need

tracing paper
soft pencil
plain paper
adhesive spray
carbon paper
scissors
plain china storage jars
cleaning fluid
cloth
clear adhesive tape
fine felt-tipped pen
water-based enamel paints: turquoise, coral, ivory, blue and yellow
fine and medium artist's paintbrushes
paint palette

1 Trace the templates at the back of the book and enlarge if necessary. Transfer the designs on to a piece of plain paper. Spray the back of the paper with glue and stick it on to a sheet of carbon paper, carbon side down. Cut out the designs leaving a margin all round.

2 Clean the china storage jars, using cleaning fluid and a cloth. Tape some of the designs on to one of the jars. Go over the outlines lightly with a fine felt-tipped pen to transfer the designs to the jar. Remove the carbon paper designs and repeat the process for the other jars.

3 Using a medium paintbrush, paint in the turquoise background colour between the vegetable designs on the sides of the storage jars and their lids. Allow the paint to dry completely before proceeding to the next stage – this may take several days.

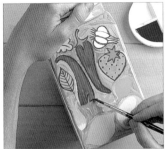

4 Mix up some red paint from the coral and ivory and paint the chillies. Mix the blue and yellow paint and paint the green of the vegetable leaves. Allow to dry.

5 Using a fine paintbrush and the blue paint, sketch in the detailing for the vegetables.

6 Paint the jar rims with the yellow paint and add some small ivory dots in the turquoise background area for decoration. Allow the paint to dry completely before using the jars.

Decorating Tiles

Plain white glazed tiles offer perfect blank canvases for decorating with paint, and their flat surface makes it so easy to do. Use single tiles for pot or pan stands, or plan a small-scale panel design over four or six tiles to add decorative details to plain walls, floors and splashbacks. Like ceramics, tiles can be decorated in a myriad ways, using different techniques and finishes, depending upon their intended use.

The history of tiles is as ancient as that of pottery, and it is possible that they originated as fragments of broken pots, for which an alternative use was found.

The History of Painted Tiles

The earliest ceramic glazes, developed in the 9th century BC, were applied to decorative tiles many centuries before glazed pots came into use. Ancient people all used decorative tilework, but its greatest flowering was during the Ottoman period, when tiles painted with scrollwork and floral designs covered the walls of mosques and palaces on the grandest scale.

Islamic decoration

The centre of Ottoman ceramic production was Iznik in north-western Turkey, and in the 15th and 16th centuries, white tiles of the finest

Below: A stylized Persian carnation is inspired by ancient Ottoman tiles.

quality were decorated with motifs such as peonies, clouds and leaves, showing the influence of Chinese Ming pottery. The tiles were often hexagonal or rectangular. At first painted in dark blue, later examples also incorporated lighter blues and turquoise, and were sometimes embossed in red. Against the background of dazzling white produced by the high proportion of quartz in the ceramics, the colours are jewel-like – resembling lapis lazuli, emerald and coral The flowing, disciplined designs blend with the architecture of the tiled buildings.

Below: Sgraffito is a simple means of adding texture to painted tiles.

The hand-painted, tin-glazed Talavera tiles of Puebla in Mexico were first made in the 16th century, when Dominican monks brought the techniques and designs of the Islamic potters to the new world from Moorish Spain. Later, the influence of Italian majolica and Chinese imports inspired new designs and added colours such as yellow, green and black to the original blue and white palette. Talavera tiles were used extensively in Poblano architecture, decorating house walls and interiors, church façades and courtyards, and were rediscovered in the early 20th

Below: A stencilled rose in the style of Charles Rennie Mackintosh.

Right: Sponged designs add a quick makeover to any plainly tiled wall.

Below: Découpage is an unusual surface covering for tiles.

century by the Californian Mission school of architects, who integrated the traditional style into their designs. The tiles are still hand-moulded from local clay in Puebla and are hand-painted using natural pigments.

Geometric patterns

The small size and regular shape of wall tiles tends to impose a discipline and regularity on the patterns used to decorate them, and designs in the Islamic style largely use symmetrical or repeating motifs. In Europe another early decorative technique for ceramic tiles, using designs of similar formality, involved incising or stamping the surface and filling the

resulting hollows with clay of a contrasting colour. Medieval inlaid tiles were often used for floors, and the style came back into use during the Gothic revival in Britain, when inlaid or "encaustic" tiles, generally in strictly geometric patterns, became very popular for domestic flooring. Many of these 19th-century floors are were made to last and are still in place today, and their distinctive appearance is quite easy to reproduce with ceramic paints on unglazed terracotta. Echoing the impressed patterns of the original tiles, intricate designs can be applied in paint using a rubber stamp, in characteristic colours such as yellow, brown and black.

Freehand style

Blue-and-white Delft wall tiles have been popular since they were first produced in the 16th century, gracing kitchens, nurseries and fireplaces. They are a universally popular pattern and are recognised the world over. The most charming designs use freehand paintings of animals, flowers, children, boats or buildings in the centre of some tiles, with tiny curling motifs in the corners, which are repeated on the otherwise plain surrounding tiles. The overall effect is light and delicate.

At the other extreme are ambitious murals in which each tile is painted with a small fragment of the overall design, the elements fitting together like a jigsaw. Italian majolica panels of this type were painted in bold colours and an exuberant style, while the Pre-Raphaelite ceramic designer William de Morgan used the glowing blues and purples and stylized, interwoven shapes of medieval Islamic painters.

White, glazed tiles are inexpensive, making this craft truly accessible to everyone. Painted tiles can add instant cheer to a room and help to complement existing features and fittings.

Materials

Ceramic wall tiles

Glazed wall tiles are waterproof and hardwearing, though brittle. They are thinner than floor tiles, usually about 5mm (¼in) thick, and come in a huge range of colours, designs, finishes and sizes. The tiles used the most in this chapter are plain white tiles as they allow plenty of scope for decoration.

Cold-set ceramic paints

Ceramic paints that are non-toxic, water-based and cold-set are the choice recommended for painting tiles. They are available in a wide range of colours and can be mixed or thinned with water. The paints set to a very durable finish after 48–72 hours drying time, but they are not as durable as unpainted glazed tiles. Care must be taken when grouting – keep the grout to the edges of the tile only. Do not clean the tiles vigorously but wipe them with a damp cloth. If more permanent decoration is required, heat-fixable paints that are set in a

domestic oven are available. Make sure your tiles are sturdy enough to be heated in this way.

Masking tape

This removable paper tape is available in different widths. It is used to mask off areas to be painted, and also to hold stencils and tracings in place.

PVA (white) glue

Use this to attach decoupage images.

Ready-mixed and powdered grout and colorant

Powdered grout is more economical than ready-mixed grout. Mix with water to a creamy paste, following the manufacturer's instructions. Powdered grout comes in different colours, or can also be coloured with grout colorant. Wear a protective face mask, safety goggles and rubber (latex) gloves when handling or mixing powdered materials.

Stencil cardboard

This manila cardboard has been impregnated with oil and is available in several thicknesses. It is durable and water-resistant and it makes strong stencils with crisp edges that last well. The cardboard is easy to cut with a craft knife and cutting mat.

Tile adhesive

Use this to glue tiles to the wall.

You will not need to purchase many items of equipment for painting tiles, but try to ensure you buy good quality paintbrushes for the most professional finish.

Equipment

Self-healing cutting mat
Use this mat to protect your work surface when cutting anything with a craft knife.

Set square
Use to align guide battens and to check that each row of tiles is straight.

Spirit level
This will ensure a straight line when you are fixing a guide batten.

Sponge
Use a damp sponge to remove excess tile adhesive and grout from tiles.

Tile spacers
These are small plastic crosses that are placed between tiles to create regular gaps for grouting. They are useful if you are using tiles without in-built spacer lugs. Some spacers are removed before grouting after the adhesive has dried. Others are much thinner and can simply be grouted over.

Tracing paper
Use to trace motifs from the back of the book and transfer to plain tiles.

Craft knife
This tool is very useful for making clean, precise cuts. Always cut away from your body and use a metal ruler to cut against.

Lint-free cloth
Use for polishing tiles after grouting.

Metal ruler
This is very useful for marking out guidelines for cutting stencils or for other decoration.

Notched spreader
Use to spread tile adhesive on tiles.

Paint-mixing container
Make sure you have enough mixed paint for the work, as it is impossible to match colours later.

Safety goggles
These should always be worn when handling powdered materials, such as grout or grout colorant, as well as for cutting tiles.

You will also find the following items useful: face mask, hammer, hand-held tile cutter, leather gloves, paintbrushes, pencils, rubber (latex) gloves, tile-cutting machine, tile file.

Tiling a wall with your completed painted tiles can be challenging depending on the size of area you are tiling and the number of tiles that have to be cut. The following tips will help the beginner.

Techniques

Cutting tiles

1 To use a hand-held tile cutter, first measure the width required and deduct 2mm (⅟₁₆in) to allow for grout. Mark the cutting line on the tile. Place the cutting wheel against a short metal ruler and score the line once only to pierce the glaze.

2 Wearing protective leather gloves and safety goggles, place the tile as far as it will go into the jaws of the cutter with the scored line positioned in the centre, then close the handles of the cutter to snap the tile in two.

3 Manual tile-cutting machines will cut tiles up to about 5mm (¼in) thick quickly and accurately, and they have a useful measuring gauge. Adjust the gauge to the correct width, then pull the wheel once down the tile to score a cutting line. Snap along this line.

4 Wearing protective leather gloves, a face mask and safety goggles, use a tile file to smooth along the cut edge of the tile if desired.

Right: Tile cutters, grout, tiles and a straightedge are just a few of the items you will need to tile an area.

Mixing grout

When colouring grout, mix enough for the whole project, as it is difficult to match the colour in a second batch.

1 When mixing up powdered grout, add the powder to a measured amount of water, rather than the other way around, otherwise the mixture may be lumpy. Mix the powder thoroughly into the water. Always wear rubber gloves, a protective face mask, old clothing and goggles.

2 Grout colorant can be added to the powdered grout before mixing it with water. Wear protective clothing as for powdered grout, and then mix with water in the proportion advised by the manufacturer.

Removing grease

You many wish to decorate tiles that are not in pristine condition. It is essential to start with a clean surface to ensure an even application of paint. To remove grease and fingerprints from the surface of tiles before you paint them, wipe with a solution of 1 part malt vinegar to 10 of water.

Below: Single painted tiles can be used to break up a plainly tiled wall.

Transferring a design

Cut a piece of tracing paper the same size as the tile. Centre the design, then trace it. Centre the paper design-side down on the tile, matching the edges. Scribble over the lines to transfer to the tile. If the design is not symmetrical, scribble over the lines on to a piece of paper. Place the tracing design-side up on the tile and redraw over the original lines.

Tiling a Wall

It is vital to prepare the surface to be tiled properly so that the tiles will adhere well. As with most techniques, the more you practise, the more skilled you will become.

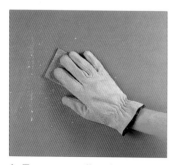

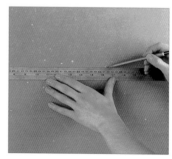

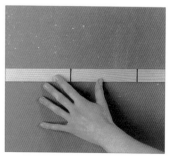

1 To prepare wall surfaces, remove wallpaper or flaking paint, and fill cracks and holes. Leave new plaster to dry for 4 weeks and seal it before tiling. Wash emulsion (latex) paint with sugar soap then sand, wearing a protective face mask, to provide a key (scuffed surface) for the tiles.

2 It is important to calculate the number of tiles before you begin. Using a long metal ruler or metal tape measure, first find the centre of the wall. You usually need to cut some tiles to fit the wall. Set the cut tiles in the corners or at the edges of walls, where they will be least noticeable.

3 Mark a wooden strip with divisions one tile wide plus an extra 2mm (⅟₁₆in) for grouting either side. Place in the centre of the wall, holding it first vertically, then horizontally. If the edges of the wall fall between two divisions on the strip, you can see the width of the cut tiles needed.

4 Wall tiles are applied upwards from a baseline, usually one tile up from a skirting (base) board, sink or the side of a bath. Draw the baseline, then attach a batten with the top edge along the line. Hammer the nails in part-way, then check with a spirit level that it is straight.

5 Use a plumbline to establish a true vertical at the side of the batten. Using a set square, draw a second line at this point to mark the side edge of the first complete tile in each row. Attach a batten along the outside of the line, hammering it in place with nails as before.

6 Wearing rubber gloves, spread a thin layer of tile adhesive, approximately 3mm (⅛in) deep, over the wall, inside the battens. Work on a small area at a time, otherwise the adhesive will dry before you have time to tile the wall.

7 Using a notched spreader, "comb" the tile adhesive to provide a key to the surface so that the tiles will adhere well. If you do not provide a good surface, the finished result will be less successful.

8 Starting in the bottom corner, position the first tile in place, where the two wooden battens meet. Push it into position with a slight twisting movement of the wrist, to ensure that the back of the tile is completely coated with tile adhesive.

9 Some tiles have built-in spacer lugs. If not, use plastic spacers at the corners of the tiles so that the grouting lines are regular. Remove excess adhesive with a damp sponge before it hardens. As you go, check the tiles with a spirit level every few rows to make sure that they are straight, and adjust as necessary.

10 When the tile adhesive is dry, remove the battens. Add cut tiles at the edges of the tiled areas if necessary. Leave for about 24 hours. Using the rubber edge of the spreader, apply grout to the gaps between the tiles. It is important to use the right type of grout depending on where the tiles are used. Make sure that the gaps are completely filled, or small holes will appear as the grout dries.

11 When the grout has hardened slightly, pull a round-ended stick along the gaps between the tiles to give a smooth finish to the grout. Add a little more grout at this stage if you notice any small holes in the previous layer.

12 Leave the grout to set for about 30 minutes, then remove the excess with a damp sponge. When the grout is completely dry, polish the surface of the tiles with a dry, lint-free cloth to remove any remaining smudges and to give a glossy finish.

Plain white tiles can be painted with individual design themes and colours of your choice for a fraction of the price you would have to pay for shop-bought ones.

Starburst Bathroom Tiles

you will need
plain white tiles
cleaning fluid
cloth
tracing paper
soft pencil
acrylic paints: white, royal blue,
light blue, deep violet, burn umber,
yellow and red
paint palette
artist's paintbrushes
acetate sheet
kitchen paper
matt acrylic varnish

1 Thoroughly clean the tiles. Trace a rectangle on to the middle of a tile as a background shape. Roughly paint the background shape in dark blue. The paint mix used here is white, royal blue, light blue, deep violet and burnt umber. Allow the paint to dry .

2 Use a soft pencil to draw a freehand star inside the rectangle on the tracing paper, and then transfer the star to the acetate. On the other side of the acetate, paint the star in yellow, using a mix of the white, yellow and red paints.

3 Tidy up the star with a damp piece of kitchen paper and retouch with the paint until you are happy with the shape. Before the paint dries, press the star lightly on to the background. Peel the film off and wipe it clean if you wish to reuse it. Leave the paint to dry.

4 When you have printed the star, check that you are happy with the shape on the tile. If the star did not print well the first time, retouch the shape with the mixed paint. Allow the paint to dry.

5 When the paint is completely dry, varnish over the painted area and leave to dry.

The rough texture and colour of hand-made terracotta tiles makes a perfect background for these naive images based on Mexican designs. Alternate the painted tiles with plain terracotta tiles in your scheme.

Mexican Animal Tiles

you will need

scrap paper

metal ruler

pencil

coloured felt-tipped pens

tracing paper

scissors

small unglazed terracotta tiles

matt, non-toxic, water-based, cold-set ceramic paints in black and a variety of colours

fine and medium artist's paintbrushes

matt varnish or terracotta tile sealant and brush

1 On paper, draw a square the same size as the tile. Trace the designs in the picture below on to scrap paper and fill them in with coloured pens.

2 Place tracing paper over each design, trace the outlines and details on to paper. Cut around the outline of each motif to make templates.

3 Centre each template on a tile and draw around it. Copy the details freehand. Paint the designs following your original coloured drawings. Leave to dry. Using a fine paintbrush outline each motif with black. Leave to dry. Seal the surface of the tiles following the manufacturer's instructions.

Turn your kitchen into a Spanish cantina with these witty tiles. The hand-made white tiles have a slightly uneven texture that adds to the rustic effect. They look good in a panel on a wall.

Cactus Tiles

you will need
chinagraph pencil
tracing paper
pencil
hand-made white glazed ceramic tiles
non-toxic, solvent-based,
cold-set ceramic paints: light green,
mid-green and golden yellow
fine and medium artist's paintbrushes
old saucer
varnish, as recommended by the
paint manufacturer

1 Using a chinagraph pencil, draw the outline of a cactus on the tile. Enlarge the template provided, if you like and transfer to the tile. Using a medium paintbrush, fill in the cactus shape with light green paint. Leave to dry.

2 Using a fine paintbrush and mid-green paint, outline the cactus, then add ridges and spines.

3 Starting in the middle of the tile, fill in the background with golden yellow paint, leaving a white outline around the cactus to accentuate the shape. Leave to dry. Seal with varnish, following the manufacturer's instructions.

The elegance of Roman numerals is timeless. Assemble these tiles inside a porch and use them to make up a particular date, such as the year your house was built.

Roman Numeral Tiles

you will need

scissors

scrap paper

stencil cardboard

clean, plain white glazed ceramic tiles

metal ruler

pencil

self-healing cutting mat

craft (utility) knife

non-toxic, water-based, cold-set ceramic paint: blue

small stencil brush

spray ceramic varnish

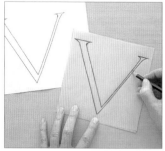

1 Cut a piece of scrap paper and a piece of stencil cardboard the same size as the tile. Using a ruler and pencil, draw the numeral on the scrap paper. Transfer the numeral on to the stencil cardboard.

2 Place the stencil cardboard on a cutting mat. Using a craft knife, carefully cut away the cardboard inside the pencil lines. Place the stencil on the tile, aligning the corners, and stipple blue paint on to the tile. Leave to dry.

3 Working in a well-ventilated area, place the painted tile on a large sheet of scrap paper. Holding the spray can about 30cm (12in) from the tile, spray it all over with an even layer of the ceramic varnish.

Trace these jolly designs from the back of the book, outline the shapes in a dark colour, then fill them in with jewel-bright shades. The bold designs are ideal for a child's bathroom.

Cartoon Tiles

you will need

tracing paper

pencil

clean, plain white glazed ceramic tiles

non-toxic, water-based, cold-set

ceramic paints in various colours

fine artist's paintbrush

paint palette

1 Trace the motifs provided and transfer to the tile. Using dark green, paint over the outlines. Add spots to the background area. Leave to dry.

2 Colour in the design. Paint spots on the fish. Leave to dry thoroughly.

Make it summer all year round with these fresh-as-a-daisy tiles. They would make a wonderful border to a wall of plain white tiles, or add individual spots of interest to a wall.

Daisy Tiles

you will need

plain white glazed ceramic tiles

chinagraph pencil

tracing paper

pencil

non-toxic, solvent-based, cold-set ceramic paints: yellow, green, warm grey and dark blue

fine and medium artist's paintbrushes

old saucer

varnish, as recommended by the paint manufacturer

1 Using a chinagraph pencil, draw a daisy and leaves on the tile. Alternatively, enlarge the templates from the back of the book and transfer to the tile.

2 Paint the flower centre yellow. Mix some green paint into the yellow make light green, the fill in the leaves. Leave to dry.

3 Add veins to the leaves with dark green paint. Add a darker yellow shadow to the flower centre, to give it depth. Outline one edge of each petal with warm grey paint. Leave to dry.

4 Fill in the background with dark blue paint. Start in the centre, painting carefully right up to the edges of the daisy, and work outwards. Leave to dry thoroughly, then seal with varnish.

Small, shaped tiles were used to decorate the floors of medieval churches with geometric patterns. This style of tiling was revived by the Victorians to create patterns on paths, doorsteps and hallways.

Medieval Floor Tiles

you will need
unglazed terracotta tiles
ceramic sealant and brush
metal ruler
pencil
non-toxic, water-based, cold-set
ceramic paints in a variety
of colours
medium paintbrushes
old saucer
rubber stamp with star motif

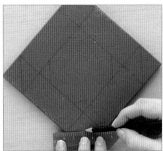

1 Seal the porous surface of the tile with a coat of ceramic sealant. Leave to dry. Draw the geometric design on the tile, using a ruler and pencil.

2 Paint the design, using rich medieval-style colours. Leave to dry thoroughly between colours.

3 Using a paintbrush, apply an even coat of paint to the rubber stamp, then press it down firmly on to the centre of the tile. Leave to dry completely.

The details on these tiles are incised into the wet paint in a traditional form of decoration known as sgraffito. Paint a set of tiles one at a time so that the paint does not dry before you add the sgraffito.

Sgraffito Fish Tiles

you will need
chinagraph pencil (optional)
clean, plain white glazed ceramic tiles
tracing paper (optional)
pencil (optional)
non-toxic, water-based, cold-set ceramic paints: dark blue and turquoise
medium artist's paintbrushes
paint palette
engraver's scribing tool or sharp pencil
varnish as recommended by the paint manufacturer

1 Using a chinagraph pencil, draw the outline of the fish on to the tile. Alternatively, enlarge the template from the back of the book and transfer to the tile.

2 Fill in the fish shape with dark blue paint using a medium paintbrush. While the paint is still wet, scratch decorative details on to the fish shape with an engraver's scribing tool or sharp pencil.

3 Fill in the background with turquoise paint, leaving a fine white outline around the fish. Scratch a swirl at each corner, as shown. Leave to dry, then seal the surface with a coat of the recommended varnish.

These deliciously pretty tiles are sponged in two tones of pink, then painted with tiny rosebuds. Sponging is simple and an ordinary bath sponge will suffice, provided it has a well-defined, open texture.

Rosebud Tiles

you will need

non-toxic, water-based, cold-set ceramic paints: pink, white, red and green

paint palette

natural sponge or highly textured nylon sponge

clean, plain white glazed ceramic tiles

medium artist's paintbrush

1 Mix the pink paint with white to give a very pale pink. Dip the sponge in the paint and apply randomly over the tile, leaving white spaces here and there. Leave to dry.

2 Add more pink to the mixed paint to darken it. Sponge this colour over the tile, allowing the first colour to show through. Leave to dry, then sponge a little white paint on top.

3 Using red paint and a paintbrush, paint rosebud shapes randomly on to the sponged tile. Using green paint, add three leaves to each rosebud as shown. Leave to dry thoroughly.

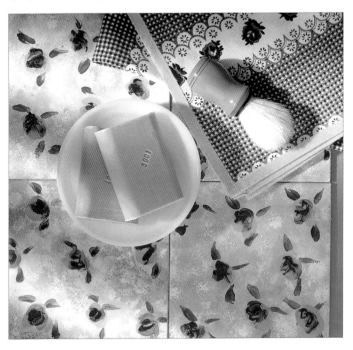

These bright and breezy tiles with their seaside-inspired motifs would look great in a kitchen or bathroom. The charming, naive designs evoke memories of salty air, sand between the toes and rock-pool gazing.

Seaside Tiles

you will need
tracing paper
pencil
carbon paper
plain white glazed ceramic tiles
tube of non-toxic, water-based black
outline paint
medium paintbrushes
non toxic water-based cold-set
ceramic paints
old saucer

1 Trace the designs from the picture below, enlarging to fit your tile. Place a piece of carbon paper face-down on the tile. Place the tracing on top. Redraw over the lines to transfer the design. Draw over the outline in black. Leave to dry.

2 Fill in the designs using the water-based ceramic paints and your choice of colours. You may have to apply two coats to get a good, opaque finish.

3 Add decorative details, such as dots, freehand, and leave the paint to dry thoroughly, following the manufacturer's instructions.

In the 15th century, magnificent tile friezes were an important element in Ottoman Turkish architecture. Stylized flower designs were popular, especially carnations and tulips.

Persian Carnation

you will need
tracing paper
pencil
plain white glazed ceramic tiles
non-toxic, acrylic paint: light pink,
dark pink, light blue, dark blue,
light green, dark green and
lemon yellow
fine and medium paintbrushes
old saucer
water-based acrylic varnish and brush

1 Trace the carnation design from the back of the book, enlarging it if necessary, and transfer on to the tile. Paint the flowers in the centre and corners light pink. Leave to dry, then emphasize the petals with dark pink.

2 Add light blue petals, then leave to dry, then emphasize the petals with dark blue paint. Paint the stems and leaves light green. Emphasize all of the stems and the leaves with dark green paint.

3 Fill in the flower centres and corners of the leaves with lemon yellow. Paint the small half-flowers with light pink and light blue paint. Leave to dry, then emphasize with dark pink. When dry, seal with varnish.

Four plain ceramic tiles combine to make a striking mural, reminiscent of Japanese art in its graphic simplicity and clear, calm blue-and-white colour scheme.

Maritime Tile Mural

you will need

soft and hard pencils

tracing paper

masking tape

4 clean, plain white glazed 15cm (6in) square ceramic tiles

chinagraph pencil

non-toxic, water-based, cold-set ceramic paints: mid-blue, dark blue and black

fine artist's paintbrushes

paint palette

1 Trace the template from the back of the book and enlarge, if necessary. Tape the tracing to the four tiles, positioning it centrally. Transfer the outline to the tiles with a hard pencil.

2 Trace over the outline again with a chinagraph pencil. Draw the border freehand, and add any extra details to the fish. Follow the finished picture as a guide.

3 Keep the tiles together as you paint. Using the ceramic paints, fill in the fish shape. First, paint the main part of the fish mid-blue.

4 Paint the detail and the border dark blue. Highlight the scales with black. Set the paint following the manufacturer's instructions. The painted tiles will withstand gentle cleaning.

This quirky cherub tile panel will add cheery individuality to any wall. Decorated in the style of Majolica ware, with bright colours and a stylized design, this romantic cherub is easy to paint.

Cherub Tiles

you will need

pencil

tracing paper

4 clean, plain white, glazed, square
ceramic tiles

non-toxic, water-based, cold-set
ceramic paints: dark blue,
yellow and red

fine artist's paintbrushes

paint palette

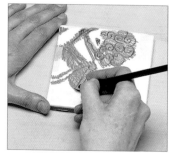

1 Trace the template from the back of the book. Enlarge the design on to a piece of tracing paper. Use a pencil to transfer a quarter of the design to each ceramic tile.

2 With a fine brush, and dark blue paint, paint over the main outline on each tile. If required, heat the tiles in the oven for the time specified by the paint manufacturer, to set the outline.

3 Fill in the wings, hair and drapery with yellow paint. Allow the paint to dry. Mix yellow with red to add darker tones, using the finished picture as a guide. Bake the tiles again, to prevent the colours from smudging.

4 With diluted blue paint, mark in the shadows on the cherub's face and body. Go over any areas that need to be defined with more blue paint. Paint the corner motifs freehand and then bake for the final time.

This is a great idea for decorating plain ceramic tiles, which could then be framed and hung on the wall. Alternatively, you could break up a plain white tiled surface with random floral tiles.

Floral Tiles

1 Trace the template at the back of the book and enlarge it. Turn the paper over and rub over the outline with a pencil. Tape the transfer to the tile and draw over the outline with a hard pencil to transfer the motif on to the tile.

2 Using a medium paintbrush and thin layers of paint, colour in the leaves and petals. If required, bake in the oven to set the paint, according to the paint manufacturer's instructions.

3 With a fine paintbrush and blue paint, draw in the outline and detail of the petals, leaves and stalk. Paint dots in the centre of the flower. Transfer the corner motifs, and paint them blue with a fine paintbrush. Set the paint by baking the tile. The tile will withstand gentle cleaning.

These Florentine-style tiles are based on ceramic decoration of the Renaissance. A single tile could be a focal point in a bathroom, or you could arrange several together to form interesting repeat patterns.

Italianate Tiles

you will need

clean, plain white glazed square tiles

tracing paper

soft and hard pencils

masking tape

non-toxic, water-based, cold-set ceramic paints: mid-green, dark blue-green, rust-red and dark blue

fine and medium artist's paintbrushes

paint palette

1 Wash and dry the tiles thoroughly. Enlarge the template at the back of the book to fit the size of your tiles. Trace the main motif (and also the border if you wish) and rub the back of the tracing with a soft pencil. Position the tracing on each tile, secure with tape, and draw over the outline with a hard pencil.

2 Paint the leaf in mid-green paint and allow to dry. You may need to mix colours to achieve the shades you require. Using a dark blue-green, paint over the outline and mark in the leaf veins. Paint a dot in each corner of the tile in the same colour.

3 Paint a border of rust-coloured leaves and a slightly larger leaf in each corner. Paint a curved scroll at both sides of the large leaf in dark blue. When the paint is completely dry, if required, set it in the oven according to the manufacturer's instructions.

This delightful vase of flowers is based on a tile design from the Urbino area of northern Italy, where the majolica style of pottery decoration developed in the 15th century.

Majolica Tiles

1 Trace the vase of flowers design from the back of the book, enlarging it if necessary, and transfer it on to the tile. Begin to paint the design with a fine paintbrush, starting with the palest tones of each colour.

2 Carefully paint in the foliage with light and dark green paint, leaving each colour to dry before applying the next. Add white to orange paint to create a paler shade. Use this to paint the top and bottom of the vase. Using darker orange, fill in the flower centres and emphasize the shape of the vase.

3 Using royal blue paint, outline the shapes of the flowers and vase. Add the vase handles and decorative details to the flowerheads. Leave the tile to dry, then seal the surface with two coats of acrylic varnish, allowing the first coat to dry before applying the second, if required.

Translucent ceramic paints give this exotic tile the rich, glowing colours associated with Byzantine art. The decorative bird motif is taken from a cloisonné enamel panel originally decorated with precious stones.

Byzantine Bird Tile

you will need

tracing paper

pencil

clean, plain white glazed ceramic tile

non-toxic, water-based, cold-set ceramic paints in a variety of rich colours

fine artist's paintbrushes

paint palette

fine gold felt-tipped pen

1 Trace the bird design from the back of the book, enlarging it if necessary, and transfer on to the tile. Paint the bird's head and legs, then start to paint the features, using bright colours.

2 Paint the plants, using your choice of colours. Leave to dry completely.

3 Using a gold felt-tipped pen, draw an outline around every part of the design. As a final touch, add decorative gold details to the bird's feathers and the plants.

The tile-making centre of Puebla in Mexico has been famous for its vibrant, colourful designs since the 17th century. These tiles take their inspiration from the colourful patterns of the Mexican style.

Pueblan Tiles

you will need

pencil

metal ruler

clean, plain white glazed ceramic tiles

non-toxic, water-based, cold-set ceramic paints:

orange, yellow, royal blue and turquoise

medium artist's paintbrushes

paint palette

1 Using a pencil and ruler, lightly draw a narrow border around the edge of the tile. Draw a square in all four corners. Paint the borders orange and the squares yellow.

2 Using the same colours, paint a design in the centre of the tile, as shown. Leave to dry completely.

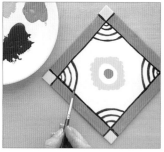

3 Outline the borders and squares in royal blue paint. Then, starting just inside the border at each corner, paint a series of blue arcs, as shown.

4 To decorate the central motif, paint blue circle and diamond shapes over the orange and yellow design, as shown. Add a scalloped edging around the circle and diamond.

5 Using orange paint, paint a small quarter-circle in each corner of the tile to form the repeat. Finally, fill in the background with turquoise paint. Leave to dry completely.

These elegant and highly stylized designs are inspired by the work of Scottish artist Charles Rennie Mackintosh and the Glasgow School of Art at the turn of the 20th century.

Art Nouveau Tiles

you will need

tracing paper

pencil

clean, plain white glazed ceramic tiles

scissors

stencil cardboard

craft (utility) knife

self-healing cutting mat

repositionable spray adhesive

non-toxic, water-based, cold-set ceramic paints: dark green, light green, deep red and white

fine and wide artist's paintbrushes

paint palette

water-based acrylic varnish

1 Enlarge the designs at the back of the book to fit your tiles. Cut two pieces of stencil cardboard to the size of the tiles and transfer one design to each. Using a craft knife and a cutting mat, cut away the centre of each design. Coat the back of the stencils with adhesive. Place the stem stencil on a tile. Using a dry wide paintbrush, apply dark green paint to the stems and light green for the leaves.

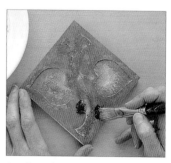

2 Allow the paint to dry completely, then use a clean, dry paintbrush to add a little deep red paint to pick out the thorns on the stem. You might also like to try reversing the stem stencil on some of the tiles, which will make the overall effect more symmetrical.

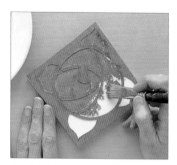

3 Mix deep red paint with white to make a dusky pink shade. Use this colour to stencil the rose motif on to another tile with a dry paintbrush. Leave the paint to dry.

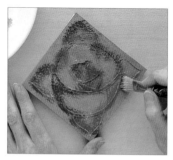

4 Add deep red around the edges of the petals to emphasize the rose shape and give it depth.

5 Using a fine paintbrush, add green dots in the centre of the rose. Leave to dry, then seal the surface of the tiles with two coats of varnish, allowing them to dry between coats, if required.

This cheerful panel is painted freehand across a block of tiles. The paint is applied in several layers, working from light to dark, to give depth and to intensify the colours.

Underwater Panel

you will need

clean, plain white glazed ceramic tiles

soft pencil

non-toxic, water-based, cold-set ceramic paints: orange, blue, green, white, red

fine and medium artist's paintbrushes

paint palette

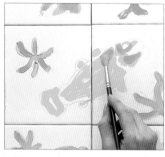

1 Arrange the tiles as close together as possible. Use a soft pencil to sketch your design on the tiles, leaving room around the panel for the border.

2 Starting with the lightest tones of each colour, paint in the fish, shell and seaweed motifs. Allow patches of the white background to show through. Leave to dry.

3 Using medium tones of each colour, loosely paint darker areas to give depth to the sea motifs.

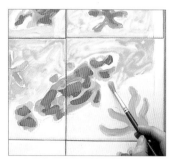

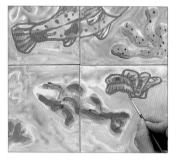

4 Fill in the background sea with diluted blue paint, allowing some of the white to show through.

5 Using a fine paintbrush and a darker tone of each colour, outline the fish, shell and seaweed motifs. Add decorative details, as shown.

6 Using a broad paintbrush, paint a border around the panel. Take the paint over the edges of the tiles where they butt up so there are no ugly gaps. Leave to dry.

This sumptuous and decadent tile is not intended for practical use but to be displayed. The surface is covered with a composite metal leaf, then decorated with a decoupage image photocopied from a book.

Silver Decoupage Tiles

you will need

plain white glazed ceramic tile

cleaning fluid

cloth

water-based Italian size and brush

aluminium composite loose leaf

wide, soft brush

purple water-based ink

black and white photocopy

scissors

PVA (white) glue

ceramic tile varnish

1 Clean the tile surface thoroughly to remove any grease. Apply a thin, even coat of size, making sure that the whole surface is covered. Leave it for 15–20 minutes until the size is tacky.

2 Carefully lay the aluminium leaf on the tile. Use a large, dry, soft brush to burnish the aluminium leaf flat and remove any excess.

3 Paint a thin wash of diluted purple ink over the photocopy and leave to dry. Cut out the image. Apply a thin coat of PVA (white) glue to the back and position it on the tile, smoothing the paper down gently in order to remove any air bubbles.

4 Leave the image to dry thoroughly. Seal the surface of the tile with two thin coats of ceramic varnish, allowing the first coat to dry for about 30 minutes before applying the second.

Based on a design by William Morris in 1870, the flowing lines of the flower painting are typical of his bold style. Morris's tiles were often manufactured by designer William de Morgan.

William Morris Tiles

1 Enlarge the design from the back of the book so that each square fits on to one tile. Cut it into four separate patterns. Transfer each pattern on to a tile, drawing over the lines with a ballpoint pen.

2 Dilute some of the blue paint, then fill in the two main flower shapes with a medium paintbrush. Leave the paint to dry before proceeding to the next stage.

3 Using undiluted blue paint and a fine paintbrush, work the detailing on the flower petals as shown, to add definition.

4 Using a medium paintbrush, fill in the leaves with dark green paint. The slightly streaky effect that is left by the bristles will add movement to the design. Leave the paint to dry. Highlight the leaves with white veins.

5 Paint green leaves on the flower tiles. Leave to dry, then highlight with white veins as before. Add detailing and fine outlines to the flowers. Leave the tiles to dry completely.

Painting

Glass

In recent years a wide range of glass paints, in a glorious array of colours, has been made available to the amateur. These paints do not require kiln firing to set them, and they can be applied easily to glassware. So whether you want to recreate the effect of a stained-glass window in your home, or add delicate colour to perfume bottles and champagne flutes to celebrate a special occasion, there are plenty of ideas here to inspire you.

Glass has been made for millennia, and although its precise origins are unknown, by 1500BC coloured glass was being made in Mesopotamia and Egypt, where the decorative qualities it offered were highly valued.

The History of Painted Glass

In ancient Egypt coloured glass was used to make highly prized beads and jewellery for adornment long before the appearance of practical and decorative glass vessels. The Romans developed ornamental glassmaking to a high degree, making ornate and complex containers of every kind and creating some of the earliest, though small. stained glass windows. An outstanding example of Roman glass, now in the British Museum in London, is the Lycurgus Cup, a "cage-cup" in which the vessel itself is enclosed within a tracery of glass strands in the form of a vine.

Stained glass, created by adding metallic salts and oxides to molten glass, was used throughout Europe to produce the great windows of the medieval cathedrals and churches. Early designers probably drew on skills such as jewellery-making and mosaic to develop their techniques, and as buildings became taller and windows wider, they were able to create huge, jewel-bright pictures that flooded the interiors with dazzling coloured light.

Stained-glass work again became prominent during the Gothic revival of the 19th century, and in both Britain and America it was among the traditional crafts taken up by Arts and Crafts designers. John La Farge and Louis Comfort Tiffany carried out extensive work on the chemistry of glass for exquisitely coloured and layered windows, and developed many of the unusual varieties available today. In Britain, William Morris took his inspiration from 12th-century survivals, and his richly coloured designs were much in demand for church windows.

Decorative stained glass was integral to the buildings of the American architect Frank Lloyd Wright, who called his leaded and delicately

Below: Delicate designs can be hand-painted on to the smallest surfaces.

Below: A special medium can be applied to glassware to give the effect of etching.

Below: Glass, film and plastic can all be decorated with today's glass paints.

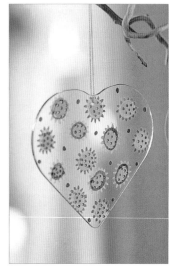

coloured windows "light screens" and used them to blur the boundaries between the interior and the landscape beyond.

Painting with light

Over the centuries, the use of stained glass panels in ecclesiastical windows gave way to glass painting, in which the colour was applied to the surface of the glass and then made permanent by firing in a kiln. Many medieval windows combined examples of both techniques. Using paint allowed for the addition of detail to stained glass, from the shading of folds of clothing, to facial features; by the Renaissance the decoration often consisted entirely of coloured paint applied to plain glass. Leading, which had formed an intrinsic part of the design in Gothic windows, became a structural necessity that the artist did his best to disguise. Paler colours allowed in more light, and coloured glass windows became fashionable elements of private homes, often painted with elaborate coats of arms. In the 20th century many artists made use of the potential of glass as a means for exploring colour. Wassili Kandinski made glass paintings inspired by Russian and Bavarian folk art, and the French artist Marc Chagall produced a famous series of windows for the synagogue of the Hadassah Hospital in Jerusalem. The last thirty years have seen an explosion of interest in the art of decorating glass, not least as a hobby, thanks to the wide availability of paints, contour pastes, etching creams and all the other materials needed to turn a plain vase or panel into a scintillating work of art.

Above: Accurate hand-painting is the key to success with this folk-art design.

Left: This plain glass bowl has been decorated freehand with delicate flower and butterfly motifs, which give it a contemporary look.

A variety of materials is needed for painting glass including glass paints and etching paste, available from specialist glass shops, and self-adhesive vinyl, which is available from craft shops.

Materials

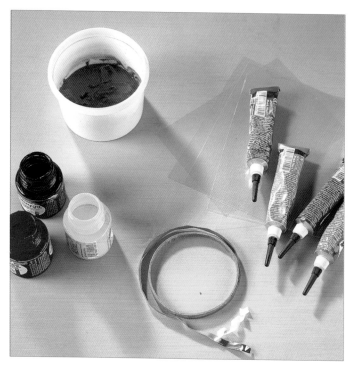

colour. They are not washable, and are designed purely for decorative use. Oil-based and water-based glass paints are available: the two types should not be combined. Ceramic paints can also be used on glass for an opaque effect.

Kitchen paper
These are useful for cleaning glass and brushes, and wiping off mistakes.

Masking tape
This is ideal for making straight lines for etching and painting.

Reusable adhesive
This is useful for holding designs in place on the glass.

Self-adhesive vinyl
Vinyl is used to mask off large areas when painting and etching the glass.

Acrylic enamel paints
These are ideal for use on glass.

Clear varnish
Mix with glass paints to produce lighter hues.

Contour paste
Use to create raised lines on glass. This gives the look of leaded windows and also acts as a barrier for paints. It can be used to add details within a cell of colour, such as the veins on a leaf.

Epoxy glue
Use this strong, clear glue to attach hanging devices to glass. It takes just a few minutes to go hard.

Etching paste
This acid paste eats into the surface of glass to leave a matt "frosted" finish. Use on clear and pale-coloured glass.

Glass paints
Specially manufactured, glass paints are translucent and give a vibrant

Toothpicks
Use to scratch designs into paintwork.

Ultraviolet glue
This glue goes hard in daylight. Red glass blocks ultraviolet rays, so you should let the light shine through the non-red glass when sticking two colours together, or use epoxy glue.

White spirit (paint thinner)
Use as a solvent to clean off most paints and any errors.

A well-lit workplace and a paintbrush are all that are needed for many of the projects in this chapter. However, the items listed below will make the job easier.

Equipment

Paintbrushes

Use a selection of artist's paintbrushes for applying paint and etching paste. Always clean brushes as directed by the paint manufacturer.

Paint palette

Large quantities of glass paint can be mixed in a plastic ice-cube tray.

Pencils and pens

Use a pencil or dark-coloured felt-tipped pen when making templates. A chinagraph can be used to draw guide-lines on the glass and wipes off easily.

Rubber gloves

A pair of gloves is vital to protect your hands from etching paste.

Ruler or straightedge

These are essential for measuring, or when a straight line is needed.

Cloth

A piece of cloth or towel folded into a pad is useful to provide support for items such as bottles or bowls while they are being painted. Paint one side of a vessel first, then allow it to dry thoroughly before resting it on the cloth while you paint the rest.

Cotton buds (swabs)

Use these to wipe away any painted mistakes and to remove chinagraph pencil marks.

Craft (utility) knife

A craft knife is useful for peeling off contour paste in glass-painting and etching projects. Ensure the blade is sharp and clean.

Nail polish remover

Before painting, always clean the glass on both sides to remove all traces of grease or fingerprints. Household glass-cleaning products can be used but nail polish remover is just as good. Use with paper towels.

Scissors

A pair of small, sharp scissors is useful for various cutting tasks, including cutting out templates.

Sponges

Cut sponges into pieces and use them to apply paint over a large area of glass. A natural sponge can be used to give the paint a decorative mottled effect, whereas a synthetic sponge will give a more regular effect.

On the following pages you will find useful step-by-step descriptions of some of the basic glass-painting techniques. They will help you to perfect your skills and achieve beautiful and successful results.

Techniques

Preparing the glass

It is essential to clean the surface of the glass thoroughly to remove any traces of grease or fingermarks, before beginning glass painting.

Clean both sides of the glass thoroughly, using a glass cleaner or nail polish remover and kitchen paper.

Using templates and stencils

There are many different templates and stencils suitable for using on glass. Choose the type that is most useful for the size and style of glassware you are decorating.

1 If you are working on a flat piece of clear glass, a template can simply be taped to the underside or attached using pieces of reusable putty adhesive, to ensure it does not move.

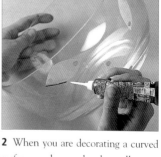

2 When you are decorating a curved surface, such as a bowl, small paper templates can be attached to the inside, following the curve. Use adhesive tape.

3 When working on a small, curved surface, such as a drinking glass, it may be easier to apply the template to the outside and then draw around it using a chinagraph pencil to make a guide.

4 Cut straight-sided stencils using a craft (utility) knife and metal ruler and resting on a cutting mat. Always keep your fingers well away from the blade and change the blade frequently to avoid tearing the paper.

5 When you are cutting a stencil that includes tight curves, cut what you can with a craft knife, then use a small pair of sharp-pointed scissors to cut the curves smoothly.

Transferring a design

In addition to using templates and stencils, there are several other ways of transferring a design on to glass. You can trace it, sketch with a pen, use carbon paper or even use water.

Tracing through the glass

Stick the design in position on the back of the article you wish to transfer it to with reusable putty adhesive or masking tape. For curved vessels cut the design into sections. Trace the design directly on to the surface of the vessel with the tube of contour paste.

Felt-tipped pens

A water-based overhead-projection pen is ideal for sketching freehand on to glass. Many felt-tipped pens will also work. When you are happy with your design, apply contour paste over the lines.

Water-level technique

To draw even lines around a vase, bowl, or other circular vessel, fill with water to the height of the line. Turn the vessel slowly while tracing the waterline on to the surface of the glass with contour paste.

Using carbon paper

Place a sheet of carbon paper over the article and then put the design on top. With a ballpoint pen, trace over the lines of your design, pressing it fairly firmly. Some carbon papers will not work on glass – handwriting carbon paper is the most suitable.

Using contour paste

Contour paste is easy to use, but it takes a little practice to get the pressure right. As it is the basis of much glass painting, it is worth persevering.

1 Squeeze the tube until the paste just begins to come out, then stop. To draw a line, hold the tube at about 45° to the surface. Rest the tip of the tube on the glass and squeeze it gently while moving the tube.

2 Occasionally air bubbles occur inside the tube. These can cause the paste to "explode" out of the tube. If this happens, either wipe off the excess paste straight away with kitchen paper, or wait until it has dried and use a craft knife to remove it.

Mixing and applying paint

Glass paints come in a range of exciting, vivid colours, and produce beautiful translucent effects. Practise painting first on a spare piece of glass to get used to the consistency of the paint.

1 Mix paint colours on a ceramic palette, old plate or tile. To make a light colour, add the colour to white or colourless paint, a tiny amount at a time, until you reach the required hue. Use a separate brush for each colour so that you do not contaminate the paint in the pot.

2 If you want the finished effect to be opaque rather than translucent, add a small amount of white glass paint to the transparent coloured paint on the palette, plate or tile.

3 Always use an appropriately sized paintbrush for the job. A large, flat brush will give a smooth and even coverage over larger areas of glass, as well as making the job quicker.

4 Use a very fine brush to paint small details and fine lines. Let one coat of paint dry before painting over it with another colour.

5 To etch a design into the paint, draw into the paint while it is still wet using a toothpick or the other end of the paintbrush. Wipe off the excess paint after each stroke to keep the design clean.

Applying paint with a sponge

Sponging produces a mottled, softened effect on glass surfaces. Experiment first on scrap paper.

1 Use a dampened natural sponge to achieve a mottled effect. Dip the sponge in the paint then blot it on a sheet of paper to remove the excess paint before applying it to the glass.

2 Use masking tape or small pieces of reusable putty adhesive to attach the stencil to the glass for sponging.

Free-styling

Rather than using contour paste to define individual cells of colour, apply a coat of varnish over the article and brush or drop colours into the varnish, allowing them to blend freely.

3 Add texture and interest to sponged decoration by adding a second colour when the first has dried. This is most effective when both sides of the glass will be visible.

4 Sponge a neat, decorative band around a drinking glass by masking off both sides of the band with strips of masking tape.

Flash drying with candles

It is possible to flash dry paintwork over a heat source. A candle is ideal, but take care not to burn yourself. Turn the article slowly about 15cm/6in above the flame.

Correcting mistakes

If you don't get your design right the first time, it doesn't matter with glass painting. All you need is a cotton bud (swab) or kitchen paper and you can simply wipe off the paint before it dries.

1 Use a cotton bud (swab) to remove a small mistake. Work while the paint is still wet.

2 To remove a larger area of paint, wipe it away immediately using a damp paper towel. If the paint has begun to dry, use nail polish remover.

3 If the paint has hardened completely, small mistakes can be corrected by scraping the paint away using a craft knife.

Etching glass

This technique is easy but very effective and produces a quick, stylish finish. Etch simple shapes such as flowers or leaves for the best results.

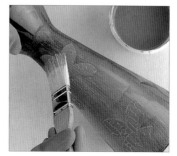
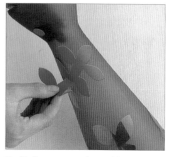

1 Self-adhesive vinyl makes a good mask when etching. Cut out shapes from self-adhesive vinyl. Decide where you want to position them on the glass, remove the backing paper and stick down.

2 Wearing rubber gloves, paint the etching paste evenly over the glass with a paintbrush. Make sure you do not spread it too thinly, or you will find the effect quite faint. Leave to dry for 3 minutes.

3 Still wearing the rubber gloves, wash the paste off with running water. Then wipe off any residue and rinse. Peel off the shapes and wash again. Dry the glass thoroughly with a clean cotton rag.

For this year's Christmas tree, buy plain glass baubles and decorate them yourself with coloured glass paints to make beautiful, completely original ornaments.

Christmas Baubles

you will need

self-adhesive spots
clean, clear glass baubles
glass-fetching medium
paper clips
gold contour paste
fine glitter
scrap paper
bright yellow glass paint
fine artist's paintbrush

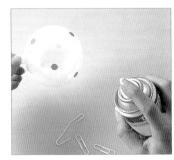

1 Stick self-adhesive spots all over the baubles. Spray on an even coat of glass etching medium. Hang up each bauble to dry using paper clips.

2 Peel off the paper spots to reveal clear circles all over each bauble. Outline each circle with gold contour paste, then draw a second circle around the first. Add some squiggly lines radiating from the neck of the bauble. While the contour paste is still wet, sprinkle it with glitter, holding the bauble over a sheet of paper to catch the excess. Hang the bauble up to dry.

3 Fill in between the inner and outer gold circles with glass paint in bright yellow, and hang the bauble up to dry, using paper clips as before. Repeat for any remaining baubles.

Glass paint and relief outliner can be used very successfully on acetate sheet, so you can use it to make unbreakable, lightweight decorations. Here, the painted design has been mounted in a card frame.

Celebration Card

you will need
scrap paper
pencil
acetate sheet
masking tape
relief outliners: silver or pewter, green, pink and yellow
glass paints: yellow and white
medium artist's paintbrush
paint tray
ruler
craft (utility) knife
cutting mat
stiff card (card stock)
all-purpose strong glue

1 Draw a freehand design of your choice of motifs and numbers on to scrap paper. Secure a piece of acetate over the drawing using masking tape. Outline the number and both edges of the border, using silver or pewter outliner. Leave to dry.

2 Draw a second line inside the outer border of each shape, using green outliner. Fill in the numbers, using pink outliner, and the border, using yellow. Leave to dry.

3 Detach the acetate from the template and turn it over. Draw a pink outline just inside the border on the back of the sheet. Mix yellow glass paint with white to make it opaque, and fill in the square on the back of the design. Leave to dry.

4 Trim the acetate, leaving a border about 2.5cm (1in) wide all around the design. Cut out a card in which to mount it, and measure and cut a window in the front of the card, about 5mm/¼in smaller all around than the acetate sheet.

5 Apply all-purpose strong glue around the window and glue the acetate sheet into the card.

White glass paint is opaque and can be used to create an etched effect. using a fooproof stencil technique, it's easy to decorate a wine glass with a classic monogram to make an elegant personalized gift.

Monogrammed Wine Glass

you will need
pencil and plain paper
scissors
ruler
wine glass
nail polish remover or glass cleaner
kitchen paper
masking tape
clear sticky-back plastic (contact paper)
soft cloth
craft (utility) knife
glass paint: white

1 Using the templates provided, draw your chosen initials to size for the required glass. Cut out the initials leaving a large margin all around.

2 Clean the outside of the glass with nail polish remover or glass cleaner to remove any traces of grease. Secure the template inside the glass with masking tape.

3 Cut a rectangle of sticky-back plastic large enough to cover the letters. Remove the backing paper and stick it to the front of the glass. Smooth over with a cloth.

4 Using a craft knife, cut out the initials, following the outlines. Peel away the plastic inside the letters to make a letter stencil.

5 Apply white glass paint over the stencil, dabbing it on with a soft cloth to create a frosted look. Leave to dry. Peel off the letter stencil carefully. Leave the painted letters to dry completely, then bake the glass, if necessary, to harden the paint, following the manufacturer's instructions.

Craft suppliers stock a range of glassware especially for painting, and these small glass hearts would look beautiful catching the light as they twirl in a window.

Heart Decoration

you will need
clean, clear glass heart shapes
nail polish remover or glass cleaner
kitchen paper
etching paste
medium artist's paintbrush
sponge
contour paste: light gold, dark gold
and bronze

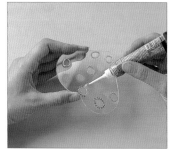

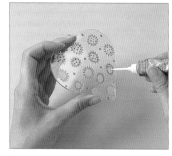

1 Clean both sides of the glass shapes to remove grease. Paint etching paste in small circles all over one side of the glass. Leave to dry, then wash off the paste with warm water and a sponge.

2 Outline alternate etched circles using light gold contour paste. Leave to dry. Add short "rays" all round each outline using dark gold contour paste, then add rays in light gold. Leave the contour paste to dry.

3 Use bronze contour paste to add a few dots between the circles. Turn the heart over and cover the etched areas in dots of bronze contour paste. Leave to dry. Bake the glass to harden the paint if necessary, following the manufacturer's instructions.

Transform plain, everyday glasses with patterns of gold relief outliner. Add clear, stained-glass colours for a jewelled effect and you will give your festive dinner the air of a medieval feast.

Festive Wine Glasses

you will need
plain wine glasses
clean cloths
cleaning fluid
gold contour paste
oil-based glass paints
fine artist's paintbrush
old glass or jar
kitchen paper

1 Wash the glasses and wipe over with cleaning fluid to remove all traces of grease.

2 Pipe your design directly on to the glass with gold contour paste. Leave to dry thoroughly for at least 24 hours.

3 Check the colour and get the feel of the glass paint, which is rather viscous, by practising on an old glass or jar first. Use a fine paintbrush to colour in your design, and be careful not to get paint on the gold contour paste. Try to finish with each colour before changing to the next one. Clean the brush between each colour.

Create a conversation piece at meal times with these contemporary salt and pepper pots, which have been simply decorated with circles, squares and dots in a variety of bright colours.

Painted Salt and Pepper Pots

you will need

clean glass salt and pepper pots

contour paste: black and gold

glass paints in various colours

medium artist's paintbrushes

clear varnish

1 Draw a few loose circles on to the pots with black contour paste.

2 When the lines are dry, colour in the background with glass paint.

3 Fill in the circles with a different coloured paint from the one used for the background. If you prefer, use a variety of different colours.

4 Apply dots of black contour paste over the background colour to add texture to the design.

5 When dry, paint squares over the circles using the gold contour paste. Leave to dry, then paint with clear varnish. Allow to dry.

The decoration on this double-layered glass frame has been painted on to the inside of the glass. This means that you need to paint the details on the leaves first, and the background colour second.

Leaf Photograph Frame

you will need
tracing paper
double-layer glass clip-frame, with cleaned glass
scissors
masking tape
photograph
felt-tipped pen
nail polish remover or glass cleaner
kitchen paper
glass paints: dark green, light green and pale blue
fine and medium artist's paintbrushes

1 Cut a piece of tracing paper the same size as the frame. Using small tabs of masking tape, stick your chosen photograph in place and mark its position, then draw a selection of leaves around it, following the leaf templates at the back of the book.

2 Thoroughly clean the glass that forms the front of the frame. Remove the photograph and turn the tracing paper back to front. Attach it to the glass using small pieces of masking tape, as shown.

3 Using a fine paintbrush, fill in the leaf stems of the design with the dark green paint. Again using the dark green paint, fill in the small triangle shapes that represent the veins in the leaves. Leave the dark green paint to dry completely.

4 Paint the leaf shapes in light green. Leave the light green paint to dry, then paint the background colour in pale blue. Leave to dry. Remove the template. Bake the glass frame to harden the paint, if necessary. Follow the manufacturer's instructions.

5 Attach your chosen photograph to the second glass sheet, checking its position against the marks on the template. Assemble the frame.

Etching cream creates an elagant frosted effect that is perfect for glasses used for iced drinks. The flowers are applied as reverse stencils: when the sticky-back plastic is removed, the motifs are revealed.

Frosted Highball Glasses

you will need

tracing paper

pencil

carbon paper

sticky-back plastic (contact paper)

scissors

highball glasses

nail polish remover or glass cleaner

kitchen paper

rubber gloves

glass etching cream

medium artist's paintbrush

warm water and sponge

1 Trace the template provided, or draw a flower freehand, and use carbon paper to transfer it to the paper backing of a sheet of sticky-back plastic.

2 Draw the motif three to five times for each glass, depending on the size of the design. For any detailed shapes, cut out the design. Use small, sharp-pointed scissors.

3 Clean the outside of each glass, using glass cleaner or nail polish remover to remove traces of grease. Remove the backing paper from the motifs and stick them at regular intervals around the glass, varying the heights of the flowers. Trim the stems, to add interest to the design.

4 Wearing rubber gloves, paint the etching cream evenly over the outside of one glass. Leave the glass to dry in a warm, dust-free area for 30 minutes.

5 Wash the cream off the glass with warm water and let dry. For areas where the cream has not worked, paint the glass again and leave for another 30 minutes. Peel the sticky-back plastic off the glass to reveal the motifs. Wash each glass again to remove any sticky smears caused by the plastic.

Ordinary glass jars make useful windproof containers for candles to light the garden during summer evenings; using glass paints, you can turn them into magical lanterns.

Glass Lantern

you will need
glass jar
nail polish remover or glass cleaner
kitchen paper
black relief outliner
tape measure
chinagraph pencil
tape reel
glass paints: red and orange
fine and medium paintbrushes
toothpick (optional)
fine wire
wire cutters
8 beads
round-nosed (snub-nosed) pliers

1 Clean the outside of the glass jar carefully to remove traces of grease and fingermarks, then stand it upside down and draw all around the base using the black relief outliner.

2 Measure 2cm (¾in) up from the base of the glass and mark this level using a chinagraph pencil. Using the outliner draw a horizontal line around the jar following the reference measurement. Draw two more horizontal lines at 2cm (¾in) intervals.

3 Measure around the jar and mark 2cm (¾in) intervals with the chinagraph pencil. Referring to these marks, draw vertical lines with the outliner to divide the rings into squares. Leave to dry thoroughly.

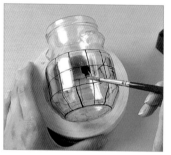

4 Support the jar on its side on a tape reel to stop it from rolling around as you work. Paint one of the squares with red paint. Using the end of a fine paintbrush or a toothpick, etch a small star through the centre of the red square. Wipe the paint off the brush after each stroke.

5 Paint the next square orange and etch a star as before. Paint and decorate all the squares, alternating the colours. Work only on the uppermost area so that the paint does not run, and wait for the paint to dry before turning the jar to continue. Bake the glass to harden the paint as required.

6 Cut a 30cm (12in) length of wire and thread the beads on to it. Use a pair of round-nosed pliers to bend each end of the wire into a small loop.

7 Cut a second wire 3cm (1¼in) longer than the circumference of the jar. Thread it through the loops in the handle and wrap it around the jar.

8 Bend one wire end into a loop and and thread the other end through it. Pull it tight, then bend it back and squeeze the hooks closed.

Stained glass is made for sunlight, and this sunlight catcher can hang in any window to catch all of the available light. Gold outliner separates the brightly coloured areas of orange, yellow, red and blue.

Sunlight Catcher

you will need

clean, 20cm (8in) diameter clear glass
roundel, 4mm (³⁄₁₆in) thick

paper

pencil

tracing paper

indelible black felt-tipped pen

gold contour paste

glass paints: orange, yellow, red
and blue

fine artist's paintbrush

73cm (29in) length of chain

pliers

epoxy glue

1 To make a template of the sun motif that will fit the glass roundel, start by using a pencil to draw around the rim of the roundel on to a piece of paper.

2 Trace the sun motif template from the back of the book and transfer it to the plain paper, enlarging to the size required.

4 Trace over the black lines using gold contour paste. Leave to dry.

5 Colour in the central sun motif using the orange and yellow glass paints. Leave to dry. Clean the brush between colours as recommended by the paint manufacturer.

3 Place the circle of glass over the template and trace the design on to the glass using a felt-tipped pen.

6 Fill in the rest of the design using red and blue glass paints. Leave to dry.

7 Wrap the length of chain around the edge of the glass and cut to size. Rejoin the links by squeezing firmly together with pliers.

8 Cut an 8cm (3¼in) length of chain, open the links at each end, and attach it to the chain circle by squeezing with pliers. Glue the chain circle around the circumference of the glass roundel using epoxy glue.

Get into the spirit of summer with this unusual etched lemonade pitcher. Etching is particularly suitable for eating or drinking vessels as once the piece has been washed there is no surface residue.

Lemonade Pitcher

you will need
clean glass pitcher
tape measure
tracing paper
pencil
scissors
reusable putty adhesive
black contour paste
self-adhesive vinyl or PVA (white) glue
and brush
etching paste
1cm (½in) decorator's paintbrush
washing-up (dishwashing) brush
craft (utility) knife

1 Measure the top rim of the pitcher. Trace and enlarge the template at the back of the book to fit. Cut into sections and space evenly inside the pitcher, just below the neck. Trace the design on to the glass with the contour paste. Leave to dry for 2 hours.

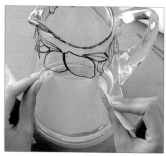

2 Cover all of the pitcher (except the design area) with self-adhesive vinyl or two costs of PVA glue. If using glue, leave the first coat to dry completely before applying the next.

3 Fill in all of the gaps between the outlines of the lemons and leaves and the vinyl with black contour paste. Apply the etching paste with the decorator's paintbrush following the manufacturer's instructions.

4 Wash off the etching paste with cold water. If the etching paste has done its job, the glass should now be evenly etched without clear patches or streaks, but if it does not seem quite right, reapply the etching paste.

5 Carefully lift the edge of the contour paste with a craft knife. Peel off the vinyl or glue and the contour paste. The paste will peel off more easily if you warm the pitcher by wrapping it in a hot towel first.

This picture frame is simply decorated using a gold felt-tipped pen and glass paints. The design is inspired by the devotional art and the patterns that adorn the Alhambra Palace in Granada, southern Spain.

Alhambra Picture Frame

you will need
clip-frame, with cleaned glass
gold permanent felt-tipped pen
glass paints: crimson, turquoise and
deep blue
fine artist's paintbrush
piece of glass
scissors
kitchen sponge
kitchen paper

1 Enlarge the template at the back of the book to fit the clip-frame. Remove the glass from the frame and place it over the design. Trace it on to the glass with a gold permanent felt-tipped pen.

2 Turn the sheet of glass over. Using a fine paintbrush, paint over the diamond shapes with the crimson glass paints. Leave a white border between the crimson and the gold outline.

3 Pour a little turquoise and a little deep blue paint on to a piece of glass. Cut a kitchen sponge into sections. Press the sponge into the paint and then apply it to the glass with a light, dabbing motion to colour in the border. Clean up any overspill with a paper towel and leave to dry.

This is a magical way to transform a plain glass vase into something stylish and utterly original. When you have etched the vase, make sure that it is evenly frosted before you peel off the leaves.

Frosted Vase

you will need
coloured glass vase
tracing paper
pencil
thin cardboard or paper
scissors
self-adhesive vinyl
etching paste
medium artist's paintbrush

1 Wash and dry the vase. Trace the leaf pattern provided, then transfer it on to a piece of thin cardboard or paper. Cut them out. Draw around the templates on to the backing of the vinyl and draw small circles freehand.

2 Cut out the shapes and peel off the backing paper. Arrange the shapes all over the vase. Smooth them down carefully to avoid any wrinkles. Paint etching paste over the vase and leave it in a warm place to dry, following the manufacturer's instructions.

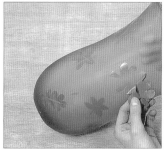

3 Wash the vase in warm water to remove the paste. If the frosting looks smooth, you can remove the shapes. If not, repeat the process with another coat of etching paste, then wash and remove the shapes.

Decorate a glass storage jar with frosting and coloured glass paints. The frosted-look background is etched first and the flowers are painted in afterwards using a selection of brightly coloured glass paints.

Kitchen Storage Jar

you will need
clean glass storage jar
self-adhesive vinyl
felt-tipped pen
small, sharp scissors
etching paste
medium artist's paintbrushes
clean cotton rag
washing-up liquid
(liquid soap)
glass paints in various colours
clear varnish

1 Draw a pattern for the storage jar on to a piece of self-adhesive vinyl with a felt-tipped pen. Alternatively trace the templates provided.

2 Cut out the individual shapes from the self-adhesive vinyl carefully using small, sharp scissors.

3 Position all the adhesive shapes on to the outside of the storage jar and lid in an even design and press them down firmly.

4 Brush a thick and even layer of etching paste over both the jar and lid. Leave to dry completely.

5 Wash the storage jar and lid thoroughly and then wipe them dry using a clean cotton rag.

6 Peel off the plastic shapes once the shapes are etched deeply enough.

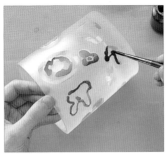

7 Remove the remains of the plastic with washing-up liquid and a clean cotton rag. Paint in the shapes with glass paints.

8 Leave to dry, then varnish the painted areas only with clear varnish. When the jar is completely dry, fill as desired.

This jazzy painted bottle will really brighten up a bathroom shelf. It is decorated with a fun bubble pattern in blues and greens, but you can experiment with designs to complement the shape of your bottle.

Patterned Bathroom Bottle

you will need
clean glass bottle with a cork
felt-tipped pen
paper
black contour paste
glass paints: blue, green, violet
and turquoise
fine artist's paintbrushes
ultraviolet glue
turquoise glass nugget
bubble bath

1 Decide on the pattern you think would look best for your bottle, then sketch your design to scale on a piece of paper.

2 Wash and thoroughly dry the bottle you have chosen. Then, using a felt-tipped pen, copy your design carefully on to the bottle.

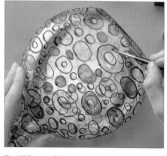

3 Trace the felt-tipped pen design on one side of the bottle with the black contour paste. Leave the contour paste to dry completely.

4 Turn the bottle over and add contour paste circles to the other side. Leave to dry as before.

5 When the contour paste is dry, paint inside the circle motifs using blue, green and violet glass paints. Clean all the paintbrushes thoroughly between colours, as recommended by the paint manufacturer.

6 Once the circles are dry, paint the surrounding area using turquoise glass paint. Leave to dry.

7 Using ultraviolet glue, stick a glass nugget to the top of the cork.

8 Fill the bottle with your favourite bubble bath and replace the cork.

Celebratory champagne bubbles were the inspiration for these gold-spotted glasses. A fine mist of white paint is applied with a sponge. This is accentuated with a raised design of gold bubbles.

Champagne Flutes

you will need

clean, clear glass champagne flutes

nail polish remover or glass cleaner

kitchen paper

flat paintbrush

white glass paint

ceramic tile or old plate

natural sponge

water or white spirit (paint thinner)

scrap paper

felt-tipped pen

gold contour paste

1 Clean the champagne glasses carefully to remove any traces of grease and fingermarks. Using a flat paintbrush, apply a thin film of white glass paint over the surface of a ceramic tile or an old plate.

2 Moisten a piece of natural sponge, using water if the glass paint is water-based or white spirit if it is oil-based. Dab the sponge on to the paint on the tile or plate.

3 Sponge white paint lightly on to the base, the stem and the lower part of the bowl of each champagne flute. Leave to dry thoroughly. Draw around the base of one glass on a small piece of scrap paper to make a template.

4 Fold the template into eighths, open it out and draw along the fold lines with a pen. Stand the glass on the template and dot along the guide-lines using a gold contour paste. Add dots in a gradual spiral around the glass stem, turning the glass slowly and working upwards.

5 Add more dots on the bowl of the glass, making the dots smaller and placing them further apart as you work up the glass. Place the final dots 2.5cm (1in) below the rim so that they do not come in contact with the lips. Repeat with the other glasses. Set the paint following the paint manufacturer's instructions.

A flurry of butterflies and flowers covers the surface of this stunning bowl. They are painted freehand, with a few brush strokes forming each wing or petal, and the details are etched into the wet paint.

Butterfly Bowl

you will need
clear glass bowl
nail polish remover or glass cleaner
kitchen paper
tape measure
chinagraph pencil
rounded fine and medium paintbrushes
glass paints: grey, violet, mauve, bright
pink, pale blue and jade green
toothpick
cotton buds (swabs)

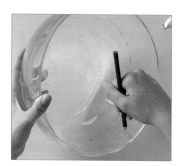

1 Clean the bowl. Measure 5.5cm (2¼in) down from the rim and mark the edge of the border with a chinagraph pencil. Divide the border into equal sections, 5.5cm (2¼in) wide.

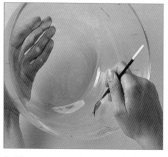

2 Using the template provided, paint a butterfly just below the border. Using a rounded paintbrush for the body and apply a single brush stroke in grey paint. Use a fine paintbrush to paint the antennae.

3 Using violet paint, paint a pair of wings on each side of the body. While the paint is still wet, use a toothpick to etch a simple design on the wings. Paint butterflies at random all over the bowl below the border, using mauve paint for some of the wings.

4 To paint the flowers for the border area, use the template provided and start with the centres. Paint a small circle in the middle of each of the measured sections with the mauve glass paint.

5 Use the medium paintbrush to paint five petals radiating out from one mauve flower centre, using the bright pink glass paint. Proceed to the next step before adding the remaining flower petals.

6 Etch a line along each petal, using a toothpick. Paint the rest of the petals and leave to dry.

7 Below the border, fill in the areas between the butterflies with swirls of pale blue paint. Leave to dry.

8 Rub off the pencil with cotton buds. Paint waves between the flowers using jade. Set the paint.

Cheap clip-frames are widely available in almost any size you need. This one is decorated with contour paste in a range of colours which have been dragged together while still wet to create an intricate design.

Geometric Bordered Frame

you will need
clip-frame
scrap paper
felt-tipped pen
ruler
nail polish remover or glass cleaner
kitchen paper
reusable putty adhesive
contour paste: yellow, bright pink,
green and orange
toothpick

1 Dismantle the frame and place the glass on a sheet of scrap paper. Draw around the edge of the glass.

2 Divide the marked edge equally and draw a double border of squares around the template.

3 Clean the glass thoroughly to remove any traces of grease. Attach the cleaned glass to the paper template with a small piece of reusable putty adhesive at each of the corners.

4 Using yellow contour paste, trace around the first square very carefully, drawing just inside the guidelines of the paper template.

5 Using the bright pink contour paste, draw a slightly smaller square just inside the yellow one. Make sure the two colours meet up exactly without any gap.

6 Draw a third line in the same way using green contour paste. Draw carefully to avoid smudging the yellow and pink paste.

7 Fill the centre of the square with the orange contour paste. Work in single strokes to prevent the orange and green paints from blending.

8 Working while the paste is still wet, use a toothpick to drag the colours from the corners of the square into the centre. Clean the excess paint from the toothpick with kitchen paper after each stroke to keep the design neat.

9 Drag another line from the middle of each side of the square into the centre. Wipe the toothpick after each stroke. Repeat on the next square: this time start with green, then use orange, pink and finally yellow in the centre.

10 Work all around the border of the frame, alternating the combinations of colours. Leave the frame to dry completely. Bake the glass to harden the paint, if necessary, following the manufacturer's instructions.

Filled with water and floating candles, this bowl becomes a magical item. Set it on the dining table with the bowl as a centrepiece, or place it in the bathroom, fill the bath, sit back and relax.

Lily Candle Bowl

you will need

masking tape

clean glass bowl

tracing paper

felt-tipped pen

scissors

reusable putty adhesive

black contour paste

glass paints: emerald, deep blue, turquoise, yellow and white

clear varnish

fine artist's paintbrushes

paint palette

piece of glass

washing-up (dishwashing) sponge

cotton buds (swabs)

white spirit (paint thinner)

1 Stick masking tape around the rim of the bowl. Trace the template from the back of the book, enlarge it and cut it into small sections. Attach it to the inside of the bowl with reusable putty adhesive. On the outside of the bowl, trace over the design with black contour paste. Complete one half of the bowl, leave it to dry, then do the other half. Draw wavy lines with black contour paste across the bowl between the lily-pads. Leave to dry.

2 Mix one part of emerald glass paint with one part varnish. Repeat with the blue, turquoise and yellow paints. Use a brush to transfer the paint on to a piece of glass. Cut a washing-up sponge into sections, one piece for each colour. Place the bowl upside down and sponge the turquoise and deep blue over the background. Then sponge emerald and yellow over each lily-pad. Leave to dry for 1–2 hours.

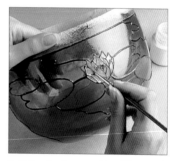

3 Dip a cotton bud in white spirit and use it to clean the coloured paint from the flower petals.

4 Paint the flowers white. Use a craft knife to peel off the contour paste from around the lily-pads, leaving the paste around the flowers intact.

Stems of French lavender, with their picturesque winged flowerheads, criss-cross over the front of this beautiful vase. Opaque paints give the flowers solidity and impact against the clear glass.

French-lavender Flower Vase

you will need
tracing paper
felt-tipped pen
straight-sided glass vase
scissors
masking tape
nail polish remover or glass cleaner
kitchen paper
high-density synthetic sponge
opaque ceramic paints: gold, white,
purple, crimson and green
paint palette
fine and medium artist's paintbrushes

1 Trace the template at the back of the book, enlarging it as necessary to fit the vase. Using masking tape, attach the tracing to the inside of the glass. Clean the outside of the vase thoroughly to remove any traces of grease and fingermarks.

2 Draw a shallow curve along a length of masking tape and cut along it. Stick the two parts to the vase, following one of the stems on the template and leaving a 3mm (⅛in) space between them. Sponge gold paint along the stem and leave to dry. Peel off the tape and repeat for the other stems.

3 Mix white with purple paint and fill in the teardrop shapes for the flowerheads in light purple. Add darker shades of purple and crimson towards the bottom end of each flower shape, stippling the paint to create texture.

4 Paint the three petals at the top of each flower in pale purple, using long, loose brush strokes. Leave the paint to dry. Indicate the individual florets on each flowerhead with small ovals in dark purple. Leave the paint to dry.

5 Using a fine paintbrush, draw spiky leaves along the stems in two or three shades of dusky green. Leave to dry completely, and then bake the vase to harden the paint if necessary, following the manufacturer's instructions.

Some bottles are too beautiful to discard. This elegantly shaped blue one has been recycled with a decoration inspired by a 19th-century original found in an antique shop.

Bohemian Bottle

you will need

tracing paper

pencil

scissors

blue bottle

nail polish remover or glass cleaner

kitchen paper

masking tape

chinagraph pencil

ceramic paints: gold, white, green, red and yellow

fine and medium artist's paintbrushes

paint palette

1 Trace the template at the back of the book and cut out the bold centre section. Clean the bottle to remove any grease and fingermarks. Tape the template to the bottle and draw all around it using a chinagraph pencil.

2 Fill in the shape with several coats of gold paint, stippling it on to create a textured effect. Leave the paint to dry. Using white paint and a fine brush, outline the shape and add swirls along the top edge.

3 Mix white with a little green paint and shade the border design with touches of pale green.

4 Paint the green leaves with loose brush strokes, and add highlights in pale green. Draw in the red and yellow dots along the curves of the border as well as for the flower centres.

5 Paint in the daisy petals around the red flower centres using white paint. Add three small hearts and one or two small yellow flowers to the design for decorative detail.

Painted glassware was a popular folk art form in Europe, with bright figures used to adorn glass, wood, fabric and ceramics. Try to find old glasses in junk or antique shops to decorate.

Folk Art Glass

you will need
tape measure
clean, tall glass
scissors
tracing paper
pencil
masking tape (optional)
soft cloth
enamel paint thinners
enamel paints: red, green, yellow, blue, black and white
fine artist's paintbrushes
elastic band

1 Measure around your glass, top and bottom, and cut a piece of tracing paper to fit in it. Trace the template from the back of the book and put the tracing into the glass, using the masking tape to secure it, if necessary.

2 Rest the glass on a cloth. Support your painting hand with your other hand. The enamel paint should be thinned just enough to flow nicely and be slightly transparent. Use light strokes and avoid overpainting.

3 When the paint has dried, place an elastic band around the glass to act as a guide, and then paint stripes of colour around it, as shown. Support the glass with a cloth and your other hand, as described in step 2.

4 Add small motifs to suit your glass; if you have a fluted base, emphasize this with a pattern. Allow one side of the glass to dry first before painting the other, unless you support the glass on its rim by splaying your other hand inside the glass.

5 Finally, introduce some individual touches by adding embellishments of your own to the design, perhaps in the form of just a few squiggles, some dots or even your initials.

This enchanting perfume bottle, with its swags of little dots and pretty little gilded flowers, is reminiscent of 19th-century Italian enamelled glassware. Use opaque ceramic paints for this project.

Venetian Perfume Bottle

you will need
round clear glass bottle with stopper
nail polish remover or glass cleaner
kitchen paper
tracing paper
pencil
scrap paper
scissors
chinagraph pencil
opaque ceramic paints: white,
red and gold
fine artist's paintbrush
paint palette
cotton buds (swabs)

1 Clean the bottle. Trace the template at the back of the book, adjusting it to fit eight times around the bottle, then cut out the scallops.

2 Use a chinagraph pencil to draw around scallop A eight times, fitting it close to the neck of the bottle. Draw in the curls, then draw around scallop B, fitting it between the first scallops.

3 Using white, paint a six-petalled daisy at the base of each upper scallop. Mix a little red paint with white, and paint eight pink daisies at the base of each lower scallop.

4 Using the template design as a guide, paint a four-petalled flower in gold paint between each scallop in the first round. Then fill in the centres of the daisies in gold paint.

5 Using the fine paintbrush, add tiny dots of white, gold and pink paint in delicate swags and lines to link the flowers. Fill in the gold ovals, and pink and white dots at the top of each heart, then complete the design with two small gold dots at the base of each pink daisy. Extend the design with rows of tiny dots up the neck of the perfume bottle.

6 Paint a large pink daisy exactly in the centre of the bottle stopper and add a gold centre to the daisy shape, as well as rows of tiny white dots radiating from the petals. Leave the paint to dry completely, then rub off the pencil marks using a cotton bud. Bake the bottle and stopper to harden the paint, if necesary, following the manufacturer's instructions.

This cabinet uses opaque enamels rather than transparent glass paints, in the tradition of Eastern European folk art. Folk art relies on basic colour combinations and simple brushwork.

Folk Art Cabinet

you will need

small, glass-fronted display cabinet

reusable putty adhesive

fine artist's paintbrush

acrylic enamel paints: white, light green, deep green, red, raw sienna, yellow

paint palette

1 Enlarge the template from the back of the book and stick it to the back of the glass door with reusable putty adhesive. Paint the design on to the front of the glass using white acrylic enamel paint. Leave to dry.

2 Remove the template from the back of the glass. Paint over the leaves with the light green enamel paint, and leave to dry.

3 Paint a line of deep green paint along the lower edge of each of the light green leaves.

4 Paint the flowers with the red paint and then carefully blend in a little white towards the tips.

5 Paint over the stalk lines, half with raw sienna and half with yellow. Leave to dry.

Working
with Glass

Glass is a versatile medium to work with and can be used to create all sorts of accessories and decorations, from trinket boxes to outdoor lanterns. Using glass that you have painted, or ready-coloured glass panels, learn to cut it safely and accurately into intricate shapes. With pieces cut to size, learn to solder them together to form three-dimensional functional pieces, or learn to add lead came to replicate stained glass windows.

Glass is essential to our comfort, yet it often escapes our notice. It can be used to make ordinary household items such as windows, mirrors and bottles, or precious works of art. It is hard and resistant, yet fragile.

The History of Stained Glass

The origins of glass are lost in prehistory, but a myth recounted by Pliny the Elder states that it was discovered on the shores of the eastern Mediterranean, where the River Belus ran into the sea. Some Phoenician traders in soda, who had landed there to cook a meal, used lumps of soda from their cargo to balance their cooking pots on the sand. As these were heated they fused with the sand, and molten glass began to run down the beach.

In fact, glass was known to cultures that predated the Phoenicians. Glass beads were being made about 4,000

years ago, by winding softened glass rods around a core of sand or pressing lumps of glass into moulds. By the 1st century BC glass production had been revolutionized by the invention of glass-blowing: blowing down a tube into a blob of molten glass created a bubble of glass that could be shaped into a hollow vessel.

Glass production

Many other significant advances in glass-making and decorative techniques arose in the Middle East – such as cut-glass work, gilging and enamelling – and the wares were traded

across Europe and Asia. Glass was also produced in China and India, while in Japan the earliest glass beads had a symbolic significance and were worn as jewels. By the 8th century, Japanese craftsmen were making blown glass vessels and delicate cloisonné enamel work, using wires to create tiny cells that were then filled with coloured glass.

In Europe, Venice became a major centre of glass production by the 14th century. Its craftsmen developed the art of engraving on glass with a diamond point and made advances in the chemistry of glass. Although the

Below: Figurative designs are easy to create with strips of lead-effect.

Below: This house number uses bold colours to make a strong statement.

Below: A bathroom cabinet is a small flat surface for an abstract design.

Right: A small jewel box needs accurately cut pieces of glass.

Below: An abstract design for a window hanging incorporates an unusual shape.

death penalty was imposed on anyone divulging these trade secrets, the formula gradually found its way to other parts of Europe. The English discovered that adding lead to glass gave it a brilliant lustre and made it easier to engrave. The invention of cylinder sheet glass in the 19th century facilitated the production of large, good quality window panes, and these were used to glaze the Crystal Palace for London's Great Exhibition in 1851 and the Palais de l'Industrie that housed the rival Paris Exhibition of 1855. These structures were so remarkable that many of the visitors to the exhibitions came mainly to see the buildings themselves.

Decorating with glass

Before the 19th century, large pieces of flat glass had been difficult and expensive to make, so smaller panes were joined in latticeworks of wood or metal. From this practical solution, elegant decorative windows resulted, and remain desirable today for period properties, even though large panes are easily obtainable. Similarly, craftsmen in stained glass turned the leading they needed to support their glass into an important design element.

The structural elements of decorative windows featured strongly in the glass panels of Charles Rennie Mackintosh, in which the leading created the graphic core of the design, while colour was used relatively sparingly. For many of his interiors, Mackintosh also designed unique light fittings with panels of coloured or opalescent glass. Though his greatest work is now more than a century old, its spare, modernist style still influences 21st-century interior design.

The current vogue for maximizing space and light in the home, while making strong, clear statements with colour, makes glass more important than ever. Its ability both to reflect and to transmit light has always drawn artists and craftspeople to work with it, and the fact that plain sheet glass, mirror glass and simple vessels are so readily and cheaply available makes the medium accessible to all. With the amateur craftsperson in mind, manufacturers have developed new paints that can create the effect of stained glass without the need for the complex chemical methods of production used by the professional.

A variety of materials is needed for working with glass, which include glass paints, solder and flux, all of which are readily available from specialist glass shops.

Materials

(2¼yd) lengths. The central bar or heart keeps two pieces of glass apart when put together. The flat strips at the top and bottom of the heart – the leaf – will stop the glass from falling out. Always wear rubber gloves or barrier cream when using lead.

Self-adhesive lead

This stick-on lead strip can be used to reproduce real lead came. Ensure a good seal by rubbing the lead with a boning peg, or the back of a teaspoon. Do not smoke or handle food while using lead, and keep it away from children. Wash your hands after use.

Solder

Made up of equal parts of tin and lead.

Tinned copper wire

This can be soldered easily. You can also tin wire with a soldering iron.

Ultraviolet glue

This glue hardens in daylight. It will not harden behind red glass, which blocks UV rays.

You will need the following items: acetate, carbon paper, clear varnish, contour paste, glass nuggets, glass paints, masking tape, paper towels, cotton buds (swabs), reusable putty adhesive, silver jewellery wire, white spirit (paint thinner), stained glass.

Copper foil and wire

A self-adhesive, heat-resistant tape, copper foil comes in various widths. Use it to bind glass edges prior to soldering. Copper wire is malleable and ideal for hooks and decoration. It is compatible with tin solder.

Epoxy glue

This strong glue hardens in minutes.

Float glass

Glaziers sell this clear polished glass.

Flux

This is brushed on to copper foil to clean it and lower the melting point of the solder so it flows more easily.

Horseshoe nails

Use to hold glass pieces in place as you work. Easy to remove, they reduce the risk of damage to glass and lead.

Lead came

Use lead came for creating stained glass windows. Available in 2m

For decorative glasswork, you will need a range of tools to equip you for the basic skills of glass cutting and soldering. The most important of these are described or listed below.

Equipment

Lead knife
A lead knife has a curved blade to help when cutting lead came.

Lead vice
A lead vice is useful for stretching pieces of lead came before cutting.

Letherkin tool
This is used to open up the leaf of the lead came after you have cut it.

Protective goggles
These are vital for eye protection when cutting glass.

Scythe stone
This removes the sharp edges from cut glass. Use on every piece.

Soldering iron
Use a 75-watt soldering iron. You will need a stand for the hot iron.

Tallow stick
This is the traditional alternative to liquid soldering flux.

Boning peg
Use to smooth down the adhesive lead to ensure good contact with the glass.

Cutting oil
This oil lubricates the cutting wheel of a glass cutter and helps to prevent small particles of glass from binding to the wheel.

Fid
A fid is used for pressing down copper foil and self-adhesive lead.

Flux brush
These inexpensive brushes are used to paint flux on copper foil.

Glass cutter
Run the wheel of a glass cutter over the glass to be cut, to create a score mark. The glass will break on the line when stressed.

Grozing pliers
These are used to take off any sharp shards of glass.

You will also find the following items useful: cotton rags, craft (utility) knife, jewellery pliers, nail polish remover, paintbrushes, pencils and pens, pliers, rubber gloves, ruler, scissors, self-healing cutting mat, sponges, thick straightedge, wire cutters, wire (steel) brush, wire (steel) wool.

Before you begin to tackle any of the projects in this chapter, look through this section, which acts as an introduction to the basic skills you will need for working with glass with assurance.

Techniques

Cutting glass Measure accurately the area of glass you want to cut. There is no margin for error and mistakes cannot be rectified.

1 Hold the cutter so that your index finger is on top, your thumb and second finger grip each side, and the grozing teeth face towards your elbow. When you cut correctly with the cutter at a right angle to the glass, this position will give you movement in your arm.

2 Always cut the glass from edge to edge, one cut at a time. So start at one edge of the glass, with your cutter at right angles. Make it one continuous cut from one edge to the other.

3 Break the glass where you have made the score mark. Hold the cutter upside down between your thumb and first finger. Hold it loosely so that you can swing it to hit the underside of the score mark with the ball on the end of the cutter. Tap along the score mark. The glass will break.

4 Alternatively, hold the glass at each side of the score mark. Apply firm pressure pulling down and away from the crack. Use this method for very straight lines.

5 You could try putting the cutter on the table with the glass on the cutter and score mark over the cutter. With the base of your thumbs put pressure on both sides of the score mark.

6 Break the glass along the score mark as shown. Smooth the edges and remove any sharp points with a scythe stone. Use a little water to lubricate the stone.

Foiling glass Edging glass with copper foil allows you to solder pieces of glass together to create stained-glass effects. This technique is simple to do.

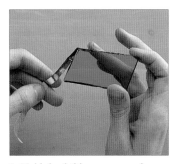 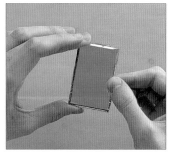 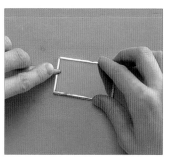

1 Hold the foil between your fingers, and use your thumb to peel back the protective backing paper as you work around the glass. Try not to touch the adhesive side of the tape – it will not stick if it is greasy or dusty.

2 Stick the foil to the edge of the piece of glass, working all the way around it, and overlapping the end of the foil by 1cm (½in).

3 Using two fingertips, press the foil down on to both sides of the glass, all the way around. Now use the fid to flatten the foil on to the glass to ensure it is stuck firmly all the way around.

Soldering glass Soldering is the technique of joining pieces of metal together, in this case copper foil-edged glass. This is a technique that requires some practice to achieve a neat, professional finish.

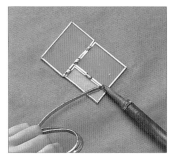 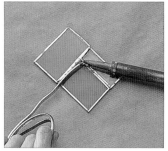 

1 Using a flux brush, apply the flux to all the copper foil showing on the first side. Take the soldering iron so the tip of the iron side faces side to side and the thin side faces up and down. Hold the solder in the other hand with 10cm (4in) uncoiled. Tack the pieces together by melting blobs of solder on to each joining edge. This holds the pieces while you solder them together.

2 Melt the solder, and allow it to run along the copper. Do not let it go too flat, but make sure you are always working with a small drop of solder. This makes it look neater and, even more importantly, is stronger. Turn the piece over and flux and solder the edges on the other side.

3 Tin all around the outer edges of the glass by firstly fluxing, and then running the soldering iron along the edges. There is usually enough solder from joining the inner edges to spread around the outside.

Using self-adhesive lead

Using self-adhesive lead is quick and easy. The skill is in the preparation: always ensure that the surface of the glass is scrupulously clean.

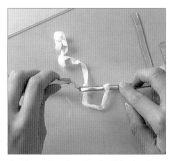

1 Clean the glass. Peel off the backing from the lead and press one end of it down gently with your fingers. Use one hand to hold the end while you bend the lead to fit the design. Always wash your hands after handling lead.

2 Trim the end with scissors. It is important that the lead strip is firmly stuck to the glass so that paint will not leak underneath it. After applying the strip, burnish it using a boning peg or the back of an old teaspoon.

Using lead came

This technique requires skill, but it is within everyone's reach. As special tools are needed for this technique, it can be expensive.

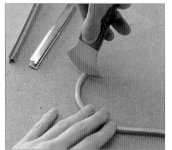

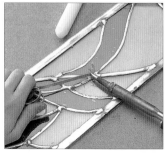

1 Draw the outline of each piece of glass that makes up the design. This outline represents the central point of the lead. Cut each piece of glass on the inside of the outline. To stretch the lead came to remove any kinks and make it easier to shape and cut, secure a spring-loaded vice to your bench and place one end of the came in it. Pull the other end with flat-nosed pliers. Do not break the lead.

2 Using a lead knife, bend the came to the shape of the edge of the glass. Using the knife blade, mark across the leaf where it will be cut (leave it a little short to accommodate the leaf of the piece crossing it). Place the came leaf on a flat surface. Position the knife and push down in a gentle but firm rocking motion until you are right through the came. Cut directly down and not at an angle.

3 Soldering wire for leaded panels contains lead, so wear barrier cream to protect your hands. Holding the soldering wire in your left hand, lower the tip of the soldering iron for a few seconds to melt the solder and join the separate pieces of lead came securely together.

This impressive panel is in the style of pictorial windows which were fashionable adornments for doors and porches in the 1930s. A gallant ship tossed on huge waves was a popular subject for this treatment.

Stained-glass Window

you will need

pane of glass to fit window

nail polish remover or glass cleaner

kitchen paper

scrap paper

felt-tipped pen

reusable putty adhesive

adhesive lead strip

tin snips or old scissors

boning peg or teaspoon

glass paints: red, yellow, dark blue, turquoise, white

fine and medium artist's paintbrushes

paint tray

1 Clean the glass to remove traces of grease. Using the template provided, draw a ship with hull and sails and waves on scrap paper to fit your panel and attach it to the underside of the glass using reusable putty adhesive.

2 Peel the backing paper off a length of adhesive lead strip and place it over the line illustrating the hull of the boat. Trim the strip at the end with tin snips or old scissors, and smooth it down firmly using a boning peg or the back of a teaspoon, to ensure a good contact with the glass.

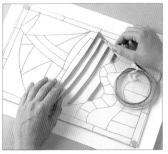

3 Repeat for the rest of the planks of the hull. Complete the outline of the boat, placing the strips over the ends of the previous ones. Trim the ends of the outline, and smooth down with either the boning peg or teaspoon.

4 Attach the lead strips for the waves, positioning the long strips first. Ease the strips around the curves with your fingers. Complete the boat mast, sails and frame in the same way. Burnish all the lines with the boning peg or spoon, carefully smoothing the fullness on the inside of the curves. ▶

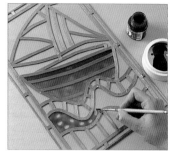

5 Mix burnt orange from the red and yellow paint and add a touch of dark blue. Paint the top plank of the hull with orange. For the next plank, mix a brighter orange. Add more of the yellow still to make light orange for the third plank, and paint the lowest plank yellow.

6 Fill in the central wave with the turquoise paint, leaving some small randomly spaced circles of clear glass.

7 Use dark blue to paint around the edge of the first panel in the lowest part of the sea. Mix the paint with white and add a pale blue strip down the middle of the panel while the dark blue is still wet. Draw the edges of the colours together for a marbled effect.

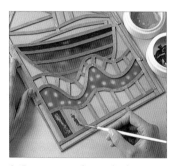

8 Repeat in each panel, alternating the colours. Above the wave, paint alternate panels dark or pale blue, leaving the remaining panels clear.

9 Mix the red with dark blue to make purple, and paint the cabin roof. Paint alternate panels of the sails yellow, then add a little blue paint to make a light green colour for the remaining parts of the sails.

10 Mix white with the light green and use to paint alternate panels of the frame. Paint the flag with the red paint. Mix turquoise with pale blue for the remaining panels of the frame. Leave the glass panel to dry completely.

Give your pictures a touch of grandeur with this richly coloured frame made from glass paints and stick-on lead in an abstract linear design. Choose colours to complement those in the picture you are framing.

Leaded Picture Frames

you will need
clean glass clip-frame
paper
pen and pencil
metal ruler
indelible black felt-tipped pen
3mm (⅛in) self-adhesive lead
craft (utility) knife
self-healing cutting mat
boning peg
glass paints
paintbrush

1 Remove the clips and backing board from the clip-frame. Place the glass on a piece of paper and draw around it to create a template of the right dimensions.

2 Using a pencil and metal ruler, draw a simple linear design on the template. Place the glass over the template and trace the design on to the glass using an indelible black felt-tipped pen.

3 Stretch the lead by pulling it gently. Cut four lengths to fit around the outside edge of the frame, using a sharp craft knife and a cutting mat. Remove the backing paper from the lead and stick the lead in place.

4 Measure the lead needed for the inner framework and cut with a craft knife by using a side-to-side rocking motion. Hold the knife blade at a 90-degree angle to the lead to ensure a straight cut. Work on a cutting mat. With the edges butted closely together, peel away the backing paper from the lead strips and press gently into place with your fingertips.

5 Once the lead is in the correct position, press firmly along its length using a boning peg to seal it to the glass.

6 With the pointed end of the boning peg, press around the outer edges of each strip of lead. This will tidy the edges and prevent the glass paints from seeping underneath the strips.

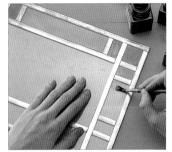

7 Colour in the design using glass paints. Leave to dry. Replace the backing board, add a picture of your choice and clip the frame into place.

This plain vase has been given a stained-glass effect with the use of vivid paints and patterns of stick-on lead. Filling the vase with water will ensure that the horizontal lines of the border will be accurate.

Banded Vase

you will need
clean, square vase
water-based felt-tipped pen
ruler
black contour paste
sponge scourer
scissors
glass paints: yellow, orange, red and violet
colourless medium
spatula
craft (utility) knife
self-healing cutting mat
3mm (⅛in) self-adhesive lead
fid

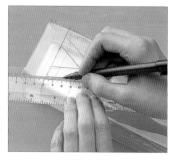

1 Gauge by eye the position of the borders. Using a water-based felt-tipped pen, draw the position of the lower border. Pour water into the vase up to this point. Stand the vase on a level surface and draw around the vase at the water level.

2 Mark the position of the top border. Top up the water to this level and draw the second line around the vase. Empty the vase. Mark the simple pattern on to the surface of the vase with the felt-tipped pen and a ruler.

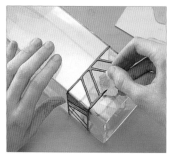

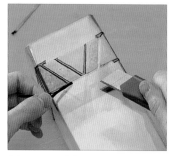

3 Go over the lines with the black contour paste and leave it to dry. Cut a sponge scourer into pieces to match the shapes of the design.

4 Mix each paint colour with an equal amount of colourless medium and sponge the paint over the vase using a different piece of sponge for each colour. Leave to dry for 24 hours.

5 Using a craft knife, score around the edge of each area of colour. Use the tip of the craft knife to lift up the contour paste and carefully peel it off the vase.

6 Cut pieces of self-adhesive lead slightly oversize for all of the shorter lines. Peel off the backing paper and press them in place. Trim the ends of each piece of lead at an angle with a craft knife.

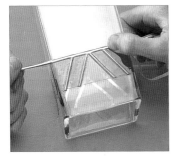

7 Cut two strips of lead for the two border lines and press them into place.

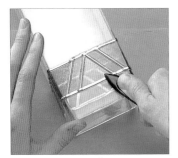

8 Rub over all the lead lines with a fid to press them firmly in place.

This piece of decorated glass creates beautiful shimmering patterns as it catches the light. The design is traced directly on to the glass with contour paste then coloured with glass paints.

Heart Light Catcher

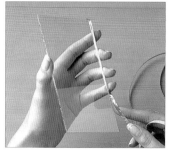

1 Enlarge the template from the back of the book and cut a piece of float glass to fit the design. Wash the glass and edge it with self-adhesive copper foil tape. Press down with a fid.

2 Bend the wire into two small circular hanging loops using round-nosed pliers. Grip the wire in the middle and bend the ends down to form an upside-down "U". With straight-nosed pliers, grip each arm of the "U" and bend up to form a 90-degree angle. Bend the arms downwards with round-nosed pliers.

3 Brush the copper-foiled edge with flux, and then tin (see Window Hanging, step 4). Solder the hanging hoops in place. Wash the glass.

4 Lay the template on a work surface and place the light catcher over it. Trace the design on to the glass with black contour paste. Leave to dry.

5 Paint the glass, following the final photograph for the colours. Use the toothpick to decorate the design with scratchwork.

The simple materials of muslin fabric, coloured glass and silver wire complement each other perfectly to create this fresh and pleasingly uncluttered decoration.

Glass Nugget Window Hanging

you will need

pencil

paper

0.5m (½yd) white muslin (cheesecloth)

sharp scissors

white sewing thread

sewing needle

copyright-free pictures of shells

acetate sheet

epoxy glue

4 large glass nuggets

fine silver jewellery wire

jewellery pliers

thick copper wire

1 Sketch your design to scale on a piece of paper. Draw the shape of the background on to the white muslin leaving extra to turn and edge the sides. Cut out the shape.

2 Using the white sewing thread, sew a single hem along each long side edge, then at the top and bottom.

3 Photocopy shell pictures on to acetate, so that they are slightly smaller than the glass nuggets. Cut out the images using sharp scissors.

4 Glue the acetate shapes on to the muslin, spacing them equally down the muslin. Then glue the glass nuggets over the images. Make sure they do not stick to your worktop as the glue may seep through.

5 Cut pieces of silver wire long enough to fit across each glass nugget, leaving a little extra at each side. Curl each end into a spiral shape using the jewellery pliers.

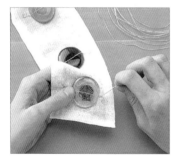

6 Sew the pieces of wire securely to the muslin rectangle at each side of the glass nuggets.

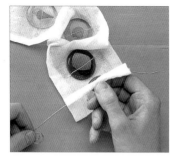

7 Take the copper wire, curl one end into a spiral using the small pliers, and slide the metal through the top hem of the muslin. Use another length of wire to do the same on the bottom. Curl the other end of both pieces of wire into matching spirals.

8 Take some silver wire and wind it round the copper wire at the top end, on both sides of the muslin, for the piece to hang in the window.

Pressed foliage and flowers are positioned on pieces of opaque blue glass and clear glass is placed on top. The wire that is wound round each pair of glass rectangles is both structural and decorative.

Flower and Foliage Wallhanging

you will need

6 pieces each of coloured glass and
matching-sized clear glass

tweezers

dried, pressed foliage

instant bonding adhesive

masking tape

1mm (¹⁄₂₅in) copper wire

ruler

round-nosed (snub-nosed) pliers

straight-nosed pliers

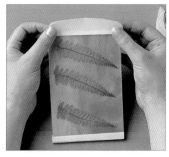

1 Get your chosen coloured glass cut to size. Lay it on the work surface and, using tweezers, position pressed leaves on to the glass, fixing with a small dab of instant bonding adhesive.

2 Place the clear glass over the leaves and apply strips of masking tape over the short edges to hold the two pieces of glass together temporarily.

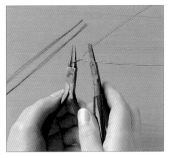

3 Cut a piece of 1mm (¹⁄₂₅in) copper wire 32cm (12½in) long. Gripping the middle with round-nosed pliers, bend the ends down and twist them together with straight-nosed pliers.

4 Use the pliers to bend out two ends of the wire horizontally, then make an "elbow" on both sides to fit over the edges of the glass.

5 Position the wire around the glass and, using your fingers, bend the two ends over the edge. Use straight-nosed pliers to twist and close.

6 With round-nosed pliers, bend the two ends up into loops, forming a strong split ring. Trim off the excess wire to 1.5cm (⅝in).

7 Cut a piece of wire 18cm (7in) long and repeat steps 3 to 6. Link the second panel by linking the top loop and split ring. Remove the masking tape. Repeat for all the panels.

8 Carefully arrange the completed wallhanging face downwards, and make sure all of the wires are aligned. Press strips of masking tape over the wire on the back to hold it in place.

This vase evokes the work of the designer Charles Rennie Mackintosh. Self-adhesive lead is used to create the effect of leaded glasswork and is simply pressed on to the glass surface for a decorative effect.

Cherry Blossom Vase

you will need

paper

pencil

vase

reusable putty adhesive

self-adhesive lead, 3mm (⅛in) and 4mm (³⁄₁₆in) wide

scissors or craft (utility) knife

fid or wooden peg

glass paints: white and pink

matt varnish

fine artist's paintbrushpaint-mixing palette

1 Enlarge the template from the back of the book to fit your vase. Stick it to the inside of the vase with reusable putty adhesive. Using the template as a guide, bend and stick the pieces of 3mm (⅛in) wide self-adhesive lead down over all of the bold lines on the template. Use scissors or a strong craft knife to trim the ends.

2 For the stem lines, cut two strips of 3mm (⅛in) wide self-adhesive lead the same length as your vase, and a further two 4mm (³⁄₁₆in) wide lead strips. Press the end of each into place to join the stems on the upper design and then run them down the length of the vase.

3 Splay the ends slightly at the base, and trim them so that they all end at the same point.

4 Cut a piece of 4mm (³⁄₁₆in) wide lead long enough to go around the vase with a little spare. Press it around the vase, just overlapping the edges of the stem lines. To smooth the joins, rub over with a fid or wooden peg.

5 Mix a little white paint with matt varnish. Do the same with a little pink paint. Apply the white paint sparingly to fill the blossom shapes, adding just a touch of pink to each area.

The etched glass panels on this old door have been painted with coloured glass paints and finished with stick-on lead strips. The finished effect has a lighter look than genuine stained glass.

Leaded Door Panels

you will need

door with two sandblasted glass panels

tape measure

paper

pencil

ruler

black felt-tipped pen

scissors

masking tape

indelible black felt-tipped pen

self-adhesive lead, 1cm (⅜in) wide

craft (utility) knife

self-healing cutting mat

boning peg

glass paints: turquoise, green, yellow and light green

turpentine

fine artist's paintbrushes

1 Measure the glass panels with a tape measure. With a pencil, draw them to scale on a piece of paper. Using a ruler, draw your design within the panel area, including 1cm (⅜in) wide dividing lines to allow for the leading. Trace over the design in felt-tipped pen, cross-hatching the lead lines.

2 Cut out this paper pattern carefully with scissors and then stick it to the reverse of one of the glass panels by applying lengths of masking tape around the edges.

3 Trace the design from the pattern on to the sandblasted side of the glass with an indelible black felt-tipped pen. When the tracing is complete, remove the paper pattern.

4 Stretch the lead by gently pulling it. Cut four lengths to fit around the edge of the glass panel, using a sharp craft knife. Remove the backing paper and stick the lead in place.

5 Measure the lead needed for the inner framework and cut with a craft knife using a side-to-side rocking motion. Keep the blade at a 90° angle to the lead to ensure a straight cut. Cut and stick longer lengths of lead first, then work the smaller pieces.

6 With the edges butted closely together, remove the backing paper from the lead and press into place with your fingertips. Then press firmly along the length of the lead with a boning peg to seal it to the glass. Press around the outer edges of the lead lines with the pointed end of the boning peg in order to create a neat, watertight finish.

7 Dilute the glass paints with 30 per cent turpentine to create a subtle, watercolour feel to the paint. Use a small paintbrush to colour in the small areas between the leading. Clean the brushes with turpentine between the different colours.

8 Once the intricate areas are coloured in, paint the remainder of the design, leaving the centre of the glass panel unpainted. Alternatively, you could paint the whole area if you prefer. Repeat for the other panel.

The fresh white and green opal glass of this planter neatly hides the flowerpot inside, while the contrasting colours of the opal glass will complement the colour of the foliage.

Opal Glass Planter

you will need
tracing paper
black pen and paper
white and green opal glass
glass cutter
straightedge
round-nosed (snub-nosed) pliers
carbon paper
ballpoint pen
scythe stone
5mm (¼in) wide copper foil
fid
solder and soldering iron
flux
flux brush
washing-up liquid (liquid soap)

1 Trace the template from the back of the book, enlarging to the size required. Place the white glass over the template and score five identical pieces for the sides with a glass cutter, using a straightedge to ensure straight lines. Use a pair of round-nosed pliers to break the glass along the scorelines. Cut strips of green opal glass for the bottom of each panel.

2 Place carbon paper over the green glass, then put the template on top. Transfer the shape for the top sections with a pen. Score the straight lines using a straightedge as a guide. Score the curved edges and break them by tapping under the glass with the ball on the end of the glass cutter. Transfer and cut out the base design. Remove sharp edges with a scythe stone.

3 Wrap copper foil around the edge of each piece and use a fid to press the foil into place. Allow the soldering iron to heat up. Brush on flux and tack-solder together the three sections that make up each side panel.

4 Lightly tack-solder one of the side panels to the base, using a minimum of solder. Position the next panel and repeat. Tack the two panels together. Continue until all the pieces are in place on the base.

5 Reflux and solder all of the joints. Wash the planter before use, with hot water and washing-up liquid.

In this unusual project, different-sized glass nuggets are gradually built up one on top of another to create a colourful wall around the mirrored base of the bottle holder. Choose a whole rainbow of beautiful colours.

Glass Nugget Bottle Holder

you will need
self-healing cutting mat
pair of compasses
indelible black felt-tipped pen
mirror glass
bottle
glass cutter
square-nosed pliers
copper foil, 12mm (½in) and
4mm (³⁄₁₆in) wide
fid
solder
soldering iron
flux
flux brush
glass nuggets

1 On a cutting mat draw a circle on mirror glass 2.5–4cm (1–1½in) larger than the base of the bottle.

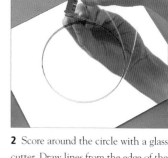

2 Score around the circle with a glass cutter. Draw lines from the edge of the circle to the edge of the mirror.

3 Tap on the reverse of the mirror with the ball of the glass cutter.

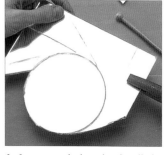

4 Loosen and then break off the excess mirror with square-nosed pliers.

5 Wrap the 12mm (½in) copper foil around the edge of the glass circle.

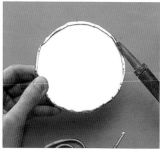

6 Press down with a fid and solder using flux and the soldering iron.

7 Select some of the coloured glass nuggets and wrap each one with the 4mm (³⁄₁₆in) copper foil.

8 Solder the nuggets and start to build up an edge around the glass circle.

9 When the border is the required height, tidy up the inside and outside with the soldering iron to smooth out any drips of solder.

Slip this glass lantern over a night-light to create a colourful glow in the evenings. The lantern is made with two plain and two panelled sections of coloured glass.

Indoor Glass Lantern

you will need
tracing paper
pencil
ruler and pen (optional)
glass cutter
sheets of clear glass
sheets of stained glass: red,
orange and yellow
etching paste
medium artist's paintbrush
clean cotton rag
5mm (¼in) copper foil
fid
flux and flux brush
solder and soldering iron
small box or block of wood
night-light
tile

1 Trace the templates for the indoor lantern from the back of the book. Enlarge to the size required using a ruler and pen or a photocopier.

2 Take a glass cutter and, using your templates as a guide, cut out two clear glass sides and the pieces of coloured glass for the other two sides. You will have four red pieces, three orange and three yellow.

4 Take the acid-etched glass to your sink and allow cold water to run freely over the glass to take the paste off. Rinse thoroughly and then dry with a clean cotton rag.

5 Wrap copper foil around the edges of all of the pieces of coloured and clear/etched glass. Using a fid, flatten all the copper foil to smooth around the edges.

3 Using the template as a guide, take each side and paint etching paste on in squares as shown. Leave the paste for 3 minutes.

6 Place the pieces next to each other as you wish to solder them, panel by panel. Flux all the copper using a flux brush.

7 Tack each side together by melting a spot of solder on each joining edge. This keeps the pieces in place, and makes soldering easier.

8 Solder each side together, and then solder around the edges to complete the four panels.

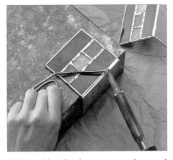

9 To solder the lantern together and make it three-dimensional you will need to balance the sides at a right angle on a small box or a block of wood. Flux and solder two corners so they can stand upright.

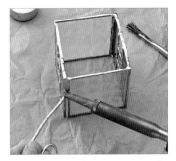

10 Solder the last two corners by fluxing and then soldering from top to bottom. Clean the glass with a clean cotton rag. Stand the night-light on a tile and place the lantern over it.

This plaque is made from pieces of stained glass and glass nuggets. Nuggets come in a wide range of colours and can add bright spots of colour among the crazy patchwork of glass.

Door Number Plaque

you will need
circle cutter
cutting oil
30cm (12in) square of 3mm (⅛in) clear glass
piece of carpet or blanket
glass cutter
tracing paper
pencil
paper
indelible black felt-tipped pen
pieces of stained glass
scythe stone
glass nuggets
ultraviolet glue
lead came
lead knife
bradawl or drill
2mm (¹⁄₁₆in) copper wire
round-nosed (snub-nosed) pliers
flux and flux brush
solder
soldering iron
black acrylic paint
tiling grout
grout spreader
clean cotton rag

Tip
Glass glue sets when it is exposed to ultraviolet light or sunlight.

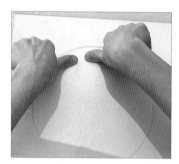

1 Set a circle cutter to cut a 20cm/8in diameter circle. Dip the cutter in oil, centre it in the glass square and score the circle in one sweep. Turn the glass over and place it on a piece of carpet or blanket on a work surface. Press down with both thumbs just inside the scoreline until the line begins to break. Repeat until the scoreline is broken all the way around.

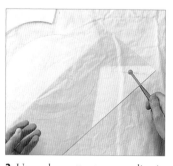

2 Use a glass cutter to score a line in from each corner of the glass square, stopping just before you reach the circle. With the ball of the glass cutter, tap behind each scored line until the glass cracks up to the circle. The side sections will fall away, releasing the circle.

3 Trace the required numbers from the back of the book, enlarging them to the size required. Draw around the circle of glass on to plain paper and write your own door number centrally using the template as a guide.

4 Score pieces of stained glass for the numerals. Break the glass by tapping behind the scoreline with the ball of the glass cutter. Remove any rough edges with a scythe stone. Centre the glass circle over the template.

5 Arrange the numerals on the glass circle and place glass nuggets around them. Cut pieces of glass in contrasting colours to fill the spaces. Working away from sunlight, apply ultraviolet glue to the back of each piece and press it into place. When all of the pieces are glued, check the position of each and slide them into place.

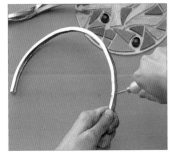

6 Use a lead knife to cut a length of lead came approximately 70cm (28in) long. Use a bradawl or drill to make a small hole in the centre of the strip of came.

7 Cut a 10cm (4in) length of copper wire. With a pair of round-nosed pliers, bend a hanging loop. Thread the ends through the hole in the came and bend them up to lock the loop in place. Wrap the came around the glass with the hanging loop at the top.

8 Trim off any excess lead came with the lead knife. Flux the joint and then lightly solder the ends together.

9 Mix some black paint with grout. Spread it over the surface, into the spaces between the glass. Remove any excess with a rag. Leave to dry, then polish with a clean cotton rag.

The type of paintwork used in this unusual window decoration is not very easy to control, and it is precisely this free-flowing quality that gives the style its appeal.

Window Hanging

you will need

paper and pencil

glass, 3mm (⅛in) thick

glass cutter

cutting oil

scythe stone

5mm (¼in) self-adhesive copper foil tape

fid

red glass nuggets

flux and flux brush

solder and soldering iron

1mm (½in) tinned copper wire

round-nosed (snub-nosed) pliers

straight-nosed pliers

black contour paste

glass paints: blue, turquoise, red, yellow, violet and white

clear varnish

fine artist's paintbrush

paint palette

1 Enlarge the template at the back of the book to a size that is suitable for the window you wish to hang the pieces in. Lay a sheet of glass on the template and cut out five sections. (Have a glazier do this if you are not confident in cutting glass.)

2 Wash all of the pieces to remove any traces of cutting oil. Remove any sharp edges with a scythe stone, then press self-adhesive copper foil tape over all of the edges. Press the foil down with a fid.

4 Brush all of the copper-foiled edges with flux. Melt a bead of solder on to your soldering iron, and run the bead along the edge of each piece of glass to "tin" it with a thin coating of solder. Repeat as necessary until all of the edges are equally coated. Cut ten pieces of tinned copper wire 5cm (2in) long for the hanging loops.

5 With round-nosed pliers, bend the ends down to form an upside-down "U". With straight-nosed pliers, grip each arm of the "U" and bend it up to form a 90-degree angle. Grip with round-nosed pliers while you bend the two arms downwards. Touch-solder the loops on the top of the glass pieces. Wash the pieces.

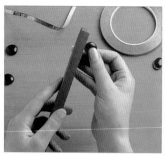

3 Using a scythe stone, lightly abrade the edge of each glass nugget. Wrap each nugget in copper foil tape.

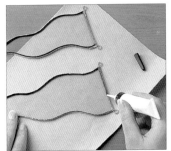

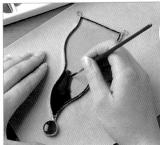

6 Apply flux to the end of one of the sections and one of the nuggets. Melt a bead of solder on to the iron and then solder the nugget in place. Melt on some more solder to ensure the nugget is secure.

7 Apply a line of black contour paste around the edge of each of the glass pieces in order to contain the glass paint solution.

8 In a mixing palette, prepare the colours you wish to use. Mix each with equal parts of clear varnish and opaque white paint. Apply the colours thickly and freely, allowing them to blend into each other. Leave to dry for at least 24 hours.

These square and triangular stained-glass pendants are decorated with motifs cut from acetate. Hang them in a line on a gauzy fabric curtain to allow the sunlight and colours to really shine through.

Curtain Decorations

1 Photocopy pictures of shells on to acetate and cut them out with small, sharp scissors.

2 Trace the triangles and squares from the back of the book. Cut out glass shapes, using the templates as a guide.

3 Wrap copper foil around the edges of the larger pieces of glass.

4 Use a fid to flatten the edges of the copper foil around the pieces of glass.

◀ **5** Flux and solder the copper foil to make it silver. The heat will make the foil turn a silver colour.

▶ **6** Take a soldered piece of glass and a smaller piece of the same shape. Glue the pieces together, trapping the photocopy between the glass.

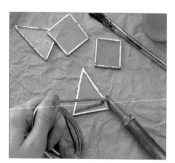

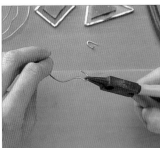

7 Using a pair of small pliers, bend the copper wire into small hooks. Make a separate hook for each decoration you have made.

8 Solder the hook to the copper foil around the edges of the decorations, remembering to flux the wire and the soldered edges.

9 Sew the eyes from several hooks and eyes to the top of the curtain and hook on the curtain decorations. Fold the curtain over a pole so the decorations are hanging in the top third of the window, as shown.

Opal glass is available from stained-glass specialists and has an extra special lustre. As this project involves cutting and soldering lots of small pieces, it is intended for the more experienced glassworker.

Trinket Box

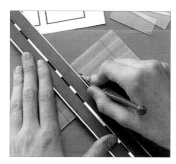

1 Enlarge the template from the back of the book to the size required. Transfer the shapes to the glass using carbon paper. Transfer the side pieces of the box on to clear glass and blue opal glass, and the octagonal base outline on to the mirrored blue glass. Score and break the glass using a thick straightedge or a cutting square.

2 Wrap the edges of the blue opal side pieces in 5mm (¹⁄₄in) wide copper foil and the edges of the thinner clear picture glass in the 4mm (³⁄₁₆in) wide copper foil. Press the foil down firmly using a fid.

3 Apply lines of 4mm (³⁄₁₆in) wide copper foil along the edges of the top surface of the mirror base to ensure that the sides bond firmly to the base. Wrap the sides in 5mm (¹⁄₄in) wide copper foil. Press the foil down firmly with a fid.

4 Brush all of the copper-wrapped pieces with safety flux and lightly tack-solder the pieces into place, adjusting them slightly if necessary.

▶

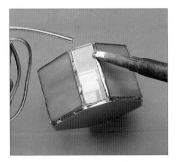  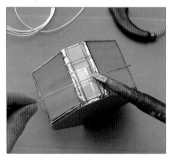

5 Reflux and solder all the copper surfaces. To give the edges a neat finish, run a bead of solder to fill the point where the side sections meet. Wash the box thoroughly to remove any traces of flux.

6 With the box balanced on one side, hold the end of a piece of wire just overlapping one of the clear sections. Brush with flux and touch the tip of the iron to the wire to solder it. Trim off the other end with wire cutters and repeat, using two vertical wires for each clear glass panel.

7 Solder two horizontal pieces of wire to each pair of verticals. Solder them on oversize, then trim them to length when they are soldered in place. Wash thoroughly to remove any traces of flux. Repeat steps 6 and 7 for each clear glass pane.

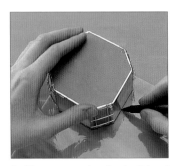 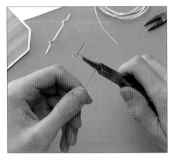 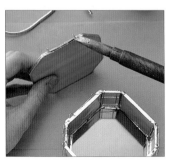

8 Choose some glass for the lid and place it with the side you want to be uppermost facing down. Place the box upside down over the glass and trace around the box with an indelible black felt-tipped pen. Score and break the glass just inside the lines. Remove any extra sharp edges with a scythe stone lubricated with a little water, then wrap the edges of the lid in 5mm (¼in) wide foil. Apply flux and plate the foil with solder.

9 Cut a piece of wire measuring about 10cm (4in) long. Bend two kinks in the wire with a pair of round-nosed pliers, using the picture as a guide. Cut another 10cm (4in) length of wire and bend two right angles in it to coincide with the kinks in the first wire. Bend the two ends into loops and trim off the excess wire with the wire cutters.

10 Apply flux to both pieces of wire. Solder the kinked length of wire to one side of the box and the looped piece to the lid. Wash both the box and the lid thoroughly to remove any traces of flux. Slot the lid hinge section into the body section to complete the trinket box.

This stained-glass project uses many glass pieces that are cut to shape to create an abstract design, ideal for the panel of a bathroom cabinet. It is an ambitious project.

Bathroom Cabinet Door Panel

you will need

tracing paper

pencil

ruler

felt-tipped pen

sheets of coloured glass

glass cutter

grozing pliers

masking tape

wooden board

three battens

hammer and horseshoe nails

lead knife

15mm (⅝in) lead came

letherkin tool

barrier cream

wire (steel) brush

tallow

clean cotton rags

solder wire and soldering iron

rubber gloves (optional)

black lead lighting putty

whiting powder

hard scrubbing brush

fire grate blackener

1 Trace the template from the back of the book, enlarging to the size required. The outer line represents the outer edge of the lead came. Go over the inner lines in felt-tipped pen. These thick lines will represent the centre of the pieces of lead came that join the glass together.

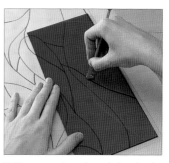

2 To cut out the coloured glass for the panel, lay a sheet of glass over the design and, starting from one corner, score along a line using a glass cutter. Carefully score along the other lines of the piece.

3 Use the ball end of the glass cutter to gently tap the reverse of the glass below the line you have scored. Tap until the two pieces fall apart. Use grozing pliers to nip off any small pieces of glass.

4 When all the glass is cut, tape your drawing to a wooden board. Nail one batten to each side edge and another to the bottom edge, along the outer pencil line of the rectangle.

▶

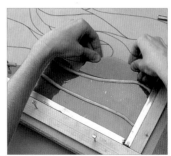

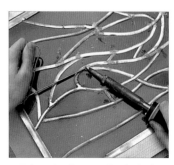

5 Using a lead knife, mark and cut a piece of lead came to fit along the side of the panel. Repeat for the bottom edge. Using a letherkin tool, open up the leaves of the lead to make it easier to insert the glass. Wear barrier cream to protect your hands from the toxic lead.

6 Build up the stained-glass design one piece at a time, cutting the lead came and inserting the glass carefully between the leaves of lead. Hammer horseshoe nails into the wooden board, as shown, to tack and hold the lead in place as you work.

7 When the design is finished, clean the lead joints with a wire brush. Rub tallow on to each joint. Place solder wire over the joint then melt into place with the soldering iron. Turn the panel over and repeat the process on the reverse.

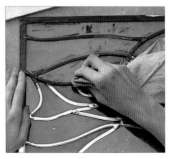

8 Wearing barrier cream, use your thumbs to press black lead lighting putty firmly into the gaps between the lead came and the pieces of glass. Work around the border and all around the individual pieces.

9 Cover the glass panel liberally with whiting powder. This will absorb the excess oil in the putty and help it to dry more quickly. Leave to harden for 1–2 hours. Use a hard scrubbing brush to clean off the whiting and excess putty. Repeat steps 8 and 9 on the reverse of the panel.

10 Wearing barrier cream, coat the lead with fire grate blackener using a clean cotton rag, then polish off the excess until you get a deep colour.

Templates

Enlarge the templates on a photocopier. Alternatively, trace the design and draw a grid of evenly spaced squares over your tracing. Draw a larger grid on to another piece of paper and copy the outline square by square. Finally, draw over the lines to make sure they are continuous.

Pot Stand, p83

Mosaic Hearts, p90

Star Wall Motifs, pp112–13

Squiggle Frame, pp118–19

Dragonfly
Plaque, p111

Love Letter Rack, pp98–9

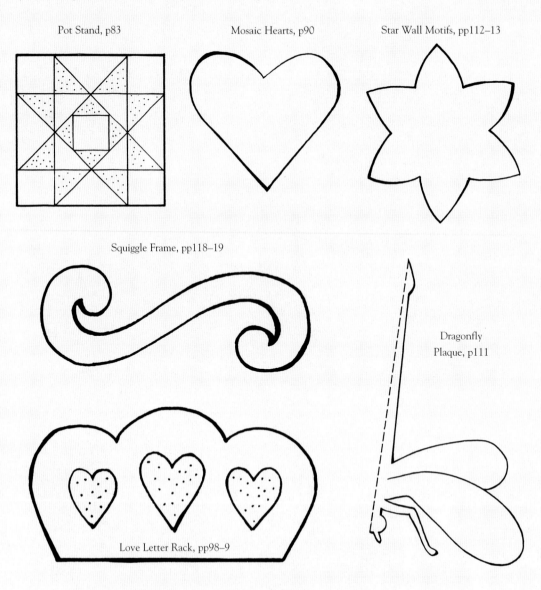

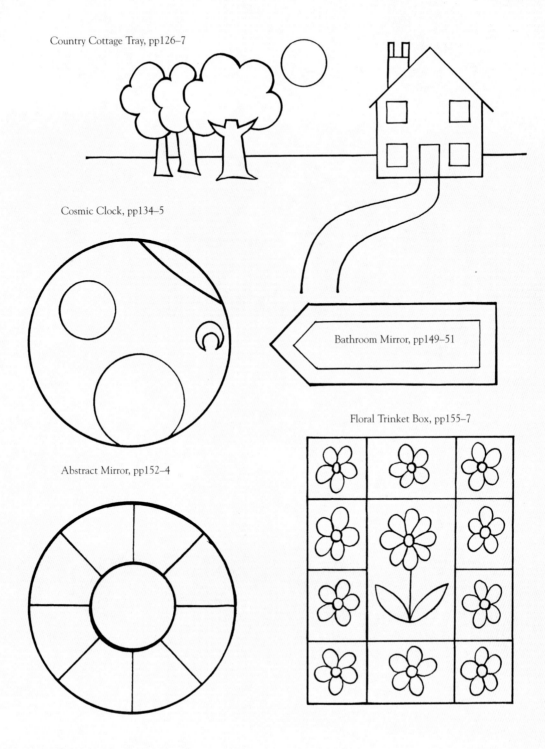

Country Cottage Tray, pp126–7

Cosmic Clock, pp134–5

Bathroom Mirror, pp149–51

Floral Trinket Box, pp155–7

Abstract Mirror, pp152–4

488

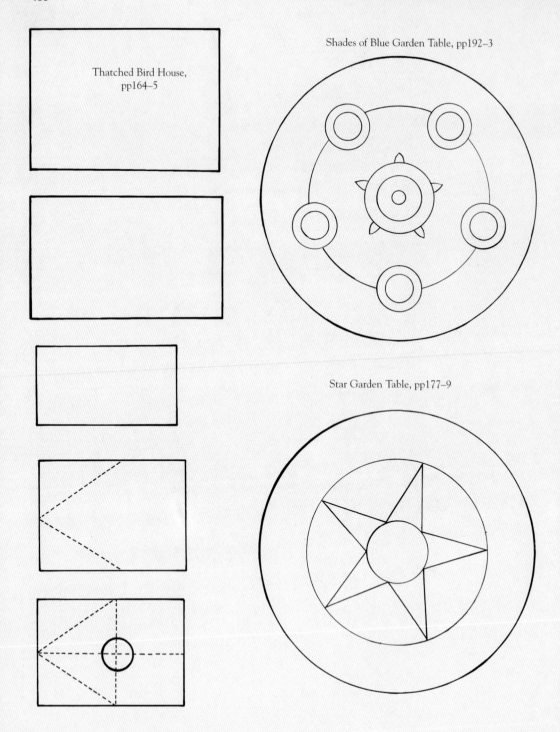

Thatched Bird House,
pp164–5

Shades of Blue Garden Table, pp192–3

Star Garden Table, pp177–9

Star Table, pp194–5

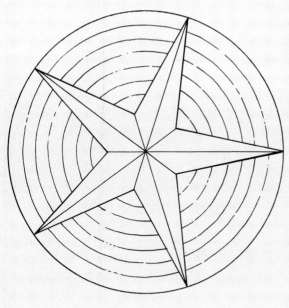

Splashback Squares, pp248–9

Rock Pool Mirror, pp124–5

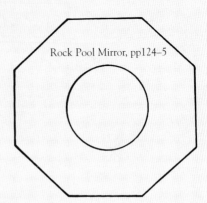

Flower Garden Table, pp196–7

Mosaic Bedhead, pp184–5

China Rail, pp242–4

Beaded Fish Splashback, pp252–3

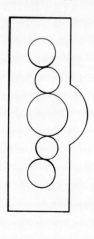

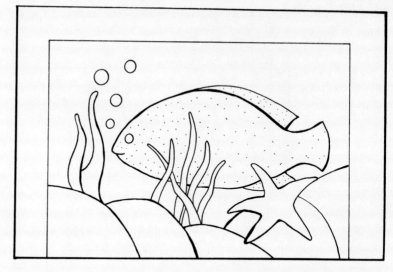

Abstract Colour Panel, pp230–1

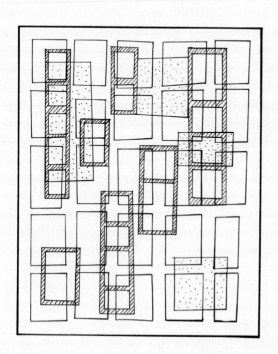

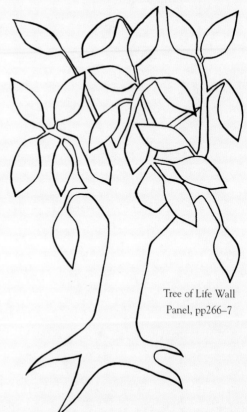

Tree of Life Wall
Panel, pp266–7

Fish Mosaic Splashback, pp255–6

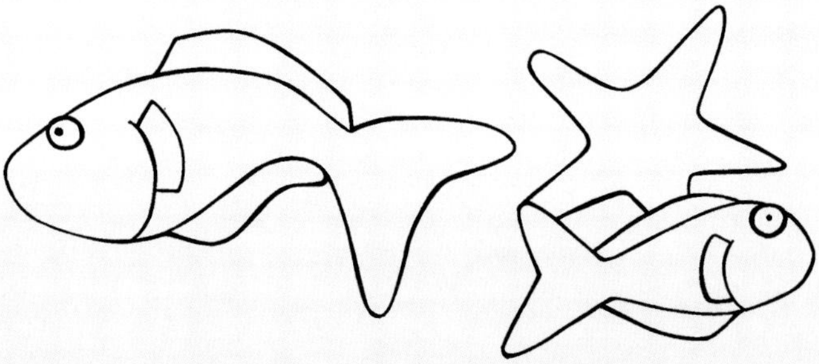

Princess Wall Mosaic, pp271–3

Black-and-white Floor, pp283–5

Bathroom Cabinet, pp232–3

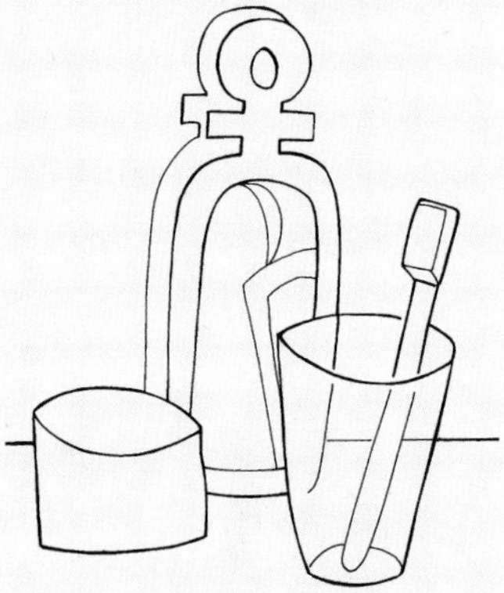

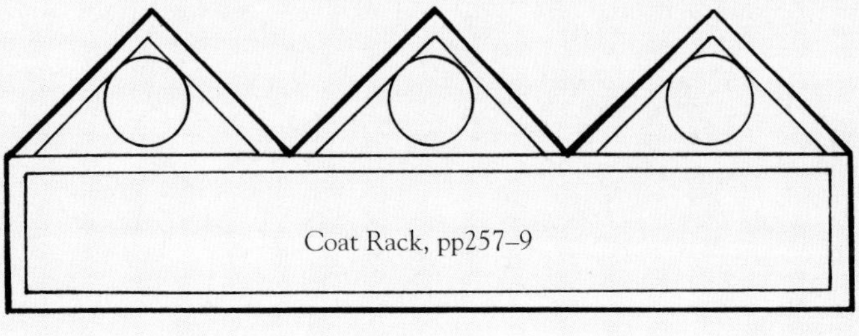

Daisy Skirting Board, pp250–1

Coat Rack, pp257–9

Boat Splashback, pp260–1

Heraldic Wall Plate, pp316–7

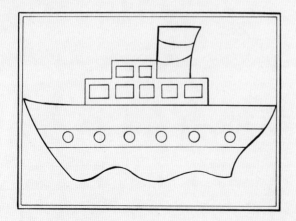

Seashore-style China, pp308–9

Stamped Spongeware, p312

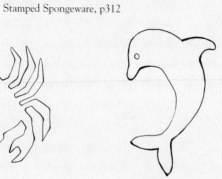

Citrus Fruit Bowl, pp306–7

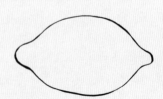

Kitchen Herb Jars, pp314–5

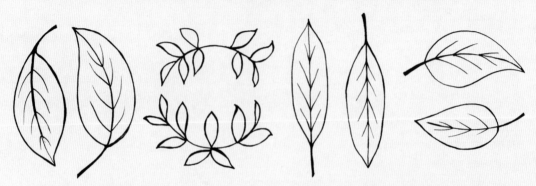

Morning Sun Face, p327

Patterned Lampbase, pp318–9

Leaf Motif Cup and Saucer, pp320–1

Sunflower Vase, pp322–3

Patterned Lampbase, pp318–9

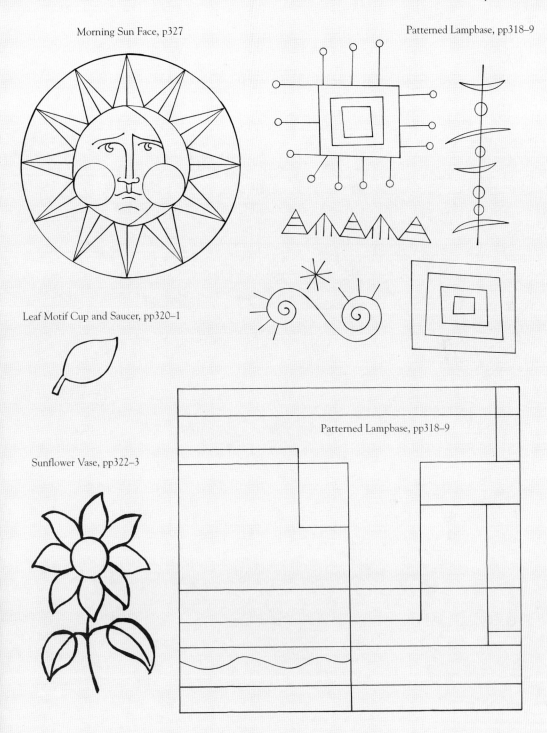

Pasta Bowls, pp330–1

Oriental Bowl, pp332–3

Espresso Cups and Saucers, pp328–9

Seashore Bathroom Set, p326

Fun Bunnies Tea Set, pp340–1

Vegetable Storage Jars, pp346–7

Paisley Teapot, pp344–5

Holly Christmas Platter, pp336–7

Fruit Bowl, pp342–3

Autumn Leaf Coffee Pot, pp334–5

Daisy Tiles, p364

Cactus Tiles, p361

Persian Carnation Tiles p9/

Summer Tea Service, pp302–3

Cartoon Tiles, p363

Sgraffito Fish Tiles, p366

Persian Carnation, p369

Maritime Tile Mural, pp370–1

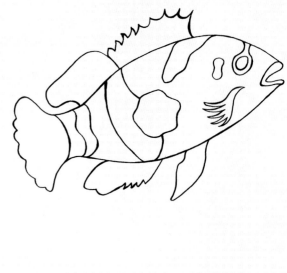

Cherub Tiles, pp372–3

Majolica Tiles, p376

Italianate Tiles, p375

Byzantine Bird Tile, p377

Floral Tiles, p374

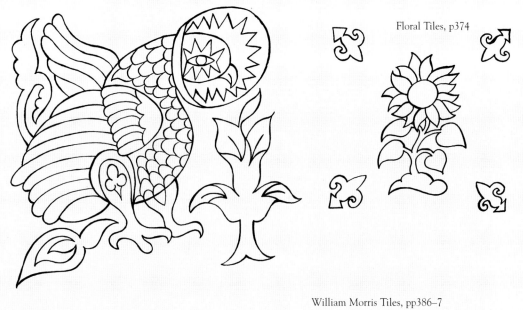

Art Nouveau Tiles, p380–1

William Morris Tiles, pp386–7

Monogrammed Wine Glass, p402

A B C D E F G

H I J K L M N

O P Q R S T U

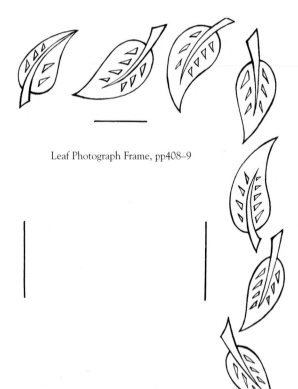

Frosted Highball Glasses, pp410–11

Leaf Photograph Frame, pp408–9

Monogrammed Wine Glass, p402

V W X Y Z &Æ

Sunlight Catcher, pp414–15

Alhambra Picture Frame, p418

Lemonade Pitcher, pp416–17

Frosted Vase, p419

Lily Candle Bowl, pp430–1

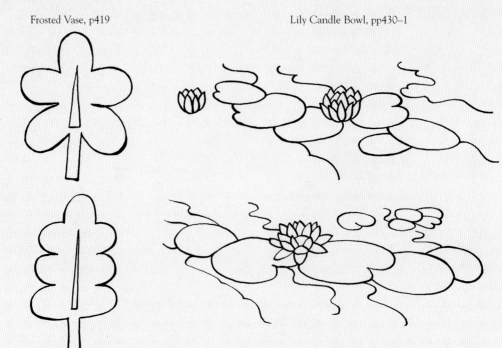

Butterfly Bowl, pp426–7

French-lavender Flower Vase, pp432–3

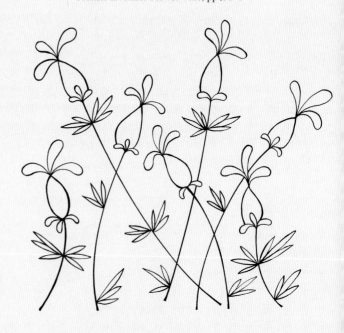

Bohemian Bottle, pp434–5

Venetian Perfume Bottle, pp438–9

Folk Art Glass, pp436–7

Folk Art Cabinet, pp440–1

Stained-glass Window pp451–3

Cherry Blossom Vase, pp464–5

Window Hanging, pp476–7

Indoor Glass Lantern, pp472–3

Heart Light Catcher, pp458–9

Opal Glass Planter, pp468–9

Door Number Plaque, pp474–5

Curtain Decorations, pp478–9

Bathroom Cabinet Door Panel, pp483–5

Trinket Box, pp480–1

Index

Acknowledgements

This edition is published by Hermes House

Hermes House is an imprint of Anness Publishing Ltd, Hermes House, 88–89 Blackfriars Road, London SE1 8HA
tel. 020 7401 2077; fax 020 7633 9499
www.hermeshouse.com;www.annesspublishing.com

If you like the images in this book and would like to investigate using them for publishing, promotions or advertising, please visit our website www.practicalpictures.com for more information.

© Anness Publishing Ltd 2006

Publisher: Joanna Lorenz
Managing Editor: Helen Sudell
Project Editors: Simona Hill and Katy Bevan
Designers: Nigel Partridge and Adelle Morris
Production controller: Pedro Nelson

Previously published in two separate volumes, *Decorating Glass & Ceramics* and *The Complete Practical Guide to Mosaics*.

10 9 8 7 6 5 4 3 2 1

The publisher would like to thank the following people for designing projects in this book:
Helen Baird for the Jazzy Plant Pot pp88–9, Mosaic Bottle pp92–3, Spiral Vase pp122–3, Country Cottage Tray pp126–7, Valentine Mirror pp128–30, Floral Lamp Base pp141–3, Spiral Lamp Stand pp146–8, Floral Trinket Box pp155–7, Garden Urn pp158–60, Star Garden Table pp177–9, Storage Chest pp180–1, Black-and-white Tiled Table pp182–3, Mosaic Bedhead pp184–6, Decorative Panel pp187–9, Daisy-covered Table pp200–02, Crazy Paving Chair pp210–12, Bathroom Cabinet pp232–3, Splashback Squares pp248–9, Daisy Skirting Board pp250–1, Fish Mosaic Splashback pp254–6, and Tree of Life Wall Panel pp266–7. **Michael Ball** for the Lemonade Pitcher pp416–17, Alhambra Picture Frame p418, Lily Candle Bowl pp430–1, Folk Art Cabinet pp440–1, Banded Vase pp456–7, Cherry Blossom Vase pp464–5, Opal Glass Planter pp468–9, Door Number Plaque pp474–5, and Window Hanging pp476–7. **Pattie Baron** for the Mediterranean Plant Pot p91. **Evelyn Bennett** for the Seaside Tiles p368. **Emma Biggs, Mosaic Workshop** for the Abstract Mirror pp152–4, and Abstract Colour Panel pp230–1. **Petra Boase** for the Frosted Vase p419. **Tessa Brown** for the Love Letter Rack pp98–9. **Victoria Brown** for the Mediterranean Mirror pp120–1. **Celia and Gregory Cohen** for the Candle Sconce pp138–40, Stained-glass Table pp203–5, and Mosaic Hearth pp262–5. **Karen Craggs** for the Decorated Pasta Bowls pp330–1, and Starburst Bathroom Tiles pp358–9. **Anna-Lise De'Ath** for the Mosaic Lantern pp86–7, Sun Light Catcher pp414–15, Patterned Bathroom Bottle pp422–3, Leaded Picture Frames pp454–5, and Leaded Door Panels pp466–7. **Ken Eardley** for the Espresso Cups and Saucers pp328–9, **Marion Elliot** for the Roman Numeral Tiles p362, Medieval Floor Tiles p365, Pueblan Tiles pp378–9, Underwater Panel pp382–3, and Silver Decoupage Tiles pp384–5. **Mary Fellows** for the Funky Condiment Set pp300–01, Sponged Snowflake Plate p313, Hand Painted Mugs pp324–5, Autumn Leaf Coffee Pot pp334–5, Carnival Vase pp338–9, Cartoon Tiles p363, Celebration Card p400–01, Heart Decoration p404, Frosted Bordered Frame pp428–9, and Stained Glass Window. pp451–3. **Lucinda Ganderton** for the Morning Sun Face p327, Persian Carnation Tiles p369, Floral Tiles p374, Italianate Tiles p375, Majolica Tile p376, Byzantine Bird Tile p377, Art Nouveau Tiles pp380–1, William Morris Tiles pp386–7, Monogrammed Wine Glass pp402–3, Leaf Photograph Frame pp408–9, French-lavender Flower Vase pp432–3, Bohemian Bottle pp434–5, and Venetian Perfume Bottle pp438–9. **Sandra Hadfield** for the Decorative Planter pp106–7, Door Number Plaque pp84–5, Funky Fruit Bowl pp115–17, Mosaic Fire Screen pp144–5, Coat Rack pp242–4, Crazy Paving Shelf pp245–7, and Coat Rack pp257–9. **Lesley Harle with Susan Conder** for the Squiggle Frame pp118–19, Low-relief Jug pp310–11, Heraldic Wall Plate pp316–17, Oriental Bowl pp332–33, Holly Christmas Platter pp336–37, Contemporary Fruit Bowl pp342–3, and Paisley Teapot pp344–45. **Tessa Hunkin, Mosaic Workshop** for the Cosmic Clock pp134–5, and Sculptural Head pp161–3. **Susie Johns** for the Christmas Baubles p399. **Francesca Kaye** for the Rosebud Tiles p367. **Mary Maguire** for the Grotto Frame pp108–9, Rock Pool Mirror pp124–5, Thatched Bird House pp164–5, Shell Table pp213–15, and Mosaic Slabs p238. **Emma Micklethwaite** for the Bathroom Cabinet Door Panel pp483–5. **Izzy Moreau** for the Stamped Spongeware p312, and Maritime Tile Mural pp370–1. **Helen Musselwhite** for the Patterned Summer Tea Service pp302–3, Lamp Base pp318–19, Seashore Bathroom Set p326, Fun Bunnies Tea Set pp340–1, and Vegetable Storage Jars pp346–7. **Cleo Mussi** for the China Tiles pp94–5, Sunflower Mosaic pp96–7, Plant Pots pp100–01, Decorative Spheres pp104–05, Part-tiled Flowerpot p110, Dragonfly Plaque p111, Star Wall Motifs pp112–14, Bathroom Mirror pp149–51, Shades of Blue Garden Table pp192–3, Mosaic Table pp216–17, Pretty Pebble Rug pp234–5, and Miniature Pebble Circle pp236–7. **Joanna Nevin** for the Stained-glass Candleholder 1pp02–03, and Stained-glass Screen pp206–09. **Christopher New** for the Mexican Animal Tiles p360. **Deirdre O'Malley** for the Glass Nugget Window Hanging pp460–1, Indoor Glass Lantern pp472–3, and Curtain Decorations pp478–9. **Cheryl Owen** for the Champagne Flutes pp424–5, and Butterfly Bowl pp426–7. **Marie Perkins** for the Citrus Fruit Bowl pp306–07, Kitchen Herb Jars pp314–15, Sunflower Vase pp322–3, Cactus Tiles p364, and Sgraffito Fish Tiles p366. **Polly Plouviez** for the Painted Salt and Pepper Pots pp406–07, Kitchen Storage Jar pp420–1, and Glass Nugget Bottle Holder pp470–1. **Tabby Riley** for the Mirror Mosaic pp131–3, Flower Garden Table pp196–9, and Mosaic Pond pp277–9. **Sarah Round** for the House Number Plaque p82, and Pot Stand p83. **Debbie Siniska** for the Heart Light Catcher pp458–9. **Tanya Siniska** for the Flowers and Foliage Wallhanging pp462–3. **Andrea Spencer** for the Seashore-style China pp308–9. **Isabel Stanley** for the Beaded Fish Splashback pp252–3, 1950s Jug and Butter Dish pp304–05, and Leaf Motif Cup and Saucer pp320–1. **Norma Vondee** for the Aztec Box pp136–7, Sea Urchin Garden Seat pp190–1, Star Table pp194–5, Slate Shelf pp240–1, Lemon Tree Floor pp268–70, Mosaic Panel pp274–6, Black-and-white Floor pp283–5, and Snakes and Ladders Floor pp286–7. **Stewart Walton** for the Mosaic Table Top pp174–6, and Folk Art Glass pp436–7.